HURON COUNTY LIBRARY

P9-CLP-007

HURON COUNTY LIB

2 008 155714

Date Due

KOSOY'S TRAVEL GUIDE
TO CANADA

by Ted Kosoy

917.104
Kos
1990

06134

KOSOY, T.

KOSOY'S TRAVEL GUIDE TO CANADA.

HURON COUNTY LIBRARY

Copyright © 1973, 1976, 1979, 1981, 1983, 1985, 1987, 1990 by Ted Kosoy

All rights reserved. No parts of this book may be reproduced or transmitted in any form or by any means electronic or mechanical including photo-copying, recording or by any information or re-trieval system, without permission in writing from the publisher.

Currency valuations, Canadian customs regula-tions, transportation schedules and other facts relative to travel in Canada are subject to change. Although every effort has been made to ensure accuracy and completeness, this guide makes no claim to infallibility and responsibility cannot be assumed for possible errors and omissions.

Photos courtesy of respective city and provincial tourist information offices. Photo on lower left corner of front cover courtesy of Minaki Lodge.

U.S. sales and distribution: Hunter Publishing Inc.
Canadian sales and distribution: Hounslow Press.

Printed and bound in Canada.

06134

CONTENTS

PART I

PART II

PART III

THE PROVINCES AND TERRITORIES

PART IV

GEOGRAPHICAL OUTLINE

Canada is an immense country. Its 3,851,809 square mile size is second only to the Soviet Union. The ten provinces and two northern territories border on 13 American states yet Greenland is a near neighbor. Cape Spear, Newfoundland is closer to Dublin, Ireland than it is to Winnipeg, Manitoba, the geographic centre of the country. Nova Scotia is closer to Venezuela than it is to Yukon Territory. Canada measures 2,840 miles in depth from its northermost extension in the Arctic (some 500 miles from the North Pole) to its most southerly latitude, a latitude south of the California-Oregon border. The big land's immensity will also be appreciated when you realize that it spans seven of the world's 24 time zones.

Canada is divided into distinct geographical regions. The Canadian Shield, formerly an impressive mountain range eroded over billions of years and today bleak tundra up north and wooded in the south, is a treasurehouse of mineral wealth. It encompasses close to half the country's land mass. The Shield begins in Labrador, encircles most of Hudson Bay, sweeps past northern Ontario, Quebec, Manitoba and Saskatchewan and extends beyond to the Northwest Territories. West of the Great Lakes are the seemingly unlimited wheat and grasslands of the Great Plains that take in southern Manitoba, Saskatchewan and Alberta and continue on past the Mackenzie River Valley as far as the Arctic Sea.

The prairies yield to the Canadian Cordillera, a series of ranges towering between the Pacific and the Great Plains. These include the Rockies, the mountain regions blanketing most of British Columbia and the giant peaks of the Yukon. Mount Logan in the Yukon (19,850 feet) is the country's highest peak. British Columbia's indented coastline has numberless fjords, glaciers, bays and islands. The ancient Appalachian region, now mostly submerged in the Atlantic Ocean, comprises the Maritime (Atlantic) provinces and southeastern Quebec.

Canada's population is about 27,000,000. Its population density is approximately five persons per square mile, one of the world's lowest. The snowy wastes of the Arctic islands are barely inhabited, mostly by Eskimos. The prairies (Alberta, Saskatchewan, Manitoba) are sparsely settled. The sense of emptiness is accentuated by the fact that most of the people live in urban areas. The narrow land strip in southern Ontario and Quebec known as the St. Lawrence Lowlands is home to more than half the population. Nine of ten Canadians inhabit a narrow hospitable land belt flanking the American border. Canada's Indian population is approximately 250,000.

This enormous land constitutes a repository of incalculable natural wealth. While the export of manufactured goods has taken on increased importance in the last 15 to 20 years, Canada's prosperity continues to be dependent on products from its farms, forests, mines and the sea. Canada is the world's leading producer of nickel, zinc, asbestos and potash, and second in the production of uranium, gold and silver. Its mineral wealth (concentrated mostly in the north) includes huge supplies of copper, cobalt, lead, iron ore and coal. The provinces and territories contain an estimated quarter of the world's fresh water supply. Lumber reserves are enormous; forests cover a billion acres. The Athabaska tar sands in northern Alberta contain virtually untapped oil reserves estimated at 300 billion barrels, equal to the known reserves of the free world producers.

AN HISTORICAL SKETCH

Although evidence has been unearthed to suggest that the Vikings established settlements in Newfoundland in the 10th century, the historical record in Canada dates back to its official discovery by John Cabot who sailed from England in 1497 to explore the New World. The discovery of Newfoundland encouraged the French to follow up on the voyages of exploration and Jacques Cartier in 1534 sailed up the Gulf of St. Lawrence to the Gaspé in modern Quebec. The first permanent settlements, however, were to be established only with the arrival of Samuel de Champlain at Port Royal, Nova Scotia in 1604 and Quebec in 1608.

The English, their colonial rivals, set up the Hudson's Bay Company to exploit the potential of the fur trade. The defeat of the French by Wolfe at Quebec City in 1759 ended France's hold in Canada and led to their expulsion from North America as a colonial power. The colonies of Canada, including Quebec, held aloof from

9

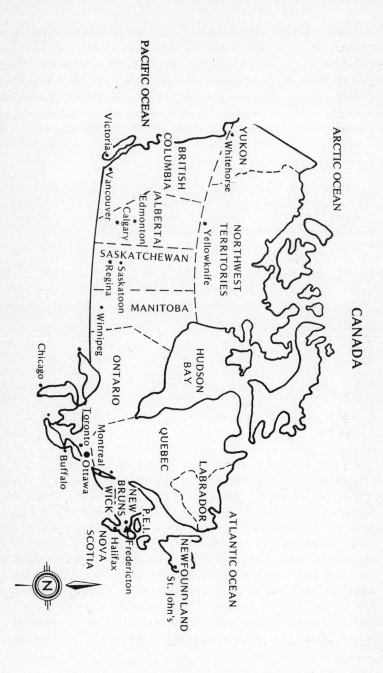

the struggle of the American colonists to gain freedom and independence during the Revolution. The war of 1812 fought against the United States created no change in the political fortunes of either antagonist but impetus had been given to the movement for unity among the colonies in recognition of the everpresent possibility of attack from the United States.

They also realized that economic benefits would follow from political co-operation and a big step to unity was taken with the completion of a railway from the Maritime provinces to Upper Canada (Ontario). The excesses of the American Civil War, the belief that the colonies had to unite to forestall the possibility of Americans carrying the war across the border, became a compelling motive for co-operation. In 1867 the British North America Act united Ontario, Quebec, Nova Scotia and New Brunswick into the self-governing Dominion of Canada. The country's conduct of external affairs, however, was still controlled by Great Britain.

Hundreds of thousands of immigrants poured into the west over the newly built (1885) transcontinental railway, drawn by the government's offer of free land to settlers who would cultivate the empty prairies. Manitoba (1870), British Columbia (1871), Prince Edward Island (1873), Saskatchewan and Alberta (1905) joined Confederation and the task of forging the former British colonies into a united Canadian state extending from the Atlantic to the Pacific was completed.

The early decades of the 20th century were marked by the Dominion's steady advance to nationhood. Britain's entry into World War One in 1914 automatically drew Canada (still a colony in foreign affairs) into the conflict. The nation's maturation as a contributor to victory in the war was marked by her entry as a separate member into the League of Nations. Canada no longer acted in consultation with Britain in the conduct of foreign affairs; the Imperial Conference of 1923 affirmed this right and during the Imperial Conference of 1926 Canada and the other members of the Commonwealth were declared to be "equal in status, in no way subordinate to one another in any aspect of their domestic or external affairs, bound by a common allegiance to the Crown." The Statute of Westminster (1931) gave legal expression to the state's attainment of independence.

The economic depression of the 1930's ended with the onset of World War II and Canada's contribution to victory was exceeded only by the United States and Great Britain. The challenge of the war forced the country into a tremendous expansion of industry and for the past 45 years Canadians have enjoyed one of the highest living standards in the world. The island of Newfoundland was admitted into Confederation in 1949.

CANADA'S GOVERNMENT

Canada broke loose from Britain nearly a century later (1867) than the Americans, during which time the English parliamentary system of government matured. Canada adopted the prevailing English system of responsible government which accounts for the different paths the two North American transplanted English speaking democracies have taken to express democratic principles. The cabinet and prime minister are responsible to the members of the popularly elected House of Commons, who in turn are responsible to the citizenry. The nation's federal system of government, which provides for the division of power between the central and provincial governments, was adapted from the American model.

Canadians elect 295 members of parliament representing constituencies or electoral districts. Canadian citizens, 18 years of age and over, are entitled to vote in a federal election. The prime minister and cabinet are normally drawn from the majority party or if there is no majority (there are currently three political parties), from the party commanding a plurality of seats in the House of Commons. The life span of every parliament is five years, less if the leader of the party in power wishes to call an early election or if the government is defeated by an opposition party non-confidence motion on a matter of importance.

The prime minister leads and selects cabinet ministers, decides which legislation to introduce, advises the Governor General when to assemble or dissolve parliament and appoints members of the Senate, foreign diplomats and key judges. Normally cabinet members are drawn from each of Canada's various regions to give the party in power a semblance of, if not the reality of, national appeal. Cabinet ministers are entrusted with the responsibilities of government departments, — e.g. finance, defence — and implement bills passed by parliament.

The Governor General is largely a symbolic political figure who attains office on the recommendation of the prime minister. He is formally appointed by the Queen and represents the Crown since Canada is technically a monarchy. The Queen symbolizes Canada's membership in the British Commonwealth of Nations. As Canada's titular head of state, Queen Elizabeth II is the Queen of Canada. The duty of the leader of the Opposition, chosen from the party with the second highest number of elected members, is to provide an alternative to the prime minister if the government falls. The Senate, consisting of 104 members, has less authority than the House of Commons; its function is to review legislation proposed by the lower house. The independent Supreme Court's influence on the nation's social and political life has become more conspicuous in recent years.

The federal government in Ottawa is entrusted with the powers, among others, of regulating foreign relations, making declarations of peace and war and issuing the currency. In recent years responsibility has been taken in formulating policies to stimulate the economy and promote full employment. The political system in the ten provinces is patterned on the federal model. Each province legislates in such defined areas as health, education, highways and the establishment of municipalities. The Queen is represented in every province by the Lieutenant-Governor. Towns and cities are governed by elected councils. The Yukon and Northwest Territories are administered by a Commissioner appointed by Ottawa and a territorial council, responsible to an elected assembly.

INFORMATION FOR AMERICAN VISITORS

In no other vacationland, covering an area as vast as Canada, is the American so at liberty to travel. One language — English — will open the door to a great degree of involvement in the nation's life. The country is known for high standards of efficiency. You will be received as friendly neighbors and few adjustments will have to be made. Nonetheless there are differences to note in the facts of everyday touring in the two countries.

ARRIVAL BY CAR No duty or tax is payable for vehicles brought in on a stay of less than six months, though motorists should carry automobile registration papers. If the vehicle belongs to someone else you must be able to furnish a letter from the owner authorizing its use and a copy of the ownership permit. Rental contracts on leased automobiles also must be furnished and if you intend leaving a car originally rented at home in Canada, customs form E 29B is to be completed. Visitors crossing the frontier in rented trailers may be asked to leave a $50. refundable deposit with border officials. American visitors should make certain to carry proof of automobile liability insurance in the form of an insurance policy or a certificate or a liability card provided by their auto insurers. This proof of financial responsibility is acceptable to police in all provinces. American guests should comply with motoring regulations in any part of Canada in the same manner they would comply with regulations in effect in their home state.

BORDER PROCEDURES Canadian customs officials are courteous and prompt at airports and border (the frontier is 3,988 miles long, not including 1,538 miles of Alaska boundary points. American visitors need no passport, visa or health certificate. Any identification will do — a driver's licence, social security card, birth or baptismal certificate, and, when appropriate, a certificate of naturalization or resident alien card. A few questions — concerning your place of birth, permanent residence, purpose and length of stay — and you will be waved along in friendly fashion. Gifts or commercial goods must be declared. Customs officials are as firmly opposed to the importation of narcotics as their American counterparts and if in their opinion a search is warranted, it will be thorough.

CANADIAN CUSTOMS REGULATIONS Almost any everyday article may be brought in provided it is evident it is meant for personal use during your stay. Canada does impose limits on the amounts of tobacco and alcohol that may be imported. Gifts, except for tobacco and alcohol may be brought in duty free provided each gift per person is valued at less than $40. A visitor can bring in free of duty 200 cigarettes, 50 cigars, two pounds of tobacco and 40 ounces of alcohol. Twenty-four 12-ounce pints of beer or ale may be substituted. Visitors under 16 cannot legally bring in tobacco. The liquor allowance does not apply to minors below the age limit prevailing in the province you are entering. Apart from these limits the visitor may temporarily import two or three cameras, a reasonable quantity of film, a musical instrument, food products, fishing and sporting gear, camping equipment, private boats, outboard motors and anything else that could be brought in for personal use. Meats, exotic plants, fruits and pets are not permitted entry into Canada unless special permission has been granted in advance. Imported animals and birds must undergo a special examination and a health certificate showing the dog has been vaccinated for rabies within the last 12 months, validated by a vet in the U.S.A., is essential for the importation of a dog. The certificate must provide a description of the pet and be initialled by a customs officer at the point of entry. No conditions are imposed on bringing in cats. All vegetable products must be presented at customs for examination since foreign agricultural produce may carry descructive insects which can cause widespread damage to farming and forest industries if they ever establish a foothold.

It's compulsory to declare firearms. You can transport shotguns, rifles and 200 pounds of ammunition over the border. Except for competitions of marksmanship, pistols, revolvers and automatic weapons are forbidden entry. Revolvers, pistols and automatic weapons may be brought in, for transit to or from Alaska and if sealed at the customs office. The seal must remain intact. Visitors under 16 cannot legally bring in firearms. Importation of hunting and fishing equipment does not confer the automatic right to fish or hunt. A permit must be obtained from the appropriate provincial or territorial government department.

AMERICAN CUSTOMS REGULATIONS Passing through customs could emerge as a psychological hurdle before your return to the U.S., though there is little to worry about if common sense rules are observed. Ease passage through customs by retaining receipts for purchases and keeping them handy in one bag. The receipts also help confirm the time you spent up here. Answer all questions clearly, courteously and truthfully.

American residents spending at least 48 hours in Canada are allowed to bring back duty-free goods worth up to $400 retail value provided the exemption hasn't been claimed in the previous 30 days. These exemptions apply only to goods purchased for personal and household use, as long as the trip was not made for the purpose of buying them and they are properly declared upon arrival in the United States. Included in the exemption is a duty free import of 100 cigars (non-Cuban), one carton of cigarettes and one liter or 32 ounces of liquor. The liquor allowance does not apply to minors below the age limit prevailing in your state. Articles manufactured in North Vietnam, North Korea or Cuba and items incorporating Cuban components won't be admitted. Items acquired in Canada must accompany you on your return to be included in the exemption. The total value of exemptions may be pooled and applied to a family. All plants, fruits and vegetables have to be declared and presented for inspection.

American residents staying less than 48 hours in Canada are permitted to import goods (which are tax free) reckoned at less than $25 retail value. The exemption may include personal or household items, with the exception of cigarettes, tobacco or alcohol. On stays of less than 48 hours, no merchandise is free from tax or duty if one of the imported items is liable to tax or duty or if the combined worth of the goods is valued in excess of $25. The total value of exemptions in this category may not be pooled and applied to a family.

Stagger purchases and avoid overburdening yourself with packages while in Canada by sending gifts to the U.S.A. free of duty for the recipient if the gift does not exceed $50 in retail value. No more than one package per person a day may be sent. To assure its clearance through American customs be certain to write clearly on it "unsolicited gift, valued under $50." This duty exemption can be used over and above the 48 hour stay duty and tax free provision and does not cover cigars, cigarettes, alcohol or perfume. These presents shipped by mail do not have to be declared upon your return.

Obscene literature, narcotics and drugs (including prescriptions and over the counter medicines) that contain narcotics are excluded from entry. Even jokes about narcotics can bring you grief. A commuter joked about the alleged cache of drugs stashed away in his attache case and customs failed to appreciate his sense of humor. Instead, on this and every trip he took thereafter, he was a marked man. His car and belongings were carefully searched, he was continually subjected to interrogation and only after many trips and some time had elapsed did customs relax their vigilance.

If you are carrying foreign goods previously purchased in the U.S.A. — for instance a Swiss watch or a German camera — you may be quizzed at customs on your return. They will attempt to ascertain if merchandise was or was not purchased at home. As a precaution against embarrassing holdups, have American bought cameras, binoculars, watches or sporting equipment identified prior to departure on certificate of registration number 4457. Also use the form to identify articles declared on a previous trip for which duty has already been paid. Without the form you could be liable to pay duty on goods you cannot prove were acquired at home.

PRICES Both prices and the quality of goods and services in Canada generally correspond to those in the States. Pay phones are plentiful, operate as in the U.S. and a call costs up to 25 cents, depending on the location of the phone booth. Cigarettes are somewhat cheaper in the U.S.A. Liquor prices are less in the U.S. but the alcoholic content in Canadian brands is sometimes higher. The price of fuel, measured in liters at gas pumps, costs a bit more than you would have to pay back home. Taxi rates are variable, averaging a basic $2.00 and another 70-80 cents every kilometer. Streetcar, subway and bus fares run about $1.00 - $1.10. Dry cleaning service is efficient and costs are approximately $1.35 - $1.90 for a shirt, $7 - $9 for a dress and $8.25 - $8.90 for a suit. A ticket to the movies costs $3.00 - $7.50, a man's haircut $6.50 - $18 and a haircut by a woman stylist ranges from around $12.00 - $50.00.

CURRENCY AND TIPPING In the last few years the floating rate for the Canadian dollar has fluctuated between $.75 and $1.03 to the U.S. dollar. Canadians are businesslike and few will attempt to gouge you. The American dollar is accepted in Canada as a matter of routine. However, owing to the regular fluctuations in exchange rates and because no establishment is obliged to accept American money or pay the prevailing rate, it's best to convert required currency into Canadian dollars. Banks (most frequently open 10-3, to 6 on Friday) offer the fairest currency conversion rates, usually about 1% for the service. You can expect to lose 1 - 2% in the difference between the buying and selling rates. Unlimited amounts of Canadian dollars may be imported or exported. A limit is strictly imposed on the amount of American money you can import or export.

The currency is composed of coins of 1 (penny), 5 (nickel), 10 (dime), 25 (quarter), 50 cents and one dollar and bills (each a different colour) of $2, $5, $10, $20, $50, $100 and $1,000 denominations. As in the States "buck" is the slang term for a dollar and "two bits" is a quarter. A supply of $1's and $5's are convenient for meeting small expenses before crossing back into the United States or for cab fare to the airport or rail terminal. Changing a $10 or $50 travel cheque to pay for a trifling amount and the consequent changing of the converted currency after you return involves costly and unnecessary procedures.

Personnel in the hospitality industry are not quite as tip conscious as their counterparts in Europe or elsewhere. Hotels and restaurants frequently do not impose a service charge. If service is not included it's customary to leave 10 - 15% to waiters, waitresses and bartenders; taxi-drivers also get 10 - 15% of the fare. It's strictly optional to tip chambermaids. Porters in rail or air terminals expect about one dollar per bag.

SHOPPING Shopping specialties not freely available in the U.S.A. are Eskimo art obtainable directly from carvers or at specialty shops in many provinces, miniature totem poles and the farmed durable Cowichan sweaters in British Columbia, Hudson's Bay blankets in the western provinces and wood carvings from Quebec. You can get furs direct from trappers at far northern outposts. The quality of clothing in Canada is quite good. Clothing sizes in all garments are the same in both countries.

MISCELLANEOUS The metric system has been adopted in Canada. Measurements are in centimetres and metres — 100 centimetres to the metre, 1,000 metres to the kilometre. One inch equals 2.5 centimetres, one foot equals 30.5 centimetres and one mile equals 1,609 metres. Conversely, a metre equals 39.3 inches and eight kilometres measure five miles. Weight is calculated in grams and kilograms (1,000 grams); one ounce equals 28.4 grams, 16 ounces equal 453.6 grams and a kilogram is 2.2 pounds. Liquids are measures in litres; there are roughly 4.5 litres to the gallon. Temperatures are now measured in degrees Celsius. In the Celsius system, zero is water's freezing point and 100° the boiling point. To reduce Celsius readings to Fahrenheit, multiply by 9/5 and add 32. To convert Fahrenheit to Celsius, subtract 32 and multiply by 5/9. Electric current is 110-120 volts, 60 cycle, alternating current and socket outlets normally require two flat prongs. Though medicines are the same, brand names are sometimes different. Water is safe to drink everywhere. Major American gasoline and other credit cards are valid here also. Daylight saving time commences the first Sunday in April and ends the last Saturday in October and comes into effect everywhere in Canada except within the province of Saskatchewan. As in the United States, timepieces are moved ahead by one hour. Abbreviations used in this guide include: R.C.M.P. or Mounties are the Royal Canadian Mounted Police, Quebec is P.Q., Prince Edward Island is P.E.I., Northwest Territories is N.W.T., British Columbia is B.C., Newfoundland is Nfld., Nova Scotia is N.S. and New Brunswick is N.B.

MAIL An airmail letter sent from nearby areas in the States should arrive in a few days though to be on the safe side, allow for a few days delay in delivery. The better hotels are usually co-operative in this respect. They are accustomed to meeting the needs of visitors and after all, are in the business of pleasing guests. They never close down, so mail can be picked up at any time. Have letters inscribed "Hold for Arrival" to ensure delivery if correspondence arrives before you do at your destination. Supply a forwarding address if you continue on your journey before anticipated mail gets there. As Canada seems so familiar to Americans, they at times forget this is a foreign country. Canadian stamps are required on all letters posted from anywhere in Canada. A custom declaration has to be affixed to packages (maximum weight 30 kilograms) posted for the U.S.A. Customs forms are obtainable at any main post office. Stamps are sold in post offices, some drug stores and in hotels. Post offices are open 8 a.m. to 5:45 p.m.

INFORMATION FOR
INTERNATIONAL VISITORS

CUSTOMS PROCEDURES Passports alone are needed by Australians, New Zealanders, Britons and West Europeans; health certificate requirements have been abolished. As the government's policies on visa requirements are regularly subject to review, and it is wise to determine them ahead of time, all other travellers should consult Canadian diplomatic representatives abroad for their respective entry requirements. Tourists may temporarily import any everyday article, provided it is intended for personal use during the stay. In addition, visitors may bring in, if declared on arrival, 50 cigars, a carton of cigarettes, two pounds of tobacco and 40 ounces of liquor.

TRANSPORTATION The road network in Canada is well developed. Traffic flows on the right hand side of the road. There are speed limits on superhighways — usually 100 kilometres per hour. Gasoline is much less expensive here than in England or Europe. Your local driving licence is valid for driving as a tourist up to 90 days in most provinces.

TRAVEL HEALTH INSURANCE An accident or illness can strike anyone, anywhere. Europeans visiting Canada are not protected under Canadian government-sponsored health insurance plans. You would be wise, therefore, to consider taking out a private, short term policy as coverage against unexpected and expensive hospital and medical treatment.

One such policy, which is both responsible in terms of its benefits and reasonable in terms of its cost, is the **Blue Cross Health Plan Visitors to Canada.** Benefits provided by Blue Cross include the payment of charges up to $50,000.00 (Cdn.) per insured person in a hospital in Canada or the U.S.A., local ambulance services and other related expenses. For an individual, the cost of a policy per day is about $3.00 (Cdn.) and for a family, the fee per day is about $6.00 (Cdn.). The policy can be purchased for a period of up to 60 days. Applications can be obtained by writing Ontario Blue Cross, 150 Ferrand Drive, Toronto, Ontario M3C 1H6. Note that policies must be purchased within five days of arrival in Canada.

Prince Albert National Park, Saskatchewan

MISCELLANEOUS The metric system of measurement was introduced some time ago into Canada. Prices on goods and services in Canada are often considerably, and surprisingly, lower than in Europe. Cigarette prices are much lower than in England and the countries of Scandinavia. Pay phones are simple to operate and local calls usually cost 25 cents. The Eastern Standard Time Zone (Toronto - Montreal) is five hours behind Greenwich Mean Time. Dry cleaning work is relatively inexpensive. The electric current is 110 - 120 volts, 60 cycles, alternating current and socket outlets take two flat prongs. A transformer is required for a hair dryer, electric shaver or travel iron. It's wise to bring along travellers cheques in dollars (preferably Canadian). Service charges are generally not imposed on hotels and restaurant bills; the standard tipping rate is 10 - 15%. The Canadian dollar is divided into 100 cents. Coins in the amount of 1, 5, 10, 25, 50 cents and one dollar and bills of $2, $5, $10, $20, $100, and $1,000 denominations are minted.

CANADIAN GOVERNMENT
TRAVEL OFFICES

The government of Canada operates official tourist information offices in most major Canadian centres, fourteen cities in the United States and seven foreign countries. They exist for one purpose — to stimulate interest in and promote the merits of the 10 provinces and two northern territories through the distribution of attractive travel brochures and leaflets. They dispense all of their travel literature free of charge hoping by this gesture to encourage the prospective tourist. If your trip is in the planning stage, talk to these representatives or read their pamphlets as a preliminary source of information. Once you get a better idea of what the province or region holds in store you will be better prepared to discuss plans with a travel agent.

Rest assured if you visit these centres that you'll be courteously received. Their personnel's job is to answer the travelling public's questions relating to a vacation project and offer tips and suggestions to help tourists make the most of time spent in Canada. If there are no representatives in your vicinity write to them at addresses listed below. Provincial or city tourist boards will also quite willingly send, again at no cost, well illustrated pamphlets and detailed maps on their respective cities and provinces. They are especially helpful in providing information that changes regularly — specific dates for upcoming events and festivals and current hunting and fishing regulations. Canada's consulates are another source of information.

Tourist information offices open in downtown areas of larger cities and in popular smaller places are also helpful. For instance, several towns in Ontario assist visitors by maintaining information booths. Toronto has several of these kiosks operating during the summer in various parts of the city. English is invariably spoken at information centres in Quebec. The following are Canadian government travel bureau locations.

CANADA

Alberta 10179 105th Street, Suite 505, Edmonton, T5J 3S3. (403) 420-2944; 220 4th Ave. S.E., Suite 630, Calgary, T2P 3C3. (403) 231-4575.

British Columbia Bentall Centre, Tower Number 4, Suite 1101, 1055 Dunsmuir St., Vancouver, V7X 1K8, (604) 661-2220.

Manitoba 400-185 Carlton St., Winnipeg, R3C 2V2. (204) 949-2300.

New Brunswick 770 Main St., P.O. Box 1210, Moncton, E1C 8P9. (506) 388-6411

Nova Scotia 1496 Lower Water Street, Halifax, B2Y 4B9. (902) 426-3458.

Ontario 235 Queen St., Ottawa, K1A 0A6. (613) 996-4610; 1 First Canadian Place, Suite 4840, P.O. Box 98, Toronto, M5X 1B1. (416) 365-3775.

Quebec 800 Place Victoria, 12th floor, Montreal, H4Z 1E8. (514) 283-5938.

UNITED STATES

California 510 West 6th Street, Los Angeles, 90014, (213) 622-1029; One Maritime Plaza, Suite 1160, Alcoa Building, San Francisco, 94111, (415) 981-8515.

District of Columbia N.A.B. Building, Suite 200, 1771 N. Street, N.W.. Washington, 20036, (202) 223-2855.

Georgia 400 South Omni International, Atlanta, 30303, (404) 577-7445.

Illinois 310 S. Michigan Avenue, 12th Floor, Chicago, 60604, (312) 427-1888.

Massachusetts 500 Boylston Street, 6th Floor, Boston, 02116, (617) 536-1730.

Michigan 1900 First Federal Building, 1001 Woodward Avenue, Detroit, 48226, (313) 963-8686.

Minnesota Chamber of Commerce Building, 15 South 5th Street, 12th Floor, Minneapolis, 55402, (612) 332-4314.

New York One Marine Midland Center, Suite 3550, Buffalo, 14203, (716) 852-7369; Exxon Building, 1251 Avenue of the Americas, Room 1030, New York, 10020, (212) 757-4917.

Ohio 55 Public Square, 10th Floor, Cleveland, 44113, (216) 771-1684.

Pennsylvania Suite 1810, 3 Parkway, Philadelphia, 19102, (215) 563-1708.

Texas 2001 Bryan Tower, Suite 1600, Dallas, 75201, (214) 922-9814.

Washington 600 Steward Street, Suite 814, Seattle, 98101, (206) 223-1777.

ABROAD

Australia Eighth Floor, AMP Centre, 50 Bridge Street, Sydney, 2000, (02) 231-6522.

England Canadian High Commission, Canada House, London, SW1 5BJ (01) 629-9492, Extension 269.

France Canadian Embassy, 37 Ave. Montaigne, Paris, 75008, (01) 723-0101.

Germany Kanadisches Fremdenverkehrsamt, Biebergasse 6-10, 6,000 Frankfurt, (611) 28-01-57.

Japan Yamakatsu Pearl Building, 5th Floor, 5-32, Akasaka 8-chome, Minato-Ku, Tokyo, 107, (03) 479-5851.

Mexico Canadian Embassy, Calle Schiller 529, Colonia Polanco, Apartado Postal 105-05, Mexico City, 5, D.F. (905) 254-3288.

Netherlands Canadian Embassy, Sophialaan 7, 2514 The Hague, Netherlands, (70) 61-41-11.

TRAVEL AGENTS

As specialists in travel planning, agents offer the benefits of their knowhow in helping you to make the most of a trip across Canada. An agent is the authorized representative of tour operators, airlines and shipping companies. He can issue tickets on their behalf only if he has demonstrated, after a considerable period of time, responsibility and skill in dealing with all phases of travel. Leave all the details to a reliable agent; he should be able to work out something suited to the limitations of your budget and time. Most fees for an agent's services are paid by the airlines and shipping companies and hotels who are saved the task of hiring additional staff to handle the increased volume of business.

Agents can often save the prospective vacationer the bother of going through reams of travel folders on Canada by giving him answers to his questions in a matter of minutes. He is authorized to purchase train, bus or air tickets, arrange hotel accommodation and car rentals or enlist a client in one of the many tours that are being steadily expanded. Part of his job may be to arrange sightseeing tours, transfer clients from terminals to hotels and obtain tickets for festivals, sporting or special events, theatre and the opera. If you wish he will enroll you in such special-interest activities as cruises along the Pacific coast, ski, student or golf tours, package tours of the Northwest Territories and combined U.S.A. — Canadian excursions. New vacation ideas are constantly being dreamed up.

For the service of getting a single air ticket or hotel reservation, agents normally ask no fee. For detailed arrangements on package or individual tours, moderate fees are sometimes charged to cover the agent's operating expenses. If you arrange trip details on your own consider going through an agent for hotel reservations on those important first few days when you're getting a footing. Many things about travel in Canada happen spontaneously or can be arranged at the last minute, but getting a room may be tricky if you plan to stay in downtown Ottawa durng the summer, in Calgary during the Stampede or at Toronto during the Canadian National Exhibition when hotels and motels are usually jammed to the rafters.

TRIP PREPARATION

Once you've decided to vacation in Canada, the next problem is to choose how you will move about the country. Basically, there are three alternatives: the conducted group tour; a planned personal holiday; and travelling alone, making impromptu arrangements.

CONDUCTED TOURS There is a growing number of tours designed for the regular or special interest tourist — anything from bus tours of the West and Rockies to combined rail-bus excursions in the Maritimes. Many tourists like this style of getting around because all details — transportation, hotels, guides, meals, tours and baggage pickups — are worked out in advance on your behalf by professional tour organizers. No detail is overlooked. Sightseeing is invariably done in a group and by the very nature of the tour individual interests take second place to collective preferences or what the tour operator *thinks* are collective preferences. After the initial experience, some vow never again to be herded down this route. Others wouldn't go any other way. They're pleased that all decisions are made for them, glad that an English-speaking guide (in Quebec) can sweep them past language barriers and happy that, with luck, there is lots of congenial company.

PLANNED PERSONAL TOUR A guided tour that isn't tailored to individual needs could become a "misguided tour". A planned personal holiday allows you to take a trip alone or in the company of friends following an itinerary worked out in advance. You gain the security of group travel since all details are prearranged by agents skilled in these matters. On the other hand, travelling alone means there is no need to place personal interests second to a group. If this more individual "middle road" style of travel seems preferable, tell a travel agent where you would like to visit, the amount of time at your disposal and the money you wish to spend. Remember, however, that expenses will be higher because you won't get the benefit of discounts available to groups. It's worth bearing a compromise in mind: planning to spend part of a holiday in a group and the rest of the time on your own.

UNPLANNED IMPROMPTU TOURING For many experienced travellers — and in particular for the motorist — holidaying this way is worth the effort involved in fending for yourself, making your own reservations and keeping track of details. You do what you want to do at the pace you decide. If you want to savor the sights in a slower fashion than the crowd, if the rush to take photos, which does happen in a group junket, upsets your holiday equilibrium or if you feel that most of the fun of travel is lost when you continually compromise with the rigors of fixed schedules and "group think", then make one trip as a spirited individualist and you'll undoubtedly become a convert. Motorists enjoy freedom and independence in getting about. Such mobility will enable you to take advantage of hotels and motels located on the outskirts of big cities and in the countryside. These byway places often offer far more value for the money than big downtown hotels, in addition to free parking space and ease in securing accommodation without a reservation.

PRE-DEPARTURE ROUTINE

You can't leave all your cares behind when you make the big getaway, but you can at least make sure that nothing foreseeable was left undone that could disturb your peace of mind and personal well being while sojourning in Canada. Here's a useful pre-departure list.

HOME UPKEEP Arrange to leave a key with a neighbor or relative who can inspect your home regularly and notify police if something is amiss. Police action can do little for you if they are not immediately informed of trouble in your home. A dwelling that isn't maintained and back and front lawns that aren't attended to during a prolonged absence, are tipoffs to prowlers. Police in the larger centres can't cope with all the requests they get to keep an eye on vacationer's homes. If you live in an apartment building, let the superintendent know you are going to be away and ask him to look in on your apartment once in a while.

DELIVERIES Items that are delivered to a dwelling on a regular basis — newspapers, bread, milk and mail — and left to stack up in front of your door are a sure sign that no one is there. Arrange in advance to have these deliveries halted or diverted in your absence. Also arrange to have all handbills and advertising material left at the front door picked up. Apartment dwellers are even more vulnerable. Newspapers stuck in the slot or left to accumulate outside the door or in the mail box are an open invitation to unwelcome visitors, who, all too often, have easy access to loosely guarded apartment buildings.

MISCELLANEOUS Let a neighbor or relative know your itinerary and forwarding address so that he can get in touch with you in case of illness or misadventure. Remove all valuables from the family car and place them in the trunk and deposit jewellery, stocks and bonds in a safety deposit box. Get your name in the society columns *after* you get back home from a vacation. Burglars scan them and know in advance who plans to be away and when. There are various electric timers available that turn lights or a radio on and off at preset hours and leave the impression that someone is about. They cost only a few dollars to install and are the cheapest security anyone can employ. Be sure all windows, doors and the mail box are secured from the inside. It doesn't serve any purpose to leave empty refrigerators plugged in or to have thermostats delivering heat to an unoccupied home. See your insurance agent for taking out travel and baggage insurance. Losing a suitcase or camera far from home is disconcerting; not having sufficient coverage only compounds the disaster.

TRAVEL AND YOUR HEALTH

Often persons afflicted with a chronic health problem hesitate to embark on a lengthy voyage. Even robust and healthy tourists are legitimately concerned about possible medical emergencies. Will a doctor be available if the need arises suddenly? Will he speak English (in Quebec)? Where would he be located? Ask your family physician for names and addresses of doctors in cities you plan to visit. If he is unable to supply you with this information, refer to the hospital or provincial medical association number listed in the phone book. Medical costs, particularly specialist fees, are quite high. Total hospital charges average $1,000 - $1,200 per day. As a precaution, take out economically priced health insurance for protection against unexpected and ruinously expensive medical treatment.

A feature to note on any visitor's medical insurance plan you may decide to get is the period during which benefits are in effect — important to consider in your assessment of the true value of a policy. Some plans written for tourists terminate when the specified period of elgibility has expired. By illustration, if you were to take out 30 day coverage and entered a hospital on the 28th day of your vacation, you would only be protected for the two days remaining on the policy. The type of plan to buy is one that spells out clearly what you're getting. Buy a policy that specifies that if you were to enter hospital on the 20th day of your holiday and you had purchased 21 days insurance, benefits would continue to flow from the medical plan until discharge from the hospital.

One such health insurance policy that fits the needs of persons touring the country (it is not made available to Canadian residents, immigrants or persons intending to apply for immigrant status) is offered by **Ontario Blue Cross.** The **Ontario Blue Cross Health Plan for Visitors to Canada** is both responsible, in terms of its benefits, and reasonable, in terms of its cost. The Blue Cross insurance coverages provides for the payment of charges up to $50,000.00 (Cdn.) per insured person in a hospital anywhere in Canada or the U.S.A., local ambulance services and other related expenses. For an individual, the cost of a policy per day is about $3.00 (Cdn.) and for a family, the fee per day is about $6.00 (Cdn.). The policy can be purchased for a period of up to 60 days. Applications can be obtained by writing **Ontario Blue Cross**, 150 Ferrand Drive, Toronto, Ontario M3C 1H6, or phoning 1-800-668-6262 from inside Ontario, within five days of your arrival.

If you have a history of chronic illness that could be aggravated by the change of routine that rigorous travel entails, get a health check-up and have your family physician enter into a record of some kind, your medical history — illnesses, record of surgery, your blood type and allergies and even his phone number. This information could be priceless for an attending doctor far from home if an emergency arises. If your medical history is quite detailed carry with you a document completed by a doctor or hospital noting the particulars.

Do you regularly require prescription medicines? Do you wear glasses? If you came to see the sights, nothing will erode the enjoyment of a vacation more than the loss of a pair of prescription glasses. A second pair of glasses, handy to have at any time, is worthwhile bringing along on a journey, particularly if you intend doing all or part of a tour by car. As a minimal precaution ask a doctor for a lens prescription. The medicines you regularly require may or may not be available just when you need them. Take enough to last an entire vacation.

Lighthouse near Yarmouth, Nova Scotia.

PACKING TO MEET YOUR NEEDS

If you disregard an axiom of the experienced traveller and take more than essential baggage you may do so at some cost to the pleasure of a vacation. Taking too many suitcases for too few hands is contrary to the instincts of sound planning. Among other things it means you'll be lugging those extra suitcases yourself when porters are unavailable and have additional packing and unpacking to do in moving from hotel to hotel. You can quite safely limit the changes of clothing to carry on extensive journeys, since laundromats and dry cleaning stores give efficient and inexpensive service across the country. Also take into account at the outset the space requirements for purchases of gifts and souvenirs.

By using lightweight luggage of nylon or canvas construction and by improvising — i.e. co-ordinating clothes around one color scheme so that you can mix and match them — it is possible to pack a suitable wardrobe and accessories for a couple of weeks or months' journey and still stay within a reasonable space and weight limit, important to consider whether you go by plane or as one of a group of passengers in a car.

In addition to clothing pack a first-aid kit and bandaids; sewing kit; insect spray (if you are going camping or heading to the far north), sunglasses; paperbacks (including the one you are now reading) for your spare time; facial tissue; a notebook; a plastic bag for separating a wet bathing suit and items that need to be laundered; ball point pen and refill; your driver's licence for car rentals; a small flashlight for reading maps at night; soda pop coolers and lunch boxes for picnics.

TRAVEL TIP Excess passenger and baggage weight puts undue stress on car springs. Distribute the weight burden evenly by placing the heaviest pieces of luggage in the forward section of the back trunk. If you travel by plane, affix a distinctive tag with your name on your suitcase. Many bags are lookalikes and mixups occur at baggage collection points. While you make a connection for Victoria, B.C., someone who took your bag in error could be on his way to San Francisco.

TRAVELLERS CHEQUES AND CREDIT CARDS

Tourists who fail to convert most of their dollars into travellers cheques (preferably Canadian) are taking an unnecessary risk. Such cheques are well worth the 1% service charge. They are almost universally accepted across Canada and money is refunded on unsigned cheques that are lost or stolen. Some travellers find it convenient to take along a reserve of one, five, and ten dollar bills that add a measure of security if it happens (and it does on rare occasions and in out of the way places) that travellers cheques are rejected and it is a Sunday or holiday when banks are closed.

Credit cards are a useful supplement to travellers cheques and carrying both gives you virtually foolproof insurance against financial disaster on a trip. The better known credit cards — Diner's Club, Visa and American Express — may be used in hotels, airlines, car rental offices, restaurants and shops — covering almost as many avenues of spending as exist. Businessmen who journey on expense accounts or on income-tax deductible trips use the vouchers for providing a running account of expenses. The disadvantages in using the well known cards is they are obtainable only for an annual fee and individual credit cards are not universally accepted ordinarily. One caution: keep a record of all credit card expenses so that you are not billed in error for expenses which you did not incur.

An alternative is getting credit cards from major oil companies. They cost nothing and are normally easy enough to obtain. They are especially useful in an interim period until you get restitution if cheques are lost or stolen or if travel cheque funds are depleted. They can also be used for the unexpected emergency — e.g. repair of a car — covering a sizeable outlay that otherwise would be needed for accommodation, meals and fuel. They give credit across North America for gasoline, oil, repair or part replacements and meals and lodging at affiliated hotels and motels.

One of Contestants in Williams Lake Stampede, Williams Lake, B.C.

MOTORING IN CANADA

Probably the most rewarding holiday is experienced by those who have the good fortune to tour Canada by car. By train you see a good deal of the countryside but only from the vantage point of the contours of the track at predetermined speeds and on fixed schedules. Little allowance is made for spontaneous urges to explore the nooks and crannies of the country. The amount of luggage you take is necessarily limited by the need to search unfettered for hotels within walking range of rail or bus terminals. Flights make few physical demands but nothing is seen of the towns, hamlets, the interesting sights and countryside in between. A drive by car through rural areas offers refreshing relief to the demands of city touring.

Running costs needn't be discouraging. For a party of two or more the cost per individual still compares favorably with other forms of transportation, and today, motoring is easier than it has ever been.

By and large, Canada's highway system is quite adequate. Canada's longest continuous road, the Trans Canada Highway, extends nearly 5,000 miles coast to coast from Newfoundland to British Columbia. This $2 billion road is described as a ribbon of asphalt binding the two ends of Canada together; it passes through six time zones and wends its way through almost every variety of scenery over a distance equal to a quarter of the circumference of the world at its latitude. Every care has been taken to meet the needs of the motorist on this well engineered highway system. Picnic tables are situated about every 50 miles off the entire length of this transcontinental highway, camping sites every 100-150 miles. Service stations and restaurants are frequently spaced alongside the road. Directions to campsites, parks and roadside rests are clearly indicated along the highway.

The driving in Canada is almost completely toll-free. There are few toll bridges. The minimum legal driving age in all provinces and territories is 16 with the exception of Newfoundland where it is 17 and Quebec, where it is 18. In Quebec the legal driving age is 16 only if a formal driver's training course has been completed.

On superhighways in Ontario and Quebec it's possible to average 55-60 miles per hour, and plan daily distances accordingly. They can be used if you're pressed for time and enjoyment of the countryside and scenery takes second place. On secondary roads connecting towns and villages and by following a normal sightseeing routine, expect to motor 225-275 miles per day in the east and 300-350 miles daily over roads in the western provinces.

Newfoundland's road system is less developed than in other provinces and driving is arduous over some roads in inland areas. Highways in the far north, if unpaved, are well maintained. The south of Ontario is criss-crossed with high speed expressways and, to a lesser extent, so is Quebec. Cruising along the uncrowded roads in the scenically rewarding Gaspé Peninsula, Cape Breton Island and Prince Edward Island is a pleasure. Motoring is fast paced over less travelled prairie routes.

Police officials can do little if out-of-province visitors park in no parking zones — for the most part. Cars can and do get towed away in the big cities. The downtown areas of Toronto and Montreal are congested with automobiles and parking costs are unacceptably high. For instance, the parking charge in downtown Toronto runs as high as $3-$5.50 for the first hour. Using the inexpensive and reliable public transportation systems in main cities and subways in Toronto and Montreal is a welcome, and at times, more efficient alternative of getting around the inner city. If you came to taste the flavor of old Montreal or historic Quebec City there is no better way to do it than on foot.

TRAVEL TIP Maps of the provinces (included in each chapter) have been designed to illustrate the relative location of touring destinations. Detailed street and road maps of cities and provinces are handed out free as a service of their respective tourist offices.

Hartland's 1282-foot-long wooden bridge

CAR RENTALS

Travellers who arrive by rail, plane, bus or ferry, but prefer to vacation by car will have no problem in locating a car hire office. There are auto rental offices in all the main cities and agencies also operate out of airports. Rentals are generally easy to arrange for the majority of everyday credit cards and involve little delay and paper work. Arrangements can generally be made (for an extra charge) to pick it up in one part of the country and drop it off in another.

There is a wide variety of rental plans. You may pay a flat daily fee for the use of the vehicle, that includes a given number of free kilometers of driving for the day. On another plan, rent and drive the car an unlimited number of kilometers for the day at a fixed rate. Vehicles are obtainable for rental on a weekly or monthly basis. Special weekend and other money saving offers are also featured. Gasoline costs are always extra.

Delivering somebody else's automobile is an alternative to the cost of renting or keeping up your own vehicle. Check the classified ads of daily newspapers for individuals seeking others to share the driving and possibly costs to various destinations in Canada. Auto delivery firms in some major cities, in business for delivering automobiles for others unwilling or unable to motor long distances across the continent, also advertise for drivers. Repair costs are borne by the owner. Little time is allotted for stopping anywhere and seeing the sights. During the peak summer season you can be expected to pay for the opportunity to drive another person's vehicle and for the gas. During the off season it's possible to get an automobile and have full expenses paid.

TOURING ROUTES

For driving peace of mind, plan ahead. Have a reputable mechanic put your car through a thorough check-up and inform him that you are planning an extended trip. Precautions include getting an engine tune-up, checking the spare tire, shock absorbers, lights, wheel bearings, steering mechanism, adjusting the brakes and changing the tires if the tread is beginning to wear thin. It's sensible to take along a

Fruit stand, Okanagan Lake, British Columbia

second spare on journeys to remote areas. Roads are unpaved and service stations are scarce in the sparsely settled far north. Items useful in an emergency are a flare, an aerosol tire inflator, first aid kit, flashlight and extra light bulb, tow rope, even a piece of wood to bolster a jack fitted on a soft road shoulder. As litter laws are enforced across the country, bring along a litter bag.

The sensible way to motor across the land is to get a head start in the early hours of the morning when you're refreshed, drive a few hours on the uncrowded roads, cover much of the mileage planned for the day when it's cool and breakfast around 9 a.m. Quit early — about 3 p.m. — to avoid rush hour traffic in the big cities and driving in dangerous twilight hours, for the opportunity to make a careful selection of hotel and motel accommodation and unwind or sightsee before the evening meal. Superhighways are crowded during summer weekends when local motorists are out in force. The vacationer who can schedule departures on a Thursday and return on a Monday will derive greater pleasure driving under more relaxed and safer road conditions.

A change of drivers or a short break at least every two hours is restorative. Keep a spare ignition and trunk key on your person at all times if a good part of the day is spent behind the wheels of a car and if you are getting out of a vehicle at fairly frequent intervals. At one time or another you could forget to take the key with you and get locked out. Don't forget to carry your driver's licence, motor vehicle insurance liability card and motor vehicle permit.

TRAVEL TIP Keep a roll of small change handy in the glove compartment for the occasional toll road or toll bridge, parking meters and soft drink machines.

Distances and average driving times are given. Note that times and distances are intended to guide, not to live by.

ST. JOHN'S — VANCOUVER via the Trans Canada Highway: Grand Falls to Port aux Basques, North Sydney, Antigonish, ferry from Cape Tormentine to P.E.I., Charlottetown, return to New Brunswick, Fredericton, N.B., diversion to the Gaspé Peninsula, return past Quebec and Montreal, Ottawa, Ontario, Peterborough, Sault Ste. Marie, Kenora, Winnipeg, Manitoba, Brandon, Regina, Saskatchewan, Calgary, Alberta, through Banff National Park, Kamloops, B.C. and Vancouver, 16-17 days, close to 6,000 miles.

TORONTO — BANFF via the U.S.A.: Detroit, Chicago, St. Paul Minnesota, Fargo, N.D., Bismarck, Great Falls, Montana, past Glacier National Park, Lethbridge, 6-7 days, 1,930 miles.

TORONTO — HALIFAX via Montreal, Quebec City, Rivière-du-Loup, Edmunston, Fredericton, Saint John, Moncton and Amherst, 1,132 miles, 3-4 days.

MONTREAL — GASPÉ PENINSULA (and return) Rivière-du-Loup, Matane, Ste. Anne des Monts, Gaspé, Percé, Bonaventure, Matapedia, Sayabec, Lac-des-Aigles, Notre Dame-du-Lac, Saint-Pascal, Montmagny, St.-Philemon, St.-Georges, Sherbrooke, Granby, 5-6 days, 1,200 miles.

WINNIPEG — CALGARY via Portage la Prairie, Brandon, Regina, Medicine Hat, 2-3 days, 820 miles.

VANCOUVER — FAIRBANKS, ALASKA via the Alaska Highway: Hope, Lytton, Williams Lake, Prince George, Dawson Creek, continue on the Alaska Highway to Fort Nelson, B.C., Watson Lake, Yukon, Whitehorse, Haines Junction, Northway Junction, Alaska, 9-10 days, 2,290 miles.

WINNIPEG — PRINCE RUPERT via the Yellowhead Highway that commences by Portage la Prairie: Yorkton, Saskatoon, Edmonton, Prince George, 6-7 days, 1,730 miles.

GRIMSHAW, ALBERTA — YELLOWKNIFE, N.W.T., via the Mackenzie Highway: Manning, High Level, Enterprise, ferry service (June-October) over the Mackenzie River to Fort Providence, Rae, 5-6 days, 955 miles.

NORTH FROM THE U.S.A.

LOS ANGELES TO VANCOUVER via Carmel, San Francisco, Yosemite Park, Oregon, Lassen Volcanic National Park, Portland, Oregon, Seattle, Washington, 4-5 days, 1,435 miles.

NEW YORK CITY TO ST. JOHN'S, NEWFOUNDLAND via Providence, Boston, Bar Harbor, Maine ferry to Yarmouth, N.S., Halifax, North Sydney, N.S., ferry to Port aux Basques, Nfld., Grand Falls, 8-9 days, 1,780 miles.

DETROIT TO CHURCHILL (Hudson Bay) via Madison, Wisconsin, St. Paul, Winnipeg, Manitoba, The Pas, railroad direct to Churchill, 7-8 days, 2,100 miles, of which 460 are by train.

BOSTON TO MOOSONEE (James Bay) via Albany, N.Y., Niagara Falls, N.Y., Toronto, Ontario, Barrie, North Bay, Cochrane, railroad direct to Moosonee, 5-6 days, 1,300 miles, of which 180 are by train.

MILEAGES BETWEEN PROVINCIAL AND TERRITORIAL CAPITALS

Approximate distances by car: To guide — not to live by

City & Province	Charlottetown	Edmonton	Fredericton	Halifax	Quebec City	Regina	St. John's	Toronto	Victoria	Whitehorse	Winnipeg	Yellowknife
Charlottetown, P.E.I.	—	3135	241	161	614	2750	950	1125	3820	4475	2270	4025
Edmonton, Alberta	3135	—	2900	3250	2540	497	4050	2200	925	1300	850	900
Fredericton, N.B.	244	2900	—	325	382	2400	1150	988	3590	4200	2050	3800
Halifax, N.S.	161	3250	325	—	796	2715	851	1305	3910	4525	2285	4150
Quebec City, P.Q.	614	2540	382	796	—	2025	1500	512	3204	3850	1645	3450
Regina, Saskatchewan	2750	497	2400	2715	2025	—	3525	1700	1225	1800	355	1400
St. John's, Nfld.	950	4050	1150	851	1500	3525	—	2000	4750	5400	3170	4950
Toronto, Ontario	1125	2200	988	1305	512	1700	2000	—	2800	3500	1310	3100
Victoria, B.C.	3820	925	3590	3910	3204	1225	4750	2800	—	1700	1560	1775
Whitehorse, Yukon	4475	1300	4200	4525	3850	1800	5400	3500	1700	—	2150	1650
Winnipeg, Manitoba	2270	850	2050	2285	1645	355	3170	1310	1560	2150	—	1750
Yellowknife, N.W.T.	4025	900	3800	4150	3450	1400	4950	3100	1775	1650	1750	—

CANADIAN ROAD SIGNS

The highway signs in use in French-speaking Quebec are designed so that you can understand them even if you aren't familiar with the language. Other provinces also use these illustrations. The signs depicted are important to know since your driving safety and pleasure could depend on recalling them instantly. In general, diamond shaped highway signs are concerned with danger, vertical rectangular ones with regulations.

NO TURNS   NO LEFT TURN   LEFT TURN ONLY   LEFT OR RIGHT TURN ONLY

STOP AHEAD   ROAD NARROWS   UNEVEN ROAD   NARROW BRIDGE AHEAD

CAUTION SHARP TURN   DIVIDED HIGHWAY AHEAD   RAILWAY CROSSING   SLIPPERY WHEN WET

ONE WAY ROAD —NO ENTRY—   NO U TURN   PEDESTRIAN CROSSWALK   REDUCED SPEED AHEAD

MOTORING IN QUEBEC

The difficulties of understanding the complexities of auto repairwork in your own language are compounded when you can't speak to a mechanic in a French language community in Quebec (or elsewhere). The following list of technical terms should enable you to impart or have imparted to you by the mechanic, repair or part replacement needs.

English	French	English	French
anti-freeze	anti-gel	hub	moyeu
axle	essieu	ignition	allumage
battery	batterie	muffler	silencieux
bearing	coussinet	oil	huile
belt	boulon	piston ring	segment de piston
brake	frein		
bulb	ampoule	pump	pompe
bumper	pare choc	puncture	crevaison
carburetor	carburateur	radiator	radiateur
clutch	embrayage	spark plug	bougie
cylinder	cylindre	spring	ressort
distributor	distributeur	switch	contact
engine	moteur	tank	reservoir d'essence
fan belt	courroie de ventilateur	tire	pneu
gasoline	essence	transmission	transmission
gears	engrenage	valve	soupape
hood	capot	wheel	roue
horn	klaxon	windshield	pare-brise
		windshield wiper	essuie-glace

Lake Louise and the Rockies

FERRY SERVICES

Canada's sea lanes afforded early explorers and fur traders a sure means of traversing the country. Rivers, lakes and sea lanes continue to play an important role for transportation in Canada. The two provinces of Prince Edward Island and Newfoundland are only accessible by air or modern steamers. Scheduled ferry services on Canada's Pacific and Atlantic coastlines are supplemented by cruise ships operating during the summer on several of the country's larger lakes and rivers. Leisurely cruises scheduled from St. John's north along the Labrador coast are an unusual travel experience.

Last year more than a million Canadians and Americans used these and other services to get to and around the ten provinces and northern territories. In some cases launches or steamers provide a quicker or less expensive method of getting from one part of the country to the other. For instance, it's much simpler to sail from Bar Harbor, Maine to Yarmouth, Nova Scotia than to follow a more circuitous route by train, bus or car. You can save time by sailing from Vancouver to Prince Rupert direct rather than by driving this route. Car ferries cruising between the Pacific Coast and Alaska offer fine sightseeing along the coastline and a chance for motorists to arrive in the north refreshed.

Many ferries take on vehicles and are equipped with lounges and restaurants.

ROUTE	SAILING TIME	FREQUENCY OF SERVICE
BRITISH COLUMBIA		
Vancouver to Alaska C.N. and B.C. Coast Steamship Service	8 days	Departures from Vancouver every week
Vancouver to Alaska Canadian Pacific	8 days	Sails practically every week in the summer
Vancouver to Victoria Tsawwassen—Swartz Bay	1 hour and 30 minutes	Departs every hour in the summer.

Sailing on Sturgeon Lake in Ontario

ROUTE	SAILING TIME	FREQUENCY OF SERVICE
Vancouver—Nanaimo	2½ hours	3 trips daily eacy way, mid May through mid October.
Port Hardy— Prince Rupert	16½ hours	Departures alternate days from either point, June to September.
Victoria—Seattle (B.C. Steamship)	4½ hours	2 sailings daily from May to October.
Victoria—Port Angeles, Washington	1½ hours	4 sailings daily in each direction from May to September, 2 sailings in each direction in October and November.

NEW BRUNSWICK

Saint John, N.B. to Digby, Nova Scotia	2 hours and 45 minutes	3 trips a day during the summer season, less frequent service in the winter.
Deer Island to Campobello, N.B.	15-20 minutes	Several trips a day in the summer.
Blacks Harbour, N.B. to Grand Manan Island	1 hour and 45 minutes	Five trips weekdays during the summer months.

NEWFOUNDLAND

Port-Aux-Basques, Newfoundland to Sydney, Nova Scotia	Slightly more than 6 hours	One trip per day, increased service in peak season.
Fortune—St. Pierre and Miquelon	1½ hours	Departures twice a week.

NOVA SCOTIA

Yarmouth, N.S.— Bar Harbor, Maine	16 hours	One sailing daily, May to October.

ROUTE	SAILING TIME	FREQUENCY OF SERVICE
Yarmouth, N.S.— Bar Harbor, Maine	6 hours	One sailing daily, May to October
North Sydney, N.S.— Argentia, Newfoundland	18 hours	A sailing every second day.

PRINCE EDWARD ISLAND

Borden, P.E.I.— Cape Tormentine, N.B	40-45 minutes	Departures every hour during the summer.
Souris, P.E.I.— Magdalen Islands, P.Q.	5¼ hours	Two trips daily, except Tuesday, during the summer.
Wood Islands, P.E.I.— Caribou, N.S.	90 minutes	Departures every 50 minutes in the summer.

QUEBEC

Riviere-du-Loup to St. Simeon, Quebec	1 hour and 15 minutes	7 round trips a day in the summer, less frequent service in the spring and fall.
Matane-Godbout, P.Q.	2 hours and 20 minutes	8-12 crossings per day in the summer.
Tadoussac to Baie Ste.-Catherine	About 10 minutes	Averages about 1 trip per hour.
Quebec City—Levis	15 minutes	Twice hourly.

Interior view of Provincial Museum, Victoria, B.C.

ANNUAL FESTIVALS AND SPECIAL EVENTS

JANUARY

British Columbia

Dawson Creek: B.C. Sports Festival — snowmobile racing, speed and figure skating, curling bonspiel.

Newfoundland

Province wide: Winter Carnivals — held in Corner Brook, Labrador City and other communities.

Quebec

Quebec City: International Bonspiel — curling events.

FEBRUARY

Alberta

Banff: Banff Winter Festival, held in the middle of the month.

British Columbia

Dawson Creek: Winter Carnival — snowmobile racing, speed and figure skating, curling bonspiel.

Vernon: Winter Carnival, first half of February.

Manitoba

The Pas: Northern Manitoba's Trapper's Festival — 150 mile world championship dog sled race, canoe and snowshoe racing, mid February.

Beausejour: Winter Farewell Festival — snowmobile racing, parade, pancake breakfast, late February.

St. Boniface: Voyageur Festival — moccasin dancing, parades, costume ball, mid February.

Ontario

Barrie: Winter Carnival — dog team races, broomball championships, mid February.

Toronto: International Boat Show, Exhibition Park, early February.

Quebec

Chicoutimi: Oldtime Carnival — townspeople relive pioneer era with dancing, costumes, parades and winter sports.

Quebec City: Winter Carnival — opening parade, snow sculptures, canoe racing, hockey competitions, dog sled derbies, street dancing, costume ball, held in early February.

Saskatchewan

Yorkton, Prince Albert and other communities: Winter Festivals — sports, dog and snowmobile races, dancing.

Yukon Territory

Whitehorse: Sourdough Rendezvous — sourdough brakfasts, dog team racing, parade, skiing, costumes of '98, mid February.

MARCH

Alberta

Edmonton: Canadian Western Farm Show.

Manitoba

Churchill: Aurora Snow Festival — dog team racing, snowshoe races, log sawing contest, beauty queen pageant, late March.

Northwest Territories

Yellowknife: Caribou Carnival — tea brewing contests, squaw wrestling, 150 mile dog derby, barbershop quartets, late March.

Fort Smith: Wood Buffalo Frolics and Northern Games — cross country ski marathon.

Inuvik: International Bonspiel, late March.

Ontario

Toronto: National Sportsman's Show — exhibits of sporting equipment, dog show, last half of March.

Quebec

Province wide: Maple sugar parties, end of March to early April.

Yukon Territory

Dawson City: Spring Carnival, end of March.

APRIL

Manitoba

Brandon: Royal Winter Fair — livestock exhibits, horse shows and events.

Northwest Territories

Inuvik: Top of the World Ski Championships, cross country skiing, Easter weekend.

MAY

Ontario

Niagara Falls: Blossom Festival — parades, dances, sports events.

Ottawa: Tulip Festival — spectacular displays of tulips across the city, second half of the month.

Saskatchewan

Moose Jaw: International Band Festival — 70 bands, 5,000 musicians attend, late in the month.

JUNE

Manitoba

Flin Flon: Trout Festival — fishing competitions, street dancing, canoe racing, end of the month to early July.

La Broquerie: Fête Franco-Manitobaine — Manitoba's celebration of St.-Jean-Baptiste Day.

Northwest Territories

Yellowknife: Midnight Golf Tournament — an 18 hole round of golf played under the midnight sun, late in the month.

Nova Scotia

Annapolis Valley: Apple Blossom Festival, held throughout the towns of this region, in the middle of the month.

Ontario

Niagara-on-the-Lake: Shaw Festival — plays by Shaw and other dramatists, mid June to late October.

Stratford: Stratford Festival — Shakespeare, chamber music, contemporary plays, opera, ballet, other playwrights, June to October.

Toronto: Mariposa Folk Festival — 3 day festival on Toronto Islands, folk singers and dancers, traditional and contemporary music. Queen's Plate — running of Canada's leading thoroughbred race, end of June.

Quebec

Montreal: Man and His World — exhibits almost as wide-ranging as in Expo '67, mid June to early September.

Province wide: St. Jean Baptiste Day — statutory holiday honoring the province's patron saint, local events and celebrations, June 24.

Yukon

Whitehorse: Annual Highland Games, third week of June.

JULY

Alberta

Calgary: Stampede — free flapjack breakfasts, rodeo, parade, fireworks' displays, chuckwagon racing, Indian encampment, nine days in the middle of the month.

Edmonton: Klondike Days — recaptures atmosphere of the 1898 gold rush, costumes of the era, livestock exhibits, late in the month.

Lethbridge: Whoop Up Days — horse races, rodeo events, mid July.

Medicine Hat: Exhibition and Stampede — farm fair, rodeo, late July.

British Columbia

Nanaimo: Sea Festival — bathtub racing to Vancouver, other events, mid July.

Vancouver: Highland Games.

Manitoba

Brandon: Provincial Exhibition and Stampede — livestock and industrial exhibits, early July.

Dauphin: Ukrainian Festival — Cossack dancing, costumes.

New Brunswick

Shediac: Lobster Festival — parades and dancing, lobster gorging contests, early to the middle of the month.

Saint John: Loyalist Days — recalls with a variety of events the arrival of the Loyalists in 1784.

Nova Scotia

Antigonish: Highland Games — athletic contests, parades, dances and pipe bands, mid month.

Pictou: Lobster Carnival — lobster feasts, early in July.

Pugwash: Gathering of the Clans — highland dances and games, July 1.

Ontario

Cobourg: Highland Games — pipe music and athletic events, early in the month.

Toronto: Caribana — a colourful festival of Caribbean music and art, on Queen's Quay, late July and early August.

Prince Edward Island

Charlottetown: Charlottetown Festival — dramatic performances, July to September.

Summerside: Lobster Carnival — lobster meals, parade, harness racing, mid month.

Quebec

Quebec City: Summer Festival — music, arts and crafts demonstrations.

La Tuque: 24 hour swimming marathon, other events, late in month.

Valleyfield: International Regatta — speedboat meet, early in July.

Saskatchewan

Saskatoon: Pioneer Days — recalls the days of the early west with pioneer exhibits, parades, one week.

Regina: Buffalo Days — rodeo competitions, songs, dances, parades in early costumes, flapjack breakfasts, late in the month.

Swift Current: Frontier Days — cowboys compete in rodeo events, dancing, five days in early July.

AUGUST

British Columbia

Dawson Creek: Fall Fair — rodeo events, middle of the month.

Kelowna: International Regatta — more than 100 aquatic events, early August.

Penticton: Peach Festival — followed by the Square Dance Jamboree, 1st and 2nd week.

Squamish: Logger's Sports Days — tree climb races, log rolling, lumber queen contest, early in month.

Vancouver: Pacific National Exhibition — a wide variety of exhibits, late in August to early in September.

Manitoba

Gimli: Icelandic Festival — songs and dances, first week.

New Brunswick

Caraquet: Acadian Festival, early August.

Saint John: Atlantic National Exhibition — midway, farm and flower displays, other events, late in the month to early September.

Nova Scotia

Bridgewater: South Shore Exhibition — rural fair, ox-pulling competitions.

New Glasgow: Festival of the Tartans — Highland gathering, early in the month.

Ontario

Brantford: Six Nations Pageant — recalls key events of Indian history, first 3 weekends.

Cornwall: Williamstown Fair — Ontario's oldest annual fall fair, late in the month.

Kenora: Lake of the Woods Sailing Regatta, early in the month.

Ottawa: Central Canada Exhibition — farm fair, midway, last part of August.

Toronto: Canadian National Exhibition — world's largest annual fair, last half of August to early September.

Prince Edward Island

Charlottetown: Old Home Week and Provincial Exhibition — livestock displays, varied exhibits, midway.

Tyne Valley: Oyster Festival — parade, fiddling and step dancing championships.

Saskatchewan

Fort Qu'Appelle: International Pow-Wow (at the neighboring Sioux Reserve).

Yukon Territory

Dawson City: Discovery Days — marks the '98 gold rush, in mid August.

SEPTEMBER

Ontario

London: Western Fair — midway, clowns, livestock exhibits, early September.

St. Catharines: Niagara Grape and Wine Festival, late in the month.

Quebec

Montreal: Grand Prix du Canada — car racing.

Trois Rivieres: International Canoe Race, early in the month.

OCTOBER

Alberta

Lethbridge: All Indian Rodeo.

Nova Scotia

Halifax: Atlantic Winter Fair — farm displays, entertainment, end of the month.

Ontario

Kitchener: Oktoberfest — German songs, bands, dancing, beer, in mid October.

Quebec

Montmagny: White Geese Festival, end of October.

NOVEMBER

Ontario

Toronto: Royal Agricultural Winter Fair — livestock and horse shows, jumping competitions, mid November.

Saskatchewan

Regina: Agribition — rodeo events, livestock displays, late in the month.

Saskatoon: Fall Fair — entertainment, livestock exhibits, end of the month.

Swift Current: Old Tyme Fiddling Championships.

DECEMBER

British Columbia

Victoria: Christmas Tree Golf Tournament.

Ontario

Toronto: Annual Craft Show, held at Exhibition grounds.

Toronto or another participating city: Grey Cup — Canadian Football championship, late in November or early in December.

TRAVEL PHOTOGRAPHY

Perfect weather and the most sensitive camera don't guarantee perfect pictures if precautions aren't taken in the care of camera and film. Color film is vulnerable to the extremes of humidity and heat. Excessive heat sometimes damages the camera. Film and camera should both be stored away from the glare of the sun, in a gadget bag or beneath the car seat, *not* on the seat, dashboard or in the glove compartment. Heat isn't the only hazard; dust or sand gathering on the lens can result in spotted pictures and possibly harm the lens. For protection, keep a case and lens cap fitted on the camera whenever it's not in use or place it in a plastic bag.

Check the camera batteries if they haven't been used for some time and have them changed about once a year. In this era of sky-jacking scares, X-rays scan baggage and film exposed to repeated scannings, even film wrapped in a foil or hidden away in your clothes, is sometimes ruined. Air travellers might consider taking the precaution of carrying all film on board in a flight bag or ask officials to examine the bag visually. You can pack in much more film (and at the same time assure customs officers that they are intended for personal use) by throwing away the boxes.

The following exposure table is intended as a guide. An exposure meter is recommended for highly sensitive cameras.

Lighting Conditions	Aperture	Film ASA25-40	Aperture	Film ASA50-64
BRIGHT SUN	1/60	f11-16	1/125	f11-16
HAZY SUN	1/60	f8-11	1/125	f8-11
CLOUDY BRIGHT	1/60	f5.6	1/60	f5.6
OPEN SHADE	1/60	f4	1/60	f5.6

		Film ASA80-160		Film ASA200-400
BRIGHT SUN	1/125	f16	1/300	f16-22
HAZY SUN	1/125	f11	1/300	f11-16
CLOUDY BRIGHT	1/125	f8	1/300	f8-11
OPEN SHADE	1/125	f5.6	1/300	f5.6

CLIMATE AND CLOTHING

There are considerable variations in temperatures prevailing in remote locations in Arctic regions, several hundred miles from the North Pole and on Lake Erie's Pelee Island, the most southerly extension of the country. At Canada's northernmost outposts only two frost-free days are recorded, while the warmest part of the country, Pelee Island on the same latitude as that of California, supports the growth of subtropical vegetation. Winters are long and severe in the west and far north (though not as snowy), less harsh in southern Ontario and coastal regions of the Atlantic provinces. Winter wear is required in most places by early or mid November and the usual accessories of cold weather clothing — overshoes, gloves and scarves — are items winter season visitors should have.

The climate is generally mild the year round on Vancouver Island. Vancouver, on the Pacific Coast, is also subject to less pronounced seasonal variations in temperatures, though seasons in the eastern part of British Columbia have more of Canada's traditionally marked weather changes. Spring thaw doesn't set in until early or mid April in the south, May in the west and June in the far north. When spring does arrive, it is short, almost too short to notice. Spring and the fall — a relatively pleasant September and early October — are both brief transition periods between the winter and summer seasons.

Summer days are surprisingly warm in the sub-Arctic, soaring into the 90's at times. In the southern latitudes, e.g. Toronto or Niagara Falls, daytime temperature ranges from early May to the middle of September are usually comfortable. Shortsleeve dress is standard for morning or afternoon wear in the summer though evenings in the west or Maritimes are often cool enough to warrant the inclusion of a lightweight sweater in your wardrobe. Hunters, campers, canoeists and fishermen sojourning in the north or Rockies should pack, in addition, medium and heavy weight apparel. Summer nights in these parts do get quite chilly. Though precipitation is slight during the summer in the prairies and Ontario, rainwear should completely prepare the visitor for any Canadian weather.

TEMPERATURE AVERAGES

AVERAGE DAILY MAXIMUM — AVERAGE DAILY MINIMUM †

Location	Jan.	Feb.	Mar.	April	May	June	July	Aug.	Sept.	Oct.	Nov.	Dec.
Alberta, Banff	22-4	29-7	38-15	49-25	54-33	65-39	73-43*	71-41	61-35	50-29	34-17	24-8
Alberta, Edmonton	16-2^B	21-2^B	34-13	52-35	64-39	70-46*	74-45*	72-47*	63-39	52-30	34-16	23-5
British Columbia, Vancouver	42-33	46-34	51-37	58-42	65-47	70-56*	70-65*	74-54*	67-50	58-45	49-39	44-35
British Columbia, Victoria	43-36	46-37	50-40	56-43	61-47	65-50*	65-50*	68-52*	68-52	57-46	49-41	45-38
Manitoba, Winnipeg	4-8^B	14-5^B	28-9	42-28	64-44	73-51*	80-57*	78-54*	66-45	52-34	30-16	15-1
New Brunswick, Fredericton	24-4^B	26-4	37-17	49-29	63-39	72-49	78-55	76-54	68-46	56-36	42-26	28-11
Newfoundland, St. John's	33-21	32-20	33-23	42-29	50-35	59-42	69-51	68-53	61-45	51-37	44-32	35-23
Nova Scotia, Halifax	32-17	31-16	38-24	47-32	58-41	67-49	74-56*	75-57	67-51	57-43	47-34	36-23
N.W.T., Yellowknife	10^B-26^B	6^B-24^B	10-11^B	29-7	49-31	61-44	69-52	65-50	52-39	36-26	14-0	6^B-21
Ontario, Ottawa	21-3	22-3	34-17	50-31	65-43	75-53*	80-58*	78-55*	69-48	55-37	40-26	25-10
Ontario, Toronto	21-18	31-17	39-25	52-36	65-46	75-56*	81-61*	78-60*	71-53	58-42	45-33	34-23
P.E.I., Charlottetown	26-11^B	25-10^B	34-8	44-12	57-29	67-50	74-59*	74-58*	66-51	55-42	43-32	31-19
Quebec, Gaspé	16-5	21-4	31-15	41-23	53-36	67-46	76-54	73-49	66-43	54-34	38-27	25-15
Quebec, Montreal	23-8	24-9	35-21	50-34	64-47	74-57	79-62*	76-60	67-52	55-41	41-30	27-15
Quebec, Quebec City	14-5	21-6	32-18	45-31	61-43	72-53	74-59	74-57	65-49	52-39	37-27	24-10
Saskatchewan, Regina	14-2^B	20-0	31-12	45-26	58-37	73-47*	81-52*	78-49	67-39	53-29	31-13	18-1^B
Yukon, Whitehorse	13-8^B	16-2^B	31-12	41-22	57-34	67-43*	67-45*	65-43	55-37	41-28	21-8	11-4

† In degrees Fahrenheit

* Minimum daily average of 8 hours sunshine in the month

^{B} Below zero degrees Fahrenheit

(Courtesy — Government of Canada Weather Bureau)

YOUTH TRAVEL BY HOSTELS

Hostels offer a rough graciousness to travel and a chance for travelling youth to roam the country without going bankrupt in the process. The Canadian Hostelling Association operates hostels in areas across the country including the Rockies, southern and northern Ontario, Vancouver, the eastern townships of Quebec and the Maritimes. Overnight stays (limited to three consecutive nights in some hotels) are quite reasonable in price. They provide a bunk bed and blanket in dormitories, separate washing facilities for men and women and, frequently, a kitchen complete with pots and pans for cooking your own meals. Some provide warm meals. Many have hot showers, and on occasion, a sauna bath.

They generally close for the day, between 9 and 5, to give houseparents an opportunity to rest from coping with the international youth who flock to Canada's 120 hostels. They are an unquestioned bargain. The usual group consists of pre-university, university and postgraduate students who put up with the curfew because these places are so inexpensive. For many, hostels are used as a base for exploring the countryside — to ski, hike, bicycle, canoe or mountain climb, to share or draw upon the travel experiences of others or to meet the young from other nations.

Many hostels remain open all year; others close for all or part of the winter. Guidebooks (available from hostel headquarters) denote which are which, the number of beds, the location, phone number and the local bus or train that serves it. Hostels range in styles from farmhouses to mountain cabins. Membership cards are issued annually and are truly international, valid for all countries of the world where member International Youth Hostel Federation hostels exist. Reciprocally, Canadian branches are open to any member of the I.Y.H.F. Family memberships (good for parents and children 8 - 18) are also obtainable annually. Parents need not accompany children but children may only use the family membership if accompanied by at least one parent. Membership in the C.H.A. is open to any Canadian resident.

The following are Canadian Hostelling Association regional office addresses:

223 Church St., Toronto, M5B 1Z1.
18 The Byward Market, Ottawa, K1N 7A1.
3541 Rue Aylmer, Montreal, H2X 2B9.
1414 Kensington Rd. N.W., Calgary, T2N 3P9.
10926-88th Street, Edmonton, T6G 0Z1.
5516 Spring Garden Rd.. Halifax, B2J 3G6.

HITCHHIKING

Though every hitchhiker has a different tale to tell where it's easiest to get lifts in Canada, British Columbia and Ontario motorists by all accounts give the best rides. Northern Ontario and the sparsely populated prairies get low ratings and Maritimers are reportedly not very sympathetic to hitchhikers. Thumbers in some places are liable to fines — up to $23 anywhere in Ontario — if caught standing off the curb (or on the highways) while trying their luck.

Girls travelling alone get rides much more often than a man travelling alone and a couple hitchhiking together — often she for the protection, he for the easier lifts — usually don't have much trouble. Groups of 3 or 4 get what lifts are left. Preference is often given to well-dressed, clean shaven hitchhikers carrying a "Winnipeg-please" sign. Others have found that the technique of seeming unwashed, outlandishly dressed and creating attention to themselves — jumping up and down on the side of the road, making mock lunges at cars — also seem to get results. The rare desperate soul who blocks the path of an oncoming car influences few motorists this way.

Keep your gear to a minimum. A driver may want to take you but will be discouraged if he thinks there is too little space in his car for your baggage. Locate yourself at access ramps to superhighways and moderate speed zones on the approaches to small towns. Never try your luck just beyond sharp curves or in front of narrow bridges. Probably the best spot to hitch a ride is by traffic lights or stop signs at intersecting roads. A driver already stopped at an intersection will be more inclined to offer a ride than if he is driving by at 60 m.p.h. and couldn't pull over even if he wanted to. Most hikers take a bus or walk to the edge of town. Lifts are generally erratic or unproductive on the way from the town or city centre to the outskirts where the real opportunity and challenge begins.

CAMPING ACROSS CANADA

Canada is superb camping country. The land, approximately 90% uninhabited wilderness, offers virtually an unlimited choice of public and private camping sites within the many hundreds of millions of acres of open spaces and wooded areas. Outdoorsmen may canoe, fish or swim in any of Canada's estimated 1,000,000 lakes, most of which in extremely remote places are nameless to this day. Campers may hike, hunt for game in regions where hardly anyone has ever before roamed or live in surroundings of wilderness at remote lakeside campsites accessible only by gravel road or bush plane. Protection — a net or repellent — is needed against black flies and mosquitoes in camp grounds from the late spring to the middle of the summer.

The federal and provincial governments have taken the needs of the average camper into account — those unwilling or unable to adapt to the demands of outdoor living in the primitive north. Campgrounds with all facilities are maintained in municipal, provincial and national parks set aside at 100-150 mile intervals along the length of the Trans Canada Highway. The advantages of this style of travel are self evident to the experienced camper. There is no need to search for suitable accommodation night after night. They are great money savers. Family groups (and individuals) can vacation this way for as little as $8-11 per person a day. Entrance fees to publicly operated camping grounds range from $3-7. Length of stay limitations vary from province to province. Pets held under control are permitted in national and a number of provincial sites.

Participants in Gimli's Icelandic Celebration

Eskimo tots, Tuktoyaktuk

PERSPECTIVE

LOCATION Alberta, the westernmost of the prairie provinces, is bounded by the Rockies, British Columbia, Saskatchewan, the Northwest Territories and the state of Montana. Calgary lies 1,240 miles north of Denver. Edmonton is located 800 miles east from Vancouver.

AREA Alberta, 246,423 square miles in size, is Canada's fourth largest province.

BACKGROUND The year 1754 marked the appearance of the first European in the area, Anthony Henday, an agent of the Hudson's Bay Company. For over a century the rival fur trading Hudson's Bay and North West Companies opened up and administered new settlements. Ottawa purchased Rupert's Land (that took in present day Saskatchewan and Alberta) in 1869 for $1,350,000. The region began to fill up with land hungry settlers from eastern Canada, the western United States, and the countries of central Europe following the completion of the transcontinental railway and in 1905 Alberta was admitted as a member province of Canada.

POPULATION Approximately 2,200,000.

CAPITAL Edmonton, estimated population 620,000. Fast growing Calgary has 535,000 inhabitants. Lethbridge is a community of 47,000.

LANGUAGES English. There are several bilingual towns north of Edmonton.

TIME ZONE Mountain Standard Time. Noon in Edmonton is 2 p.m. Eastern Standard Time.

WHEN TO VISIT Alberta is a year round vacationland. June, July and August days are pleasantly sunny, but evenings, particularly in the Rocky Mountains, tend to be cool. June and September — when tourists are fewer — are ideal months for a trip to the Rockies. Alberta also appeals to visitors in the winter who are interested in the first-rate skiing offered at the resorts of Banff and Jasper.

ALBERTA

EDMONTON Queen Elizabeth Planetarium in Coronation Park schedules shows on the solar system. Performances are given 3 times daily in summer, while winter showings are featured twice daily on weekends and 8 p.m. from Tuesday to Friday. The McDougall Memorial Shrine, the oldest Protestant (Methodist) church in the region, is a typical structure of the Old West and dates from 1874. It houses relics of the pioneer days which are displayed at 1885 Street in Fort Edmonton Park. Fort Edmonton Park is a reconstruction of an early Hudson's Bay fur Trading Post. At Fort Edmonton Park and 1885 Street, a series of special events is staged in the summer months. The Legislative Building (1913) stands on the original Fort Edmonton grounds. Walter House in Walterdale Historical Park is the first home built in Edmonton (1876). This museum of the pioneer era is open 10-6 daily, July 1-September 1. Storyland Valley Zoo in Laurier Park is worthwhile for both children and adults. It is open from 10-6 p.m., May to October. The Ukrainian Church of St. Josephat, with an ornately decorated interior, is an interesting specimen of religious architecture in the Byzantine style. The church is located at 9th St. and 108 Ave.

EXCURSIONS FROM EDMONTON The 1,300 acre Polar Park, 20 miles east, is a park designed to permit the preservation of animals inhabiting cold-climate regions and is open the year round. Several miles to the north of Edmonton is St. Albert, featuring an old wooden church (1862), a museum with exhibits on pioneer life. **Dunvegan,** in northwestern Alberta, was an early Hudson's Bay Post and fur trading centre for the Peace River region and houses a mission dating from 1867. A church built on the site in 1885 has been converted into a museum showing paintings by its first rector, Father Grouard. A Ukrainian museum is situated in the Mundare area, 55 miles east of Edmonton; medieval manuscripts are exhibited 9:15 to 5, every day. The Great Pioneer Village (seven miles from Spruce Grove on the route west to Jasper) is a preserved late 19th century community. Its sights include an early post office, homes, shops, a school, a church and other structures. The Reynolds Museum in Wetaskiwin, open from May to October, has a large collection of antique automobiles, fire engines, motorcycles, tractors and steam engines. The museum also contains exhibits of Indian and Inuit artifacts. **Red Deer** is known for its bird sanctuary and the restored Fort

EDMONTON

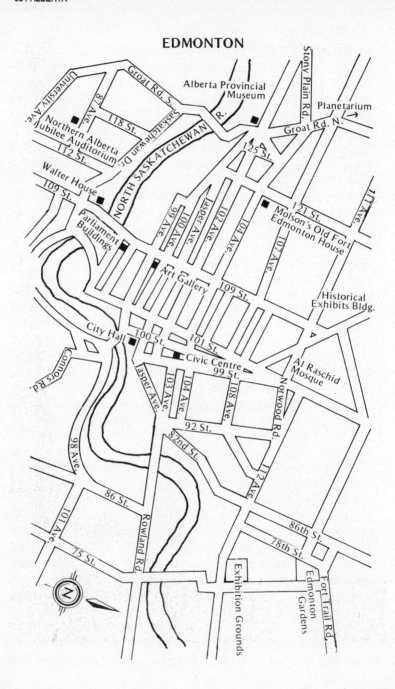

University Ave.

Groat Rd. S.

Alberta Provincial Museum

Stony Plain Rd.

Planetarium

Groat Rd. N.

87 Ave.

118 St.

Saskatchewan Dr.

R.

125 St.

Northern Alberta Jubilee Auditorium

112 St.

NORTH SASKATCHEWAN

121 St.

117 Ave.

Walter House

109 St.

99 Ave.

100 Ave.

Jasper Ave.

102 Ave.

104 Ave.

Molson's Old Fort
Edmonton House

107 Ave.

Parliament Buildings

Art Gallery

109 St.

Historical Exhibits Bldg.

City Hall

100 St.

101 St.

Civic Centre

99 St.

Al Raschid Mosque

Connors Rd.

Jasper Ave.

103 Ave.

104 Ave.

108 Ave.

Norwood Rd.

92 St.

82nd St.

112 Ave.

98 Ave.

86 St.

86th St.

101 Ave.

Rowland Rd.

75 St.

78th St.

Fort Trail Rd.

Edmonton Gardens

Exhibition Grounds

N

Fishing, Jasper National Park, Alberta

Normandeau (1885). A tour south to Drumheller (en route to Calgary) leads to the Badlands, a valley of oddly shaped hills and hoodoos, that is, mounds with a mushroom-like shape. A few reach a height of 125 feet. Bones and even skeletons of dinosaurs were found in the valley late in the 19th century. You can view what's left of a petrified forest here. You'll stop by at an oddity on the trail: a local white and pink church, which holds only six worshippers at a time. The Drumheller museum displays both prehistoric skeletons and discoveries of fossils from the valley. There are both excellent hunting and fishing opportunities and first rate camping facilities in the lake area of Alberta's northeast. There is also hunting and fishing at Lac la Biche summer resort. For visits to Lloydminster, see Saskatchewan chapter.

CALGARY began as a North West Mounted Police fort. The city probably is best known for its Stampede held during July. Events of the week-long Stampede include a colourful opening parade, fireworks displays, an Indian encampment, square dancing on city streets, chuckwagon races, stage shows and cowboys from across the continent competing for cash awards in rodeo competitions. The Calgary Zoo and Natural History Park in St. George's Island near midtown, features a wide variety of animals and birds and some two dozen lifesize reconstructions of prehistoric dinosaurs. While the attraction is open throughout the year, visiting hours vary from the winter to the summer. The Calgary tower commands a view of the city and the surrounding countryside from the observation deck and the revolving restaurant. Visit the Calgary Centennial Planetarium and Aerospace Museum, open daily in the summer months; 1:30-10 p.m., Tuesday-Sunday and Monday from 3:30-10 p.m. in the winter. The planetarium, at 7th Ave. S.W. and 11th St., illuminates the workings of the solar system. Admission is free for Reader Rock Gardens (26th Ave. and 2 St. S.E.) which displays thousands of plants and trees from the South Seas, the Orient and Europe. Open 10-5 p.m. A well preserved church (1874) is open to visitors during the summer at Morley village, 40 miles east of Calgary. Heritage Park, an authentically reconstructed townsite which depicts life in the province prior to and after the arrival of the railway, is open 10-6 p.m., daily, mid May to Labour Day. The park is located at 1900 Heritage Drive S.W.

CALGARY

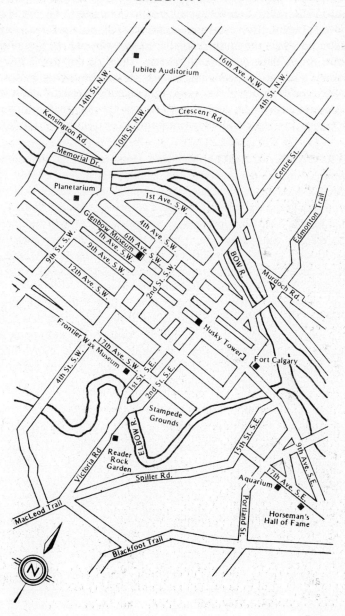

CHILDREN'S EDMONTON AND CALGARY The Old West comes alive for children at Fort Edmonton Park and at 1885 Street, Storyland Valley Zoo always appeals to youngsters. The Badlands have something for everyone — the remains of a petrified forest, hoodoos which are mushroom-shaped mounds and the Drumheller musf m of Alberta's prehistoric era. Alberta's north will suit the family interested in camping, fishing and hunting. Calgary's Zoo, with reconstructions of dinosaurs, is fascinating to tots. Rodeos, with competing cowboys, are featured across the province during the summer. In Calgary, Heritage Park should be of interest to children.

SOUTHERN ALBERTA Medicine Hat Stop in at the pioneer museum and see the stampede and fair staged at the end of July. Free tours are conducted through the Altaglass plant where you may watch skilled glassblowers at work. **Lethbridge**'s Indian Battle Park highlight is Fort Whoop Up, a trading post built in 1870 and featuring relics of the pioneer era; a rodeo takes place in town each July. Those with an interest in gardens may visit the Japanese Garden in Henderson Park. You may take an excursion from here to Waterton National Park or to Fort Macleod, site of an R.C.M.P. post (1874) and the earliest settlement in the area. Frank features the phenomenon of a two-mile-wide valley filled with rocks as big as a home. A landslide destroyed the town in 1903. An early Mormon home and temple stand in **Cardston**, a community established by Mormons immigrating here from Utah in 1888. The temple opens during the late spring and summer and the home, daily 9-5, in July and August. It closes Sunday.

HISTORIC SITES, MUSEUMS AND ART GALLERIES Edmonton The Provincial Museum and Archives, 12845 2nd Ave., is highlighted by fine natural history, pioneer history and Albertan Indian sections. Many hours could be devoted to this interesting museum, open 9-9 p.m., daily, from late spring to the end of the summer. Visiting hours are reduced during other months. The Edmonton Archives at 10,105 112th Ave., traces with its exhibits, the course of the city's history. The Edmonton Art Gallery, 102nd Ave. and 99th St., displays works mostly by Canadian artists, from 10:15-5 p.m., Monday to Saturday, and Sunday afternoons. The Reynolds Museum in Wetaskiwin, housing exhibits of old farm implements and antique cars, is open 10-5 p.m., every day, from early May to late

September. **Calgary**'s Glenbow Museum displays Indian exhibits and pioneer crafts. Also featured: a coin collection, Eskimo artwork, replicas of the Crown Jewels and weapon displays of both world wars. Glenbow Art Gallery, in the same building, features art from the western pioneer era. Both the museum and art gallery are open 11-7 p.m. daily. The Homestead Antique Museum in Drumheller depicts life in early settlements from 9-6 p.m., May-October. Other museums of early Canadian life are located at Grande Prairie (April-October), Lethbridge and Medicine Hat (late spring and summer). An open air museum of pioneer Canada stands a few miles outside of Spruce Grove.

MUSIC AND THE THEATRE Edmonton's Jubilee Auditorium, the centre of the city's cultural life, offers concerts, theatre, opera and ballet performances. Information on current production is available in the daily newspapers. The Banff Summer School of Fine Arts gives courses in dancing, creative writing and painting, while Banff's Summer Festival features ballet, concert, opera and dramatic performances by students. A two-week Sundance Festival is held every August in the Blood Indian Reservation, 19 miles south of Fort Macleod. Edmonton's Citadel Theatre is a professional group, offering half a dozen plays during the season. Theatre Calgary also performs a series of plays during the season. Drama presentations are staged in Calgary's Allied Theatre. The Calgary Philharmonic Orchestra features a series of concerts from the fall through to the spring months.

HUNTING AND FISHING Big game species in the mountains are Rocky Mountain bighorn sheep, timber wolf, mountain goat and mountain lion, antelope, stone sheep, grizzly bear, black and the occasional brown bear. The abundant upland game birds and waterfowl include geese, several varieties of grouse, quail, many species of duck, pheasant and partridge. Small game are fox, rabbit, cougar and coyote. Anglers have their choice of Arctic grayling, northern pike (as high as 35 pounds) and rainbow trout in the many lakes. Other fish yielded in provincial waters include cutthroat trout, walleye (up to 15 pounds), goldeye and whitefish. Information on recent provincial hunting and fishing regulations is available from the Fish and Wildlife Branch, Department of Lands and Forests, Natural Resources Building, Edmonton.

Indian Medicine Man at Banff Indian Days Celebration

ALBERTA

Wood Buffalo
Natl. Park

Lake Athabasca

SASKATCHEWAN

Dawson Creek

Grimshaw

Lesser Slave Lake

Grande Prairie

Lac la Biche

Vermillion

Jasper Natl. Park   Edmonton   Lloydminster

Jasper   Hinton   Elk Island Natl. Park

Wetaskiwin

Lake Louise   Banff Natl.
Park   Red Deer

N

Calgary

Brooks

Medicine Hat

BRITISH COLUMBIA

Pincher Creek   Lethbridge
Ft. Macleod

Waterton Lakes Park

Glacier Park   Cardston

MONTANA

WINTER AND SUMMER SPORTS Skiing is excellent at resorts in the Rockies. Three favorites in Banff National Park are Lake Louise, Sunshine and Mount Norquay. Sunshine Village, a top ski area 16 miles southwest of Banff, provides chalets, 5 chair lifts, 3 T-bars, 1 tow and 1 Gondola. Marmot Basin in Jasper National Park has 3 double chair lifts and 2 T-bars. The season runs from late November to April. Skiing facilities operate at Fortress Mountain in the Kananaskis region. Skiing is also a feature of the Edmonton and Calgary districts. Other winter sports are curling, snowmobiling, skating, cross country skiing, snowshoeing, tobogganing and hockey. The several golf courses in Edmonton and Calgary are a few of more than 100 in operation in Alberta. Tennis courts are open to the public in Jasper, Banff, Edmonton and Calgary. Swim facilities are provided in the main cities and at provincial and national parks; most recreation areas offer boating facilities. You may hike, ride and climb at Banff and Jasper. Canadian Football League games are played in Calgary and Edmonton from July to late November. There are two National Hockey League teams in Alberta: the Calgary Flames and the Edmonton Oilers. Professional soccer (NASL) is played in both cities. Other spectator sports include cricket, horse racing in Edmonton (July, August) and Calgary (July, September), hockey, baseball and auto racing.

NATIONAL PARKS Banff is Canada's best known national park, one of the scenic splendors of North America. It's situated approximately 75 miles west of Calgary and contains many of the Rockies' peaks in its 2,500 square mile area. The town of Banff features a museum with displays of local fauna and flora and rock samples; open all day during the summer. The Buffalo Paddocks, on the edge of town, offers views of buffalo. Other interests include the Upper Hot Springs, with swimming pool and steamchamber, a few miles south of Banff, daily cruises for sightseeing in Lake Minnewanka, summer courses at the Banff School of Fine Arts, lifts to Sulphur Mountain, Mount Norquay and visits to the lovely Lake Louise surrounded by the Rockies. Other attractions include Bow Falls, glaciers, wooded valleys, rivers and streams, Sundance Canyon (a four-mile hike from Banff), numerous lakes, animals roaming free and drives to Moraine Lake. **Jasper National Park** (1907), on the eastern half of the Great Divide, is 4,200 square miles in size. The park boasts trails, beautiful mountain lakes, exceptional scenery and wildlife (moose, deer, bear). The park's administrative centre is in Jasper with restaurants, motels, lodges and hotels. The townsite is a base of departure for visiting Lake Maligne and canyon, 30 miles east. Sightseeing cruises features views of spectacular mountain scenery. Tours lead to Miette Hot Springs whose springs bubble forth at 132°; the outdoor pool is supplied with mineral waters. Columbia Icefield (120 square miles of ice) is frozen thousands of feet deep in parts, the source of diverse rivers. Three mile snow-mobile rides are a highlight of a summer tour. A cable car lifts sight-seers from a 4,000 to a 7,500-foot level of Whistler's Mountain. Here you can picnic, take tea, lunch, hike and observe the view. Other interests are trips to Mount Edith Cavell (11,000 feet), Medicine Lake, Lake Pyramid and Athabasca Falls. The park opens through-out the year. **Waterton Lakes National Park** (1932) is the Canadian half of the combined Waterton Lakes-Glacier National Park of Montana. Its 200 square miles feature hiking trails, a buffalo herd, valleys, lakes, camp sites and waterfalls. Buses drive by way of Akamina Highway to Cameron Lake in the park's southern sector. Waterton town, overlooking Waterton Lake and surrounded by peaks, is the park's administrative centre. It features restaurants and hotels. **Rocky Mountain House National Historic Park** in central Alberta is 50 miles west of Red Deer. Fur trading posts were erected here in the first half of the 19th century. On display are chimneys, all that remains of the fort built in 1866. **Elk Island National Park** isn't far from Edmonton. The 75 square mile park, open all year, offers wildlife, a buffalo herd, picnic grounds, camp-sites, many lakes and wooded areas. Accessible by way of the Yellowhead Highway which runs past this recreation area. The parkland's administrative centre is situated by Astotin Lake.

FOOD AND DRINK Alberta restaurants are well-known for deli-cious ribs and thick, succulent steaks. The delicious Arctic char (shipped from the north) is served locally. Enjoy free servings of flap-jacks and bacon for breakfast in the centre of town during the Cal-gary Stampede. In the past several years, (as in other major centres in Canada), a number of fine new restaurants have opened in both Edmonton and Calgary. Try any of the excellent Canadian ales, beers and whiskies. You may purchase beer or liquor (in individual bottles or cases) in provincial liquor outlets. Bars and beverage rooms remain open to midnight, dining rooms usually to 11:30 - 2 a.m. The legal drinking age in the province is 18.

TRANSPORTATION IN ALBERTA Alberta has a good road system, leading to major destinations in all directions. On rural roads there is usually no traffic congestion. A particularly fine highway connects Calgary and Edmonton and on this route the motoring is fast paced. Cars are available for hire from major auto rental companies in major tourist centres. Rail service connects Calgary (and Banff) and Edmonton (and Jasper) by train with the rest of Canada. Rail service is furnished from principal cities in eastern Canada on a daily basis. Air service between Calgary and Edmonton and from Calgary and Edmonton to other centres is provided on a frequently scheduled basis every day of the week by major airlines. Buses operate in rural areas, between main centres, to the north, points in the U.S. and to the rest of Canada on the trans Canada bus route.

SHOPPING Good buys in Alberta are furs and Hudson's Bay point blankets, produced since the fur trading years of the pioneer era of Canada. You've a good choice of Eskimo and Indian handicrafts— baskets, totem poles, moccasins, dolls and leatherwork. Western attire (cowboy boots, hats) is readily available. Eskimo carvings imported from Arctic regions make a unique gift or souvenir and their artwork is becoming progressively more valuable. Top department stores are Eaton's, Simpons-Sears, Woodward's and The Bay. Most shops remain open 9-6 p.m., to 9 p.m. Wednesday, Thursday and Friday evenings. Oil-rich Alberta is the only province that hasn't had to impose a sales tax on goods purchased. **West Edmonton Mall** is perhaps the most impressive shopping centre in Canada, and indeed, North America. The mall features many hundreds of stores along with varied amusement facilities to keep youngsters entertained while adults shop.

ACCOMMODATION Banff Voyager Inn, 555 Banff Ave., Box 1540, (403) 762-3301, convenient to downtown, 85 rooms, colour TV, satellite TV, parking, coffee shop, dining room serving buffet of Chinese foods daily, outdoor pool, sauna, hot tub, major credit cards, nightly entertainment. **Brooks** Heritage Inn, 1303 2nd St. W.

(403) 362- 6666, 64 rooms, colour TV, phones, air conditioning, satellite TV, coffee shop, dining room, lounge, sauna, swimming pool, parking. **Calgary** The Westin, 4th Ave. at 3rd St. S.W., (403) 266-1611, 550 rooms, colour TV, downtown location, shops, barber and beauty shops, health club available, heated indoor parking, lounge, indoor swimming pool, sauna, room service, car rentals, 2 fine restaurants. Sheraton Cavalier, 2620 32nd Ave. N.E., (403) 291-0107, near airport, 251 rooms, coffee shop, restaurant, 2 lounges, indoor heated pool, sauna, no smoking rooms available, disabled facilities, pets permitted. Holiday Inn Downtown, (403) 263-7600, 8th Ave. at 6th St. S.W., 201 rooms, radio, TV, heated car parking, no smoking floor, outdoor swimming pool, gift shop, fine restaurant, close to museum. Holiday Inn, (403) 287-2700, on 42nd Ave., MacLeod Trail, 159 rooms, radio, TV, indoor pool, restaurant, lounge, parking, not far from downtown, major credit cards. **Edmonton** Westin Hotel, 101st Ave. and 100th St., (403) 426-3636, 420 rooms, non smoking floors, located in city center, specialty dining room, 2 lounges, restaurant, indoor swimming pool, sauna, exercise room, colour TV, car rentals, beauty shops, 24 hour room service, indoor parking. Nisku Inn, at international airport, 148 rooms, air conditioning, parking, pool, sauna, whirlpool, coffee shop, dining room, night club, major cards accepted, free transportation to and from airport 24 hours a day. Relax Inns, Edmonton South, 10320 45th Ave., (403) 436-9770, 227 rooms, colour TV, heated indoor pool, restaurant, major credit cards, whirlpool, free parking, offers good value. Relax Inns, 18320 Stony Plain Rd., (403) 483-6031, 228 rooms, colour TV, air conditioning, parking, major credit cards. Sheraton Plaza, 10010 104th St., (403) 423-2450, 140 rooms, downtown, near sightseeing attractions and West Edmonton Mall, coffee shop, no smoking rooms available, disabled facilities, 2 restaurants, sauna, lounge, heated indoor pool. Holiday Inn Edmonton (403) 429-2861, 107th St. and 100th Ave., downtown, near Government Buildings, 15 floors, 186 rooms, coffee shop, dining room, lounge, outdoor swimming pool, gift shop, parking available, major credit cards. Hilton Hotel 10235 - 101 St. (403) 428-7111, near City Hall, Edmonton Convention Centre and shops, spacious guest rooms have colour TV, mini bar, non smoking floors, twice daily maid service, excellent restaurants and lounges, lobby lounge, English Pub, concierge, indoor swimming pool, whirlpool, health club, first rate service, 24 hour room service. **Jasper** Sawridge Hotel, 82 Connaught

Drive, (403) 852-5111, a beautiful and modern property, features 154 rooms, colour TV, air conditioning, indoor pool, whirlpool, sauna, hot tub, cable TV, dining room, coffee shop,nightly entertainment, parking, major credit cards, lounge. **Lethbridge** Pepper Tree Inn, 1142 Mavor Magrath Drive, (403) 328-4436, 56 rooms, colour TV, air conditioning, parking, ice machine, restaurants nearby, close to Japanese Garden, coffee shop, hot tub, open all year, major credit cards. **Slave Lake** Highway Motor Inn, Box 1519, (403) 849-2400, 76 rooms, colour TV, room phones, parking, main credit cards accepted, friendly service. **Vegreville** Wild Rose Inn, 6001 50th Ave., (403) 632-6263, 51 rooms, colour TV, air conditioning, satellite TV, water beds, parking, restaurants nearby, open all year, free coffee, all credit cards accepted. **Red Deer** Red Deer Flag Inn, 4217 Gaetz Ave., (403) 346-6671, 63 rooms and suites, each room has TV, dining room, lounge with live entertainment, steak pit, licensed coffee shop, sauna, free parking.

Barkerville, British Columbia

PERSPECTIVE

LOCATION British Columbia, Canada's westernmost province, lies between the Rockies, the Yukon Territory, the Northwest Territories and the Pacific Ocean and the states of Alaska, Idaho and Washington. Vancouver, on the Pacific coast, is 5,000 road miles from St. John's, Newfoundland, at the eastern extremity of the country.

AREA B.C., 344, 817 square miles in area, ranks third in size among the provinces.

BACKGROUND British Columbia was first sighted by Sir Francis Drake in 1759. The territory was governed by the Hudson's Bay Company until 1849 when Vancouver Island was ceded to England and declared a British colony. The discovery of gold in the Fraser River in the late 1850's drew a great many newcomers to the mainland and it too was declared a colony. The two colonies united and agreed to enter Confederation as a Canadian province in 1871 on the condition that a transcontinental railway be built to link the east with the Pacific coast. That condition was fulfilled by 1885.

POPULATION 2,800,000, third highest in Canada.

CAPITAL Victoria, estimated population 226,000. Close to half of B.C.'s population reside in Vancouver, Canada's third largest city, population 1,200,000. Penticton has 22,000 residents.

LANGUAGE English is the medium of expression of virtually everyone.

TIME ZONE Pacific Standard Time. Noon in Vancouver is 3 p.m., Eastern Standard Time.

WHEN TO VISIT The climate in communities along the Pacific coast is fairly mild the year round. Many times the weather is pleasant enough in Victoria and Vancouver during January for a round of golf. On the other hand, the colder interior of British Columbia is outstanding for winter sports from December through March. Summer days are comfortably warm but, at times, rainy along the coast. The Okanagan Valley can be quite hot on occasion in the months of June, July and August.

BRITISH COLUMBIA

VANCOUVER The main attraction in Vancouver is **Stanley Park.** Its 1,000 acres offer picnic grounds, totem poles, a view of the city and harbour, quiet pathways, and golfing. Also see the acquarium, a zoo, take tea or a meal, bicycle, ride a train, watch cricket or play tennis. Stanley Park's aquarium houses the usual array of sea life gathered together in an exhibit of this sort — sharks, turtles, alligators, tropical fish and even killer beluga whales. Open 10 to 6 p.m. in the summer months. Chinatown is interesting as one of the largest Chinese communities in North America. **Gastown** in old Vancouver is a renovated district now comprised of restaurants, boutiques and antique shops. The city's several gardens include the Japanese Friendship Garden (in New Westminster suburb) with flower-bedecked paths and cherry trees, the Century Gardens Park and Central Park in the suburb of Burnaby, and Queen Elizabeth Gardens with its Bloedel Conservatory on Little Mountain. The conservatory houses a wide variety of plants. The Van Dusen Botanical Display Garden contains native and exotic plants. Open daily at 10. British Properties is a fine residential section of West Exhibition Park at East Hastings, has the British Columbia Pavilion with its impressive B.C. relief map, seven years in the making and with its impressive B.C. relief map, seven years in the making and the Indian museum. The Pacific National Exhibition is held here. One reward of an excursion to Burnaby and Burnaby Mountain Park is the great view you get of the modern Simon Fraser University on Burnaby Mountain. The 1,000 acre campus of the older and equally fine University of British Columbia (1914) is noted for its Nitobe Gardens and the Museum of Anthropology, with its fascinating collection of native totem poles and native Indian art. Capilano Canyon is interesting: you can walk along the scary 450 foot-long suspension bridge 230 feet above the Capilano River. Things to do outside of the city include joining a harbor tour, operated at least once a day out of the Denman St. pier. More frequent service is scheduled in the summer. Catch the Super Skyride, a cablecar to the top of Grouse Mountain 3,700 feet above sea level, and take in a marvellous view of the area. Other possibilities include taking an excursion to Vancouver Island or driving to scenic Horseshoe Bay or Whitecliff Park where you may swim and picnic in summer, and ski during the winter.

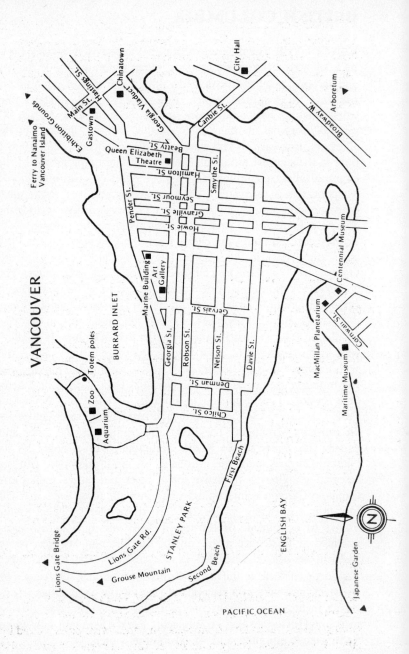

VICTORIA on Vancouver Island enjoys Canada's mildest climate. The main attraction is **Butchart Gardens**, the floral showpiece of North America, featuring four gardens in one (Italian, English rose, Japanese and sunken) within a space of 32 acres. It's located at Brentwood and stays open throughout the day and evening with the entire gardens illuminated at dusk, May to September. The Parliament Buildings (1898), near the waterfront, are open on weekdays 8:30-7:30 p.m. in summer, 8:30-4 p.m. weekdays in winter. Nearby **Thunderbird Park** is noted for its Indian totem poles, carvings by coastal tribesmen and displays of native arts and crafts. Many of the poles date back to the late 1800's. Carvers constantly create new poles on the site since the old ones have a limited life span. Undersea Gardens is in the neighborhood; it displays a variety of marine life on view, 9 a.m. to 9 p.m., daily from late May to the middle of September. Craigdarroch Castle (on Joan Crescent), erected 1888, is interesting for its interior and stained glass windows. Open daily in the summer, 9 a.m. to 9:15 p.m. Beacon Hill Park's 154 acres, in the city centre, houses one of the world's highest totem poles. Helmcken House, by Thunderbird Park, is one of Victoria's original homes (1852). It is maintained as a museum, open every day but Mondays, 10-5 p.m., May to September. Visiting hours are reduced the balance of the year. Point Ellice House at Pleasant and Bay St. is a century old, charming home depicting life in the Victorian period (open 10-5 in the summer, 12-4 in the winter). Sealand on Oak Bar Marina offers additional glimpses of sea life and has 2 killer whales performing in the interesting Killer Whale show. Bastion Square is noted for its refurbished mid 19th century buildings. The Dominion Observatory on Little Soanich Mountain, featuring one of the world's largest telescopes, accepts visitors 9:30-4:30 p.m. English village on Lampson Street has the world's only replica of William Shakespeare's home (furnished in the 16th and 17th century styles), in addition to Anne Hathaway's thatched roof cottage. Both open from 9-9 p.m., May to October. A new attraction to visit is Crystal Garden, a tropical garden under glass roof, filled with exotic plants and birds.

CHILDREN'S VANCOUVER AND VICTORIA Stanley Park in Vancouver provides interests for every member of the family — golfing, hiking, a tea house, an aquarium and totem poles carved by gifted B.C. Indians. Many families will find Victoria's Thunderbird

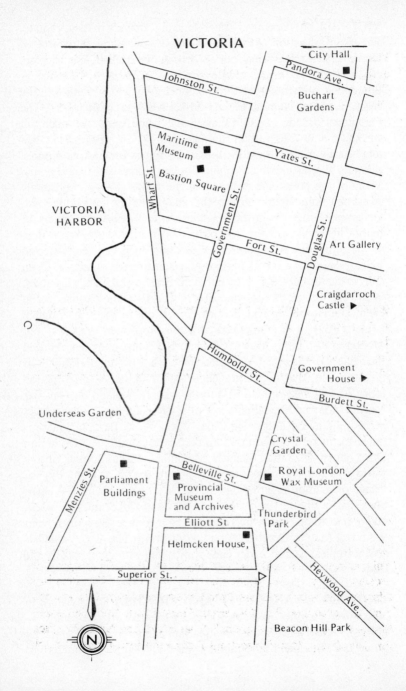

Park with its totem poles very interesting. Vancouver's Lippsett Indian collection of artifacts is housed in the Centennial Museum.

Victoria's Wax and Classic Car museums are excellent for family outings on rainy days. **Excursions from Victoria and Vancouver.** Okanagan resorts offer family vacation pursuits: museums, the Okanagan Game Farm near Penticton, boating on the many lakes and free ferry cruises on Kootenay Lake. Barkerville has something for everyone; it recalls the way of life of the gold rush era with renovated old buildings, a saloon, barber shop and entertainment of the late 1800's.

EXCURSIONS FROM VICTORIA Fisgard Lighthouse and Fort Rodd Hill are seven miles west on Route 1. The fort was restored in 1963 after having been used as a garrison for various periods from 1898-1945. British Columbia Forest Museum, 1 mile north of **Duncan,** provides an account of the Canadian lumber industry. An ancient logging locomotive chugs its way along the site from 10-5:30 daily from mid May to mid September. Another attraction is the Old Stone Church, constructed in 1871. While it has been refurbished, services haven't been held here in close to 100 years. A century old church is found in the nearby Indian village of Tzuhalem. **Nanaimo** The Bastion is a Hudson's Bay fortress built in 1854. The museum housed in the edifice is open from late in May to the middle of September. Petroglyph park, 1½ miles south, is noted for its petroglyphs or ancient rock carvings dating from a period of ancient history too distant to calculate. Ferries sail the route between Nanaimo and Vancouver. Many of B.C.'s provincial parks are located here, including the huge Strathcona Provincial Park, with soaring peaks and offering fishing, camping facilities, skiing or hiking. Elks Falls Park, not far from Campbell River, is another fine recreation area. Excellent salmon fishing draws anglers to the community of Campbell River.

OKANAGAN VALLEY AND KOOTENAY REGION Penticton This summer resort and fruit packing centre in the Okanagan fruit growing valley is 245 miles east of Vancouver. The Penticton Museum and Archives (Main Street) is open every day, 1-9 p.m., mid June to September. The Okanagan Game Farm, five miles south, houses a variety of exotic animals from Africa and North America, on view all day. Other attractions include the Peach Festival (early

August) and the Square Dance Jamboree staged a few days later. The September Harvest and Grape Fiesta marks the annual harvest. Winter skiing is featured at Apex Alpine. The Dominion Observatory just south of here is open 2-5 on Sunday afternoons, July and August. **Kelowna** fruit farming region and vacationland features tours of its fruit-packing plants and local museums. The Kelowna Blossom Time Sailing Regatta in late July is very popular, and in the winter you can enjoy fine skiing in the vicinity. **Vernon** is another fruit-packing centre and holiday region. Highlights are summer boating in the Kalamalka and Okanagan Lakes, skiing in the vicinity and the annual February Winter Carnival. The Kootenays' 17,500,000 acres consist of wooded hills, magnificent peaks, lakes, valleys, fruit farms and national parks, including Kootenay National Park. **Nelson** The town stages the weeklong Midsummer Curling Bonspiel in early July. Other interests are the Indian Museum — open daily, June and July — and sporting facilities. Some tourists take advantage of the free ferry cruise operated from Balfour on Kootenay Lake. **Trail** Cominco operates a 2 hour tour of a metallurgical-chemical fertilizer plant. Exceptional scenery, skiing, hunting and fishing characterize the region's holiday appeal. The Kaiser Resources in Sparwood have 2 hour tours of the surface mines, underground mines, and reclamation and preparatory plant. Nearby Rossland contains the historical museum and the LeRoi mine. Both the mine, dating from 1891, and the adjacent museum receive visitors on daily tours, summers. Winter ski facilities operate here. Creston is home to the Blossom Festival every May. Boswell, 22 miles north, contains the curious dwelling made of 500,000 12-ounce bottles; the home took eight years to construct. **Kimberley** operates free daily conducted tours of the Sullivan zinc and lead mines and free morning visits of a fertilizer factory.

TO THE NORTH There are a number of places to see and things to do on the route north to Prince George, a route that corresponds to the former **Cariboo Trail.** The trail originates from Lillooet and was built during the gold rush of the early 1860's. Clinton has the South Cariboo Historical Museum on Cariboo Highway 97. Excellent hunting is a feature of the locality and lake resorts dot the area north from here. Lac la Hache town is located by a lake of the same name. This region is also noted for fine hunting and fishing. During the winter season Lac La Hache is the starting point for the

BRITISH COLUMBIA

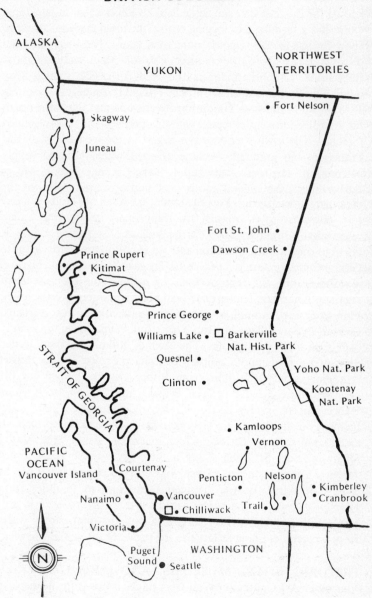

Cariboo cross country ski marathon (Canada's second largest such competition). Williams Lake, in a cattle-raising region, is primarily known for the four-day stampede held here every year in late June. Quesnel is a farming and logging centre; the town provides access to good fishing in the region's numerous lakes. The local museum displays items from the pioneer era, on view summer days. **Barkerville**, established during the gold rush, was named after miner Billy Barker who struck it rich. The gold rush began a boom in 1858 in the Fraser and Thompson Rivers area and the surge north for gold filled the entire region with prospectors. Only a few gained fortunes. The town was once the largest in the west north of San Francisco, but gradually became deserted when the gold supply petered out. The renovated church, Wake Up Jake Saloon, Moses Barber Shop, the general goods store and other reminders of the period are worth seeing. **Fort St. James,** site of an old Hudson's Bay fort, contains graves of early fur trappers. A neighboring Indian reservation is home to 5,000 Carrier Indians. Top fishing resorts lie north of the location. **Hazelton** and old Hazelton are tourist gems in Gitksan Indian country. The Skeena Treasure Home in old Hazelton is worth visiting; this reproduction of a native home is a museum of regional Indian life. Numerous totem poles add interest to the town. Plan your day around a visit to the authentically reconstructed Gitksan Indian Village of Ksan. Other Indian villages in the vicinity have even more totem poles. The town of **Kitimat** operates guided tours of the Aluminum Company of Canada Project. **Prince Rupert** is a Pacific port 470 miles from Prince George, known for the excellent Museum of Northern British Columbia on 1st Avenue. Prince Rupert is also accessible from Vancouver by ferry. The highway north from Prince George to Dawson Creek passes through exceptional scenery. Dawson Creek marks the start of the Alaska Highway. **Fort St. John** stages a three-day western rodeo every August. The ruins of an 85-year-old mission chapel stand on the town's outskirts. W.A.C. Bennett Dam, located 15 miles from Hudson's Hope, is one of the world's greatest hydro-electric projects. Williston Lake, the reservoir behind the dam, stores water from a catchment area as large as the province of New Brunswick.

HISTORIC SITES, MUSEUMS AND ART GALLERIES

Vancouver Art Gallery on West Georgia St. is noted for its displays of Canadian art, including many of the works of Emily Carr and the

Close up of 90 year old totem pole

famed (Canadian) Group of Seven. Paintings and Indian handicrafts are displayed 10-5 p.m., Tuesday-Saturday and on Sunday afternoon. The MacMillan Planetarium has daily presentations on the workings of the solar system. The Maritime Museum is visited principally for the 110 foot-long Arctic ship St. Roch (constructed in 1930), which cleared the difficult Northwest Passage en route to the Arctic Ocean. The return trip was completed over a period of four years between 1940-44. Lippsett Indian Museum in Exhibition Park (open 11-5) is noted for a fine collection of the artifacts and life of the B.C. Indian. Old Hastings Mill in Pioneer Park, dating from 1866, has been converted to a museum of pioneer Vancouver. Irving House located in New Westminster, a suburb of Vancouver, is a fine museum of Victorian life. **Victoria** The British Columbia Provincial Museum next to the Parliament Buildings (open daily) houses sections concerning natural history, B.C. Indian artifacts and modern history. The Wax Museum is a facsimile of the well known Tussaud museum in London and exhibits wax figures of historical personalities and the English royal family. The Classic Car Museum at Douglas St. and Humboldt contains other wax figures and an array of antiquated deluxe cars. Open 9-9 p.m., in the summer, 9-5 in the winter. Thunderbird Park offers varied totem poles and Helmcken House, a pioneer museum. The B.C. Maritime Museum in Bastion Square (open daily) is a worthwhile museum of its kind. Craigflower Manor, five miles from town on Island Highway, constitutes a museum of mid 19th century life in B.C. Open every day but Monday, from mid May to mid September; closed Mondays and Tuesdays during the winter months. Fable Cottage at 1587 Cordova Bay Rd. (an extension of Marine Drive) features a unique handcrafted home on a waterfront estate, open from late March to October. Parksville, on Island Highway north of Victoria, has a good museum with displays on various items, including a number of original Edison phonographs. Fort Langley was a Hudson's Bay outpost from 1828. Today it's a regional history museum, open 10-9 p.m., summer days.

MUSIC AND THE THEATRE Vancouverites support a symphony orchestra, opera association and professional theatre groups. Opera, jazz and dramatic performances are featured in the Queen Elizabeth Theatre and the Orpheum. You can enjoy outdoor summer concerts at Stanley Park. The summer Internation Arts Festival presents ballet, musicals and attracts well-known guest artists. Many small theatre groups are active in Vancouver. Current plays being offered are listed in local newspapers and magazines. Variety shows and concerts are presented summer weekdays at Victoria's Butchart Gardens. Musical performances or drama are offered at Barkerville's Theatre Royale. Summer festivals are held elsewhere in the province.

HUNTING AND FISHING British Columbia supports a wide variety of major game. Hunters may stalk caribou, moose, mountain sheep, wolf, grizzly and black bear, mule deer and black tailed deer. The west coast and interior offer good waterfowl hunting. Anglers can pit their skills against a variety of species of salmon: chinook, cohoe, pink and sockeye. Other fish species yielded by provincial waters include mountain whitefish, brown, brook, lake, Dolly Varden, steelhood and steelhead trout (up to 35 pounds) and perch. Information in detail concerning recent hunting and fishing laws in B.C. is obtainable from the Ministry of the Environment. Fish and Wildlife Branch, Parliament Building, Victoria, B.C. V9V 1X4. For information on regulations concerning tidal water fishing, contact the Marine Resources Branch, Ministry of Environment, 1019 Wharf St., Victoria, B.C. V8W 2Z1.

WINTER AND SUMMER SPORTS There is excellent skiing in many parts of the province. The season runs well into the late spring at Whistler Mountain Ski area and the facilities here are very fine. Highlights of the Big White Mountain ski area, 42 miles southeast of Kelowna, include ski lessons, a lodge, one double chairlift, three triple chairlifts and three T-bars. At Big White you'll find an entire on-mountain ski village with accommodation for over 2,000 skiers. Whistler is famous for the longest vertical drop, serviced by lifts, in North America. Courtenay's Forbidden Plateau Ski Run (13 miles to the north) offers rope tows and T-bars during its November to May season. Other skiing facilities exist in Nelson, Trail, Kimberley, Revelstoke, Rossland, Penticton, Mount Seymour and at Grouse Mountain, Vancouver. Kamloops' Tod Mountain has one of North America's longest beginner runs. It is 5 miles long. Other winter sports are skating in rinks, curling and snowmobiling. The professional Vancouver Canucks perform against competing teams in the National Hockey League during the season, which runs from the fall to early spring. The B.C. Lions Football team is a member of the western division of the Canadian Football League; the season extends from August to November. Vancouver also offers a professional soccer team, the Vancouver Whitecaps. Golfing is popular practically the year round in Vancouver and Victoria and several courses accept the visiting public. Tennis courts are open to visitors at many of Vancouver's parks e.g. Queen Elizabeth Gardens, in other main centres and in popular resort areas. Safe swimming opportunities abound at Vancouver's English Bay Beach, at Stanley Park's Third and Second Beach, municipal swimming pools at Kitsilano, Spanish Banks, provincial parks and in the Okanagan Lake resort region. Kelowna stages an aquatic festival — the Kelowna Regatta — in late July. Boating and yachting facilities are quite extensive in the many lakes of the Okanagan region, at Stanley Park, around Vancouver Island and in the provincial park system. House boating on the Shuswop Lakes is very popular during the summer months. The Bowron Lakes chain provides excellent recreation for the canoe enthusiast. Boats can be hired by the hour or day in both the Vancouver and Victoria districts. Bicycles may be rented here also. Roller skating is one of the more popular sports in Stanley Park. Unlimited trails lure the hikers in Stanley Park, in Strathcona and Garibaldi provincial parks, other B.C. and national recreation areas. Other sports are mountain climbing, lawn bowling, lacrosse, trotting and horse racing (in Exhibition Park) and baseball.

NATIONAL PARKS Fort Langley National Historic Park is located on the south bank of the Fraser River, 25 miles east of Vancouver. The fort's reconstructed palisades, buildings and authentic furnishings allow the visitor a glimpse of Canada's pioneering past. **Kootenay National Park** straddles five miles of both sides of a 60-mile portion of the Sinclair-Vermilion stretch of the Windermere-Banff Road. Its 543 square miles contain many animals including moose and deer; picnic and camping sites operated from May to the end of September; hiking trails, canyons and glaciers. (Permission to hike and booklets are available at the information office.) Canoes are permitted in Kootenay National Park. Radium Hot Springs by the park's western entrance has 112° springs; bathing is featured in outdoor mineral spring pools. Marble Canyon rates as one of the park's most spectacular canyons. **Glacier National Park** in southeast B.C. is a lovely wilderness area, containing within its 520 square miles glaciers, ice-fields, peaks, meadows, forests, canyons and waterfalls. Camp sites operate in the summer. Activities include hiking, skiing and mountain climbing (register with the park warden for this). The towns nearest to the park are Golden to the east, Revelstoke to the west. **Yoho National Park** is located west of the Continental Divide, not far from Banff. Within the 507 square-mile area are riding trails, hiking paths, picnic and camping sites. Emerald Lake, Takakkaw Falls, Natural Bridge and Lake O'Hara are prominent sights. The park headquarters are in Field. **Fort Rodd Hill National Historic Park** is located on Route 1A, 10 miles west of Victoria on the way to Sooke. The fort was used for coastal defence until 1956. The Fisgard Lighthouse close by, is one of the oldest lighthouses on the west coast. **Pacific Rim National Park**, situated on the west side of Vancouver Island, is one of Canada's newest national parks. The park contains camping grounds at present and has supervised swimming. The spectacular, 250 square mile park stretches along 65 miles of the open Pacific Ocean. **Mount Revelstoke National Park** is close to Revelstoke along the Trans Canada Highway. The parkland offers winter skiing, hiking (40 miles of hiking trails) and picnic spots. An unpaved road leads to the top of Mount Revelstoke.

FOOD AND DRINK Not surprisingly, the coastal province serves a good deal of ocean-caught seafood. Local specialties include clams, oysters, shrimp, King crab, smoked black cod, many varieties of trout and halibut. It's possible to sample five varieties of barbequed salmon. Cariboo beef, roasts and steaks are delicious. The province's orchards are famed for their great variety of fruit, their apples, cherries, peaches, berries, apricots and other delicious fruits available at low prices in fruit stands. Chinese, Japanese, Mexican, Polynesian, German and Italian foods are specialties of Vancouver. The province produces wines made of grapes, blackberries and loganberries. Liquor, beer or wines are sold in provincial liquor outlets. The legal drinking age is 19.

TRANSPORTATION IN BRITISH COLUMBIA The road system is well maintained throughout the province. Prince Rupert is the terminus of the Yellowhead Highway that begins by Portage la Prairie, Manitoba and crosses the northern section of the Canadian West. The Alaska Highway extends from Dawson Creek to Fairbanks, Alaska. June, July and August are the easiest months to travel this dusty unpaved road. It's risky to attempt the trip without a car that is completely serviced and bring along at least two spare tires. Trancontinental train service is scheduled from the east. Provincially owned trains penetrate the north country. Cars are available for hire in all tourist centres. Bus companies provide access to every community in B.C., conducted tours of the province and scheduled connections with the rest of the country and the U.S.A. Vancouver city buses give dependable service to the early morning and double decker buses brought in from London have been used for Vancouver city sightseeing. Airplanes fly to remote communities in the north. Boats sail between several coastal communities. Boat companies schedule service from Washington State, cruises are operated to the north and regular ferry crossings link Vancouver and Victoria. Sightseeing launches tour Vancouver harbor and the coast. For detailed information see Ferry Services.

SHOPPING Leading department stores are Woodward's, the Bay and Eaton's. Import shops sell a variety of wares in Vancouver's Robson Street, sometimes known as Robsonstrasse. Miniature carved Indian totem poles are sold in Vancouver and Victoria. The durable Cowichan Indian woolen sweater is a provincial specialty. Chinatown is a prime shopping locale for items of Chinese origin. Victoria's shops stock bone china, English imports, tweeds and woolens at attractive prices. Eskimo soapstone carvings, goods made of local woods and fruits from the Okanagan Valley add to the variety of shopping specials. A provincial sales tax is imposed on goods purchased.

ACCOMMODATION Burnaby Sheraton Villa Inn, 4331 Dominion St. (604) 430-2828, near airport, 275 rooms, 12 suites, coffee shop, restaurant, pub, lounge, entertainment, indoor and outdoor heated swimming pools, non smoking rooms available, parking. Holiday Inn Metrotown, 4405 Central Blvd., (604) 688-1779, 100 rooms with colour TV, parking available, Boulevard Cafe where all meals are served, shops, lounge with dart board, big screen TV and dance floor. **Campbell River** Painter's Lodge, lovely property, popular with fishermen as well as with tourists, dining area, bar, free parking, swimming pool. **Chetwynd** Chetwynd Court Motel, 5104 52nd St. on Hwy. 97, on route to Alaska Highway, downtown location, 14 rooms, colour TV, phones, cooking units, complimentary coffee, near restaurants, friendly service, Master Card and Visa accepted, parking. **Glacier National Park** Best Western Glacier Park Lodge, 51 rooms, colour TV, satellite TV, heated outdoor pool, sauna, 24 hour coffee shop, dining room, parking, open all year, major credit cards accepted, lounge, gift shop, museum and information centre next door, beautiful surroundings. **Lac La Hache** Mile 115 Lodge, on Hwy. 97 just south of Lac La Hache, 10 rooms, colour TV, pub, restaurant, weekend entertainment, close to lake and beaches, main credit cards accepted, free parking. **Manning Provincial Park** Manning Park Resort, (604) 840-8822, 41 rooms, chalets, parking, dining room, coffee shop, cross country skiing trails, canoeing, hiking, swimming, sleigh rides in winter, horseback riding offered by Manning Park riding stable near the lodge, relaxing atmosphere, lovely setting, tennis courts. **Nakusp** Selkirk Inn, 210 6th Ave. W. (604) 265-3666, 25 rooms, cable TV, kitchenettes, sports and movie channels, games room, sauna, parking, **Prince George** Holiday Inn Prince George, (604) 563-0055, 444 George St., city centre via Queensway, 140 rooms, indoor swimming pool, no smoking floor, Traders Dining Room, Coaches corner pub. den lounge, parking. Northwood Motor Inn, 2270 Hart Hwy. (604) 563-0456, 25 rooms, colour TV, phones, kitchen units, parking, pub, open all year, main credit cards accepted, restaurant next door, live entertainment nightly. **Prince Rupert** Rupert Motor Inn, central location, rooms with TV and private bath, free parking. **Terrace** Cedars Motor Hotel, 4830 Hwy. 16W (604) 635-2258, 22 rooms, kitchen units, TV, free parking, open year round, Master Card and Visa accepted. **Tumbler Ridge** Tumbler Lodge Inn (604) 242-4277, 50 rooms, colour TV, phones, kitchenettes, some suites as well, parking, lounge and pub, 2 restaurants, evening entertainment, open all year, major credit cards. **Valemount** Sarak Motor Inn, on Hwy 5, 69 rooms, colour TV, some air conditioned, swimming pool, whirlpool, dining room, coffee shop, not far from Jasper National Park, major cards accepted. **Vancouver** Holiday Inn Vancouver - Broadway, (604) 879-0511, 711 West Broadway Ave., rooms with radio, TV and phones, Cherry Tree restaurant, two movie theatres, health club, sauna, swimming pool, free parking, lounge, exercise room, airport shuttle bus. Hyatt Regency Vancouver, 655 Burrard St., (604) 687-6543, 651 rooms overlooking the harbour and surrounding mountains, in city centre, gourmet restaurant, rooftop show lounge with panoramic view, 6 restaurants and lounges, shopping mall in the complex, near Stanley Park. Four Season's Vancouver (604) 689-9333, 385 rooms on 28 floors, with mini bar, colour TV, in-house movies, 24 hour room service, same day laundry service, valet parking, health club open all day, indoor and outdoor heated pools, formal dining room, garden lounge, piano music nightly. Sheraton Landmark Hotel, 1400 Robson St., (604) 687-0511, near Stanley Park, 360 rooms, lobby cafe, revolving dining room, lounges, jacuzzi, no smoking rooms available. Sheraton Plaza 500, 500 West 12th Ave., (604) 873-1811, 153 rooms, 4 suites, near B.C. Stadium, dining room, lounge, entertainment, pub, no smoking rooms, facilities for disabled. The Westin Bayshore, West Georgia at Cardero, (604) 682-3377, 519 rooms, air conditioned, on Vancouver harbour overlooking Stanley Park, minutes from downtown, outdoor and indoor swimming pools, sauna, exercise rooms, South Seas cuisine in restaurant, colour TV, barber shop, lounge. New World Harbourside Hotel, 1133 West Hastings St., (604) 689-9211 or 1-800-663-8882, lovely rooms, Channel Bar, Lobby Lounge, excellent restaurants, Chinese cuisine, shoreline or skyline views from 4th to 18th floors, suites available, fitness centre with a year round pool, sauna, gym. Le Meridien Vancouver, 845 Burrard St. (604) 682-5511, in central Vancouver, close to shops, theatre and business district, with 397 rooms, air conditioning, colour TV, in house movies and mini bar, 24 hour room service, concierge, health club and spa with sauna, comfortable lounges, French cuisine served, informal dining area, valet parking, limo service, swimming pool. Royal Garden Hotel, 110 Howe St. (604) 684-2151, in the heart of downtown near shops and entertainment area, 210 rooms with cable TV and in house movies, non smoking rooms available, indoor heated swimming pool open all year, Royal Garden restaurant for fine dining, Ryan's Lounge, near Stanley Park and Gastown. **Victoria** Casa Linda Motel, 364 Goldstream Ave. (604) 474-2141, rooms with colour TV, free parking, near Fort Rodd Hill National Historic Park. **Wells** (Barkerville) White Cap Motor Inn, Ski Hill Rd., (604) 994-3489, 30 rooms, each room can handle 4 to 6 people, colour TV, free parking, beautiful setting, winter skiing, Ginger Jar Restaurant nearby, best place to eat in town, brunch, salads, luncheon, specialties include salmon teriyaki, open from 10 a.m.

TRIP SUGGESTION The vacationer bound for western Canada can combine a trip to mainland British Columbia with a cruise along its Pacific coast. The seven day voyage on **Admiral Cruises's M.V. Stardancer** originates from and concludes in Vancouver. These **Ad-**

miral week-long sailings, offering passengers the opportunity to view the spectacular coastal scenery, take you past the Inside Passage and Bella Coola, off northwestern British Columbia, and then continue to Juneau and Haines in Alaska. On the return portion of **Admiral's** sailing, the *Stardancer* sails past Tracy Arm's Glaciers, Ketchikan and Misty Fjords and once again voyages past the Inside Passage before docking at the end of the cruise in Vancouver. The **Admiral Cruise** sailings are scheduled every summer from June to September. Staterooms have two lower beds, a radio, closed circuit TV, and a telephone. Entertainment is featured nightly and there is a casino on board. Reservations for these popular **Admiral Cruise** sailings are recommended well ahead of time.

MISCELLANEOUS

PROVINCIAL TOURIST BUREAU Tourism British Columbia, 1117 Wharf St., Victoria, B.C. V8W 2Z2.

VISITOR INFORMATION CENTRES Greater Vancouver Visitors and Convention Bureau, 650 Burrard St. Each town and city throughout the province has a Chamber of Commerce information centre which can provide information on area attractions.

PERSPECTIVE

LOCATION The prairies begin in Manitoba, the geographic centre of North America. Manitoba is also a maritime province, with 400 miles of coastline on Hudson Bay to the north. Churchill port here offers access to Hudson Strait and beyond to the North Atlantic.

AREA Of Manitoba's 211,470 square mile area, 40,000 square miles are fresh water.

BACKGROUND The boundaries of present day Manitoba were included in the fabulous domain — called Rupert's Land — governed by the Hudson Bay Company from 1670. Until 1812 fur trading remained the main activity in the region. A group of pioneer settlers setting out from Scotland reached the present site of Winnipeg in 1812 and the scant wheat harvest in the fall of that year marked the beginning of the prairies' tradition as Canada's bread-basket. The Canadian government purchased the territory in 1869. A short lived provisional rebel government led by Louis Riel was removed and in 1870 Manitoba was admitted as the fifth member of Confederation.

POPULATION Estimated at 1,050,000.

CAPITAL Winnipeg, population approximately 600,000. Brandon has a population of close to 35,000.

LANGUAGES English. Both French and English are spoken in Winnipeg's neighboring municipality St. Boniface.

TIME ZONE Central Standard Time. When the clock reads noon in Winnipeg, it is 1 p.m. in the Eastern Standard Time Zone (i.e. in Toronto-New York), 2 p.m. in the Atlantic Standard Time Zone (Halifax), 11 a.m. in the Mountain Standard Time Zone (Calgary-Denver) and 10 a.m. in the Pacific Standard Time Zone (i.e. in Vancouver-San Francisco).

WHEN TO VISIT Ideal times to journey here are June, July and August. The first few weeks in September can also be good. The fall promises excellent duck hunting and fishing; the winter, theatre and ballet.

MANITOBA

WINNIPEG The Legislative Building is similar in appearance to many other North American legislative buildings. You may view the interior on your own or by scheduled tours (9-7:30 p.m.), every day from May to September. Visiting hours are reduced in other months. Features include the dome surmounted by the six ton Golden Boy statue, sculptures, statues and murals. The local Grain Exchange (Winnipeg Commodity Tower) conducts free guided tours of trading floor activities weekday mornings. The Winnipeg Centennial Centre on Main St. houses the Planetarium, the Museum of Man and Nature and the Concert Hall. Assiniboine Park and Zoo encompasses 390 acres of parkland with animals from around the world roaming its zoo. Also featured are picnic grounds, winter sports facilities, an English garden and flower shows in the conservatory. Kildonan Park, another fine recreation area of 90 acres, draws visitors interested in winter and summer sports as well as summer concerts staged at Rainbow Stage outdoor theatre. Both parks remain open all day. Seven Oaks House was completed in 1851; it's the oldest habitable home in Manitoba, displaying furniture of the period. The northern Gateway on Main Street is all that was left after Upper Fort Garry was demolished. It had served from the 1830's to 1881 as the regional centre of the Hudson's Bay Company. Several multi-domed Ukrainian churches are to be seen about the town.

EXCURSIONS FROM WINNIPEG St. Boniface has a city museum of pioneer Manitoba and adjoining the basilica, a cemetery contains the grave of Louis Riel, conspicuous in events influencing the history of western Canada. The Royal Canadian Mint offers tours on the half hour from 9 a.m. to 3 p.m. weekdays. **Upper Fort Garry** It's a well-preserved Hudson's Bay Company fur trading post on 14 acres of grounds. Attractions dating from the 1830's include the fur loft, blacksmith shop and the Governor's Residence. Open 9 to 6, May to late in October. **Selkirk** is a point of departure for cruises on Lake Winnipeg; five-day cruises lead to Berens River, Hecla Island and Gimli. St. Peter's Church, (a few miles north at Dynevor), was a mission to the Indians built in 1853. Whiteshell Provincial Park is excellent for hunting, camping, fishing, picnics and boating and for canoeing on its many rivers and lakes. St. Andrews Church by Lockport was constructed in the early 1800's and is still in use; buffalo skins to kneel on add an interesting touch.

WINNIPEG

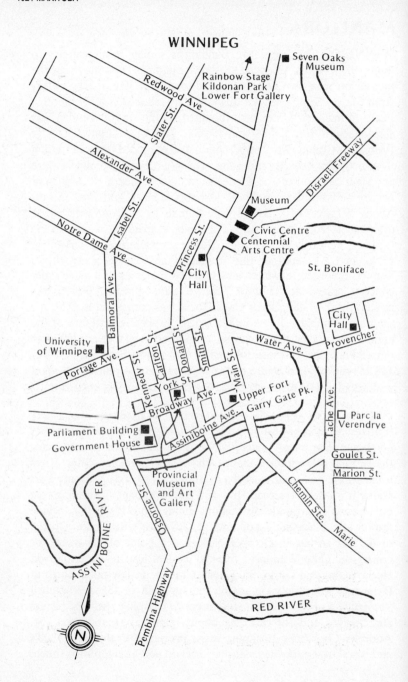

The Mennonite pioneer village of Steinbach dates from 1873, the year the Mennonites settled here.

SOUTH AND WEST MANITOBA Portage la Prairie was constructed on the site of Fort la Reine, established by the famed explorer La Vérendrye. The Yellowhead Highway starts its northward route from this point. The wheat and industrial centre of **Brandon** stages the June Provincial Exhibition, a fair with carnival and agricultural exhibits. International Peace Garden extends into North Dakota. It was created in 1933, complete with pathways, wooded areas, lakes and picnic grounds, to mark the frontier between Canada and the United States, the longest unfortified border in the world. The 50,000 acre Spruce Woods Provincial Park is noted for its sand dunes. There is a classic auto museum in **Elkhorn** near the Saskatchewan border. **Souris** in the Brandon region attracts rockhounds who pay for the right to collect rocks. The 580-foot-long footbridge spanning the Souris River is the longest in Canada; Hillcrest (pioneer) museum is nearby.

TO NORTHERN MANITOBA Dauphin is not far from Duck Mountain Provincial Park (camping) and Riding Mountain National Park (bison herd). It's also used as a base of departure for trips to the north and for boating, swimming and fishing in the region's waterways. The city is the scene of an annual Ukrainian Festival in early August. **The Pas,** 500 miles north of Winnipeg, served once as a major fur-trading centre. Events of the February Trapper's Festival include dancing, dog team racing and ice fishing. See the Anglican Christ Church built in 1839 (with its original furniture intact) or tour the local museum concerned with Indian life and fur trapping. Trains depart from The Pas for trips to Churchill on Hudson Bay. The mining centre of **Flin Flon** conducts tours of mining operations. Hunting and fishing flourish in the area (e.g., in Clearwater Provincial Park). A Trout Festival in late June and early July offers street dancing, canoe and beauty contests. **Churchill** is 530 miles north of The Pas, accessible by train or plane. A major attraction of this summer port is travelling by boat to the partially restored Fort Prince of Wales, completed from 1732-70 and noted for its 40-foot-thick walls. It was surrendered to the French without a single shot being fired in 1782 and is now cared for by the Canadian government. The Eskimo museum, the remote location and the Beluga whales in

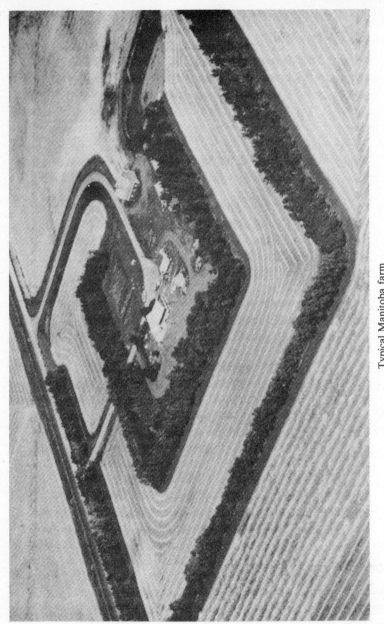

Typical Manitoba farm

MANITOBA

surrounding waters add to the town's appeal. Hunting and fishing are superb in the far north.

HISTORIC SITES, MUSEUMS AND ART GALLERIES Winnipeg's Art Gallery (at 300 Memorial Blvd.) displays Eskimo and Canadian art 11 a.m. to 5 p.m. Tuesday to Saturday, noon to 5 p.m. on Sundays and holidays. The Manitoba Museum of Man and Nature, 190 Rupert Avenue, has exhibits on the natural history and development of the province throughout its 7 galleries; new sections are being added. Open 10-9 Monday to Saturday and from noon to 9 Sunday, mid May to mid September. In winter, the museum is closed during the evenings. Seven Oaks House was erected in 1851 by fur trapper John Inkster who immigrated from Scotland. This museum of the pioneer era is located on Rupert's Land Avenue, West Kildonan and stays open 10-5 daily, June to mid September, from 10 to 5 weekends, mid May to mid June. The stone Red River House (1867) was home to Captain Kennedy, an agent for the pioneer Hudson's Bay Company. It contains items of the period and of Manitoba life in general; open 19-7 late May to late October, weekend afternoons the balance of the year. **St. Boniface**'s Museum (1847) at 494 Taché Ave. recalls early Manitoba history. It is open for tourists but visiting hours vary considerably. **Portage la Prairie** is visited for its Fort la Reine Pioneer Village and Museum which depicts life in early settlements. The schoolhouse, log cabin and church may be toured 10-6 p.m. from mid May to October. **Austin**'s Agricultural and Homesteaders Museum has a fine collection of antiquated cars and farm machinery. The village, which includes three log buildings, a church, a post office, livery barn and grist mill, is open every day from May 1 to October 30. Other museums are situated in Minnedosa, Killarney, Virden, Morden and Churchill.

MUSIC AND THE THEATRE The fine Winnipeg Symphony Orchestra gives a dozen concerts from September to May and features many celebrated guest artists. The widely acclaimed Royal Winnipeg Ballet's season extends from October to April though it often visits other cities across North America during the winter. The Royal Winnipeg Ballet also features performances in the summertime. The Manitoba Opera Association presents an exciting array of world artists in full scale productions during November, February and April. Broadway musical shows are staged in Kildonan Park's

2,500-seat outdoor theatre, Rainbow Stage, during July and August. Top Canadian actors appear in several major plays throughout the winter season at the highly rated Manitoba Theatre Centre, while the Warehouse Theatre presents popular, informal productions as well. The Canadian Ukrainian Festival is highlighted by Cossack singing and dancing. Songs, dance and drama are a feature of the Icelandic Festival held in Gimli, the first week in August.

HUNTING AND FISHING White-tail deer are found in most parts of the province; black bear and moose are plentiful in the northern forests. Game birds and waterfowl include several species of grouse, snow and blue geese, duck, pheasant, snipe, ptarmigan and partridge. The opportunities for hunting game birds are excellent in the early fall. Waterfowl abound in southern Manitoba's lakes, ponds and grain fields before they migrate south for the winter. You may be able to arrange whale hunting in northern Manitoba off Hudson Bay. Sportsmen have their choice of the exotic Arctic char, Arctic grayling, northern pike (up to 25 pounds), lake and brook trout and walleye. Information regarding current hunting and fishing laws is obtainable from the Department of Natural Resources, 1495 St. James Street, Winnipeg, Manitoba, R3H 0W9.

WINTER AND SUMMER SPORTS Falcon Lake ski area, 100 miles east of Winnipeg, provides rope tows, ski instruction, skating, tobogganing and equipment rentals; tows operate on holidays and weekends. Holiday Mountain ski resort (110 miles from Winnipeg) has two rope tows, nine slopes, two T bars, a ski school and a ski jump. Mt. Agassiz ski resort in Riding Mountain National Park offers seven slopes, two rope tows, three T-bars, ski lessons and rentals. There are 250 curling rinks in Manitoba. You can skate in Kildonan Park, St. Vital Park and Assiniboine Park. Golf in White-shell Provincial Park, Riding Mountain National Park, Hecla Provincial Park, Selkirk, on six public courses in Winnipeg, Beausejour (nine holes), Portage la Prairie, Dauphin, Brandon, Souris, The Pas, Flin Flon and in other communities. There are a number of tennis courts open to the public in the capital. Swimming is excellent (and safe) in the pure waters of many provincial parks — Whiteshell has 130 lakes — at several pools in Winnipeg, off the beaches of Winnipeg Beach on Lake Winnipeg. Canoeing is popular in northern rivers and lakes. Boating and yachting opportunities abound in

Lakes Winnipeg, Manitoba and Winnipegosis. Hiking trails are marked out in most of the provincial and National parks. The football season of the professional Winnipeg Blue Bombers of the Canadian Football League extends from July to November. Horse racing fans head to Assiniboia Downs from early May to October. The Winnipeg Jets of the National Hockey League play from September to April. Other spectator sports include (summer) lacrosse, wrestling, boxing, soccer and cricket.

NATIONAL PARKS Riding Mountain National Park is 170 miles north and west of Winnipeg. Its 1,155 square mile area offers numerous lakes, golfing, tennis, water sports, horseback riding, hiking and camping sites. The resort town of Wasagaming contains a small museum, open from the middle of May to mid September. **Prince of Wales National Historic Park** is found at Churchill, Hudson Bay. Highlights of the 40 acre park, accessible only by boat during fair weather, is the Fort Prince of Wales. This British-built fort, dating from the mid 18th century, boasts 40-foot-thick walls. **Lower Fort Garry National Historic Park:** This Hudson's Bay stone trading post was completed in the 1830's; the 14-acre site is open every day for conducted tours from mid May to mid October.

FOOD AND DRINK Dishes reflect the composition of the local population: Sample pea soup in St. Boniface, German, Italian, Chinese, Polynesian, Ukrainian and Scottish specialties. There are many good steak houses in Winnipeg. Restaurants in the city are known for goldeye, a tasty smoked fish available in few other parts of Canada. Provincial government liquor stores open 11 - 8, beer stores 10 - 8 p.m. Drinks are served 5 p.m. to 2 a.m. in cabarets, between noon and 1 a.m. in licensed dining rooms, 9 a.m. to 1 a.m. in beverage rooms and in beer parlors for men only between 11 a.m. and midnight. The legal drinking age is 18.

TRANSPORTATION IN MANITOBA An extensive highway system criss-crosses the southern part of the province. Trains and planes are the only way to get to Churchill in the far north, where a unique transport service, dog sled taxis, operates during the winter. You can rent a car at many locations throughout Manitoba. Portage la Prairie marks the beginning of Yellowhead Highway, a route that extends across the northwestern part of the country as far as Prince Rupert.

The Trans Canada Highway leads to Ottawa in the east and to Regina in the west. Small aircraft may be chartered to get to dozens of communities — charter outfits are particularly active in the remote north. Buses operate to most centres in Manitoba and bus lines connect the province with the rest of the country and points in the U.S.A. (for instance, Minneapolis and Fargo). Bus companies conduct sightseeing tours of Winnipeg and the surrounding area. Winnipeg city buses run past midnight.

SHOPPING Canadian furs are good buys. Hudson's Bay Company blankets, coats, Eskimo soapstone carvings and Indian crafts and leatherwork are other provincial shopping specialties. Fine china and woolen imports are among the quality goods stocked in specialty shops and leading department stores, Eaton's, Simpson-Sears and the Bay. Portage Avenue in the central part of Winnipeg is regarded as one of the better places to shop in Winnipeg. A provincial sales tax is levied on goods purchased.

ACCOMMODATION Brandon Victoria Inn, on Hwy. IA, 3550 Victoria Ave. W., (204) 725-1532, 104 rooms, colour TV, phones, air conditioning, pool, hot tub and sauna, lounge, cafe, free parking, room service, games area, laundry service. **Churchill** Arctic Inn, in centre of town, (204) 675-8835, 27 rooms, colour TV, phone, shower, restaurant nearby, friendly service, minutes from railway station. **Flin Flon** Kelsey Trail Flag Inn, Highway 10 North, (204) 687-7555, 60 rooms and suites, air conditioned, each room has colour TV, radio and phone, dining room, cocktail lounge, beverage room, swimming pool, sauna. **Portage La Prairie** Westgate Flag Inn, 10th St. and Saskatchewan Ave., (204) 857-7891, 25 rooms, air conditioned, each room has colour TV and phone, some rooms have fully equipped kitchenettes, water and queen size beds available, restaurant adjacent to the hotel. Gordon Motor Inn, 177 Saskatchewan Ave., (204) 857-6881, 20 rooms, air conditioned, radio and colour TV in every room, restaurant, bar, dancing, entertainment, laundry service, free parking. **Winnipeg** Sheraton Winnipeg, 161 Donald St., (204) 942-5300, downtown, near Legislative Buildings and shopping mall, 280 rooms, restaurant, lounge, entertainment programmes, indoor swimming pool, whirlpool, disabled facilities available, no smoking rooms available, pets permitted, parking, a first class property. Viscount Gort Motor Hotel, 1670 Portage Ave., (204) 775-0451, convenient to downtown and airport, rooms have colour TV and air conditioning, indoor swimming pool, whirlpool, sauna, exercise room, wading pool for children, dining room, free parking, coffee shop, lounge. Carlton Inn, 220 Carlton St., (204) 942-0881, central location, rooms have colour TV and air conditioning, dining area, close to main sightseeing attractions, open all year, major credit cards accepted. The Westin Hotel, 2 Lombard Place, (204) 957-1350, 350 rooms, lovely property, colour TV in rooms, at Portage and Main in the downtown area, airport limousine service, dining room, cocktail lounge, indoor swimming pool, sauna, colour TV, specialty shops, barber and beauty shops. Holiday Inn Downtown, 350 St. Mary's Avenue, (204) 942-0551, close to the largest indoor downtown shopping centre, 411 rooms, with phone, TV and radio, no smoking floor, coffee shop, parking, entertainment lounge, restaurant, 24 hour room service, sauna, gift shop, indoor and outdoor swimming pools, fitness facilities. Holiday Inn Winnipeg South, (204) 452-4747, 1330 Pembina Hwy., near large shopping centre, 175 rooms with phone, radio and TV, parking, indoor pool, whirlpool, lounge, no smoking floor available. **Virden** Virden Motel, at junction of Hwy. 1 and 83, (204) 748-2424, 36 rooms, colour TV, phones, air conditioning, licensed restaurant nearby is Capital Restaurant, specialties are steak, seafood and Chinese food, salad bar, open all year.

MISCELLANEOUS

PROVINCIAL TOURIST BUREAU Department of Economic Development and Tourism, Travel Manitoba, Room 101, Legislative Building, Winnipeg, Manitoba, R3C 0V8.

TRAVEL INFORMATION CENTRES are located in Winnipeg, Bossevain, Emerson, the Whiteshell area and along the Manitoba-Saskatchewan border.

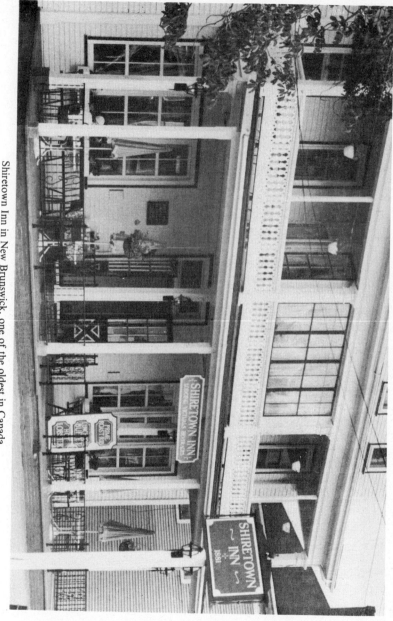

Shiretown Inn in New Brunswick, one of the oldest in Canada

PERSPECTIVE

LOCATION New Brunswick, with 1,410 miles of coastline, lies between Nova Scotia, Quebec and the state of Maine. Fredericton is readily accessible by train, plane and bus from major cities in eastern Canada and the New England states.

AREA With an area of 27,633 square miles, New Brunswick ranks as eighth in size among the ten provinces.

BACKGROUND The region was sighted on a voyage of discovery by Jacques Cartier, the French explorer. European colonization followed in the early 1600's, and by 1762, pioneers immigrating from Britain founded the settlement of Saint John. United Empire Loyalists — American colonists who were sympathetic to England and opposed to the cause of the American Revolution — arrived here from the United States in 1784. In the same year New Brunswick was separated from Nova Scotia and established as a distinct colony. New Brunswick combined with the other British colonies of Nova Scotia, Ontario and Quebec in 1867 to form the self governing Dominion of Canada.

POPULATION Estimated at 720,000.

CAPITAL Fredericton, population 40,000. The biggest city, Saint John, numbers about 120,000 residents. Moncton has a population of approximately 56,000.

LANGUAGES New Brunswick contains the largest French language minority of any province. French is the mother tongue of about a third of the people.

TIME ZONE Atlantic Standard Time. When the clock reads noon in Fredericton, it's 11 in the morning in the Eastern Standard Time Zone.

WHEN TO VISIT Vacation time extends from early in June to late September. The months of April and May are excellent for fishing in this Atlantic province. October and the early part of November are particularly good for hunting or filming the lovely autumn foliage.

NEW BRUNSWICK

SAINT JOHN Canada's first incorporated city (1785) includes among its attractions, the phenomenon of the famous Reversing Falls Rapids of Saint John River. At low tide the current descends to the sea over a gorge; the waters calm momentarily and at high tide the water surges *up* the St. John River from the Bay of Fundy. Both low and high tide may be witnessed from the tourist office's observation deck. Timetables for seeing the tides are available from the tourist bureau. The Martello Tower in Saint John West was constructed in the War of 1812 for the defence of the city, but never used; the stone walls are eight feet thick at the base. Cherry Brook Zoo is eastern Canada's only zoo inhabited by exotic animals. Many animals are on the endangered species list. The New Brunswick Museum depicts the history of the province. For some visitors it's interesting to view the workings of the city's 1,2000-foot-long huge dry docks, said to be the world's biggest. Many of the early United Empire Loyalists who left the newly constituted United States of America are buried in the Old Loyalist's Burial Ground by King Square. Trinity Church, the old County Court House, Loyalist House, Barbour's General Store and Pleasant Villa School remain from an earlier period of Saint John history.

EXCURSIONS FROM SAINT JOHN Rockwood Park in the city outskirts encompasses 2,000 acres of campgrounds, hiking trails, boating and swimming facilities. **St. Andrews** is a one hour drive from Saint John. A resort town overlooking Passamaquoddy Bay, it includes the eye catching Greenock Church (1823), the stone prison dating from 1831 and the 140 year old court house. St. Andrews has over 250 homes that date back to the 1800's. The Ross Home has recently been opened to the public as a museum featuring one of the finest antique collections in Canada. The blockhouse (with cannon) was constructed during the War of 1812. The Huntsman Marine Laboratory Museum and Aquarium on Joe's Point Rd. exhibits marine life on view summer days. **Campobello Island,** the summer home of Franklin D. Roosevelt (renovated and open to visitors) is a 3,500 acre park. A ferry connects Campobello to Deer Island and a bridge links the island to Lubec, Maine. The very large lobster pound in Deer Island is open to tourists and can be reached by ferry (free of charge) from Letete on the mainland. A bird museum accepts visitors

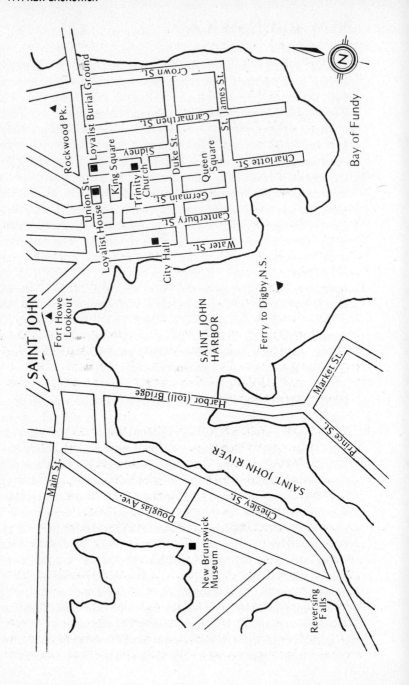

on the geologically interesting Grand Manan Island, which is accessible by ferry from Black's Harbour. Grand Manan Museum (with exhibits depicting regional history), whale and bird watching are some of the island's main attractions.

FREDERICTON sits astride both banks of the St. John River. The legislative building (1880) has portraits by the English painter Reynolds; the Assembly Hall contains pictures of George III and Queen Charlotte. The Legislative Library houses an 18th century copy of the Domesday Book on medieval England, a rare set of the Paintings of the Birds of America by John Audubon and 18th century maps. The Gothic Christ Church (Anglican) Cathedral on Church St. was completed in 1853. Note the bible presented by King Edward VII and an altar cloth of gold used for the coronation of King William IV. Visit the nearby residence of the United Empire Loyalist John Odell, dating from the late 1700's. Old Government House is a Georgian building erected in 1828. Formerly a residence of provincial governors sent here from England before 1867, it's an R.C.M.P. detachment today. The University of New Brunswick Library contains rare editions of H.G. Wells and Dickens. The Canadian Agricultural Research Station on the edge of town commands a fine view of the river valley. Other town attractions are the Beaverbrook Art Gallery, York-Sunbury Museum and free tours of pottery and weaving studios.

NORTH FROM FREDERICTON Hartland has a 1,280-foot-long covered bridge, one of the longest in North America, typical of 79 such bridges in the province. These wooden bridges were covered in order to assure them of a longer life. **Grand Falls** is near a 134-foot-high waterfall, one of the biggest cataracts in the country. Just outside of Fredericton don't miss the Opus Craft Village near Mactaquac Provincial Park. The village is well known for its locally produced handicrafts; the artists' studios can frequently be toured. **Edmundston** is a pulp and paper manufacturing centre. Pulp is made and sent by pipeline to be converted to paper at Madawaska, Maine. Observers may watch both phases of the production process. The Cathedral of the Immaculate Conception is open daily. The Cars of Yesterday Museum, located a few miles west in the new Les Jardins de la Republique Provincial Park, features antique automobiles and other interesting items. Chaleur's Museum of History contains varied

NEW BRUNSWICK

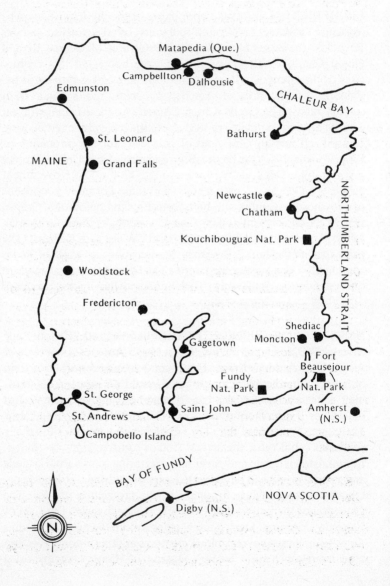

exhibits; Bathurst's paper mill operates guided tours.

MONCTON AND REGION The tidal bore is one of Moncton's two unusual attractions. The powerful Bay of Fundy tide surges up the Petitcodiac River twice a day. The river, a slow moving steam at low tide, has reached heights of 30 feet at high tide. Waves of up to five feet high are created. The Free Meeting House (1821) was used by several of the town's denominations before churches could be built. Driving on the Magnetic Hill 10 miles from town is a different experience. Park your car in neutral gear at the bottom of the hill, turn off the motor and you'll coast unaided up the hill. The experience is supposed to be an optical illusion. A game farm nearby contains animals gathered from around the province. Highlights of Animaland, situated a few miles from Sussex on Route 2, are wild animal sculptures in realistic settings and a garden with carved animals where children can scamper about. Open 8 a.m. to dusk from mid May to early in October. Fundy National Park contains eighty square miles of recreation land. Hopewell Cape by the mouth of the Petitcodiac River has interesting rock formations, mushroom shaped, carved over eons of time by the surging high tide, the winds and the chill of winter. It's best to take a close look at them at low tide, but bear in mind that high tide comes in very quickly. Visit the Albert County Museum and County Court House with displays of antiques. The museum also recalls the era of the sailing ship industry. Fort Beausejour Historic Park features the remains of a two century old French fort. Several stone homes in the surroundings of the very old village of Dorchester date from the early 1800's. It is well worth stopping in the small towns along the northeast coast, including Bathurst, Tracardie, Newcastle and Chatham. Of particular interest is Caraquet which dates back to 1757 and hosts the annual Acadian Festival in August. Nearby, visitors will find the Acadian Historical Village which recreates the way of life in the province between 1780-1880.

HISTORIC SITES, MUSEUMS AND ART GALLERIES Saint John The New Brunswick Museum on Douglas Ave. is the oldest in the country, completed in 1843. Contents include sections on Indian, French and British periods of history, the provincial archives, miscellaneous displays of ship models, stuffed birds, antique toys and dolls. Open 10-8 p.m. from mid June to the middle of September;

hours are reduced other times. Martello Tower has an old weapons museum, open 9-5, every day, June to october, to 9 p.m. in July and August and on Sunday afternoons. Note Trinity Church's (Charlotte Street) royal (House of Hanover) coat of arms carved in wood, spared and imported from Boston by Loyalists when others were destroyed during the revolution. The Court House in King's Square has an unusual unsupported stone circular staircase. The refurbished Loyalist House (1811) at Union and Germain is open to tourists every day from June to September. Other colonial homes grace the neighborhood. **Fredericton's** Beaverbrook Art Gallery includes works by the English artists Reynolds, Romney, Turner, Constable and Gainsborough, Salvador Dali, the Canadian artist Krieghoff and portraits of Winston Churchill and Somerset Maugham. Open 10-9 Tuesday to Saturday, Sunday and Monday afternoons. The York-Sunbury Museum, by Officer's square, features a number of historical exhibits, on view daily from 10-5 (and Sunday afternoon) during the summer. **Gagetown's** Tilley Museum was the home of Samuel Tilley, one of the Fathers of Confederation (creators of Canada in 1867). View items from the loyalist days 10-5, every day (evenings during the summer). Sackville, Hampton, Dalhousie, Woodstock and Moncton maintain other museums.

MUSIC AND THE THEATRE Fredericton's Beaverbrook Playhouse is the home to the New Brunswick Symphony Orchestra and the home of Theatre New Brunswick, a professional group that performs the year round. Both local and visiting theatre groups perform at the Beaverbrook Playhouse. The University of New Brunswick (Fredericton) has a chamber music and jazz festival each summer. Drama, bands, dances and folk singing are part of the province's many festivals, fairs and celebrations.

HUNTING AND FISHING Black bear, white-tailed deer, fox, bobcat, raccoon and rabbit inhabit this densely wooded province. Upland game birds to be found include several varieties of grouse, pheasant, woodcock, geese, duck and partridge. New Brunswick is noted for fine salt, fresh water and deep sea fishing. Salmon fishing is excellent and brook trout, northern pike, perch and striped bass are also given up in the province's waters. Information on current game and angling laws is available from the Director of Fish and Wildlife Branch, Department of Natural Resources, Fredericton.

WINTER AND SUMMER SPORTS The ski resort at Mont Falagne offers T-bars, ski instruction, a chairlift and equipment rentals during the season which extends from late in November to early April. Cross country skiing is a feature of Fundy National Park and Mactaquac Provincial Park near Fredericton. Sugarloaf Provincial Park (Campbellton) is the province's major ski area. Other ski facilities can be found at Poley Mountain (Sussex), Crabbe Mountain (near Fredericton), Hammond River (near Saint John) and Silverwood (in Fredericton). Other winter sporting activities in the Mactaquac Park are snowshoeing, skating, sleigh rides, tobogganing, ice fishing and snowmobiling. You can golf at courses in Moncton, Campbellton, Fundy National Park, Saint John, Fredericton and St. Andrews. Tennis enthusiasts have their choice of courts at Fundy National Park, several places in Fredericton, Moncton's Centennial Park and in St. Andrews. Swimming is excellent in this Atlantic province. There are fine beaches near Moncton, Grand Lake, on the Bay of Chaleur, St. George, Shediac, Campobello Island and in the provincial park system. The northeast coast of New Brunswick also has excellent beaches. Boating is good along the extensive coastline, on the Saint John River, inland waterways, lakes and rivers. Boats are rented in Fundy National Park. Trails invite hikers in Campbellton district and Rockwood Park in Saint John. Harness racing is scheduled regularly during the summer in Fredericton, Moncton and Saint John.

NATIONAL PARKS Fundy National Park encircles the Bay of Fundy. The park includes within its 80 square miles, cliffs carved from the sea, wooded areas, waterfalls, wildlife, hiking trails and camp sites. Outdoor interests are tennis, golf, swimming and horseback riding. The New Brunswick School of Arts and Crafts gives courses in July and August. While the park remains open the year round, facilities generally operate from late in May to the first part of September. The park's headquarters are located at Route 114, about two miles from Alma. **Fort Beausejour National Historic Park** is a few miles east of Sackville. This partially restored fort was constructed by the French in 1751, beseiged by English invaders in 1755 and renamed Fort Cumberland. It was used for defence against American invaders in 1776. The fort museum opens every day from the middle of June to mid September. **Blockhouse National Historic Park** is in St. Andrews next to Centennial Park. The fortification dates from 1812 and was used by the townspeople for defence against invading Americans. Open every day from mid May to mid September. **Kouchibouguac National Park** is located on the northern side of Northumberland Strait. Features of the 93 square mile park are bathing in peaceful bays and lagoons and offshore sand bars; campsites are now in operation. It's accessible from Kouchibouguac, 25 miles south of Chatham.

FOOD AND DRINK Local seafood is tempting. Lobster, scallops, crab, oysters, clams and Atlantic Ocean salmon are served in coastal communities. Seafood can even be bought fresh from fishermen at reasonable prices. Shediac has lobster gorging contests during its July Lobster Festival. Dulse, in case it's offered, is an edible dried seaweed from Grand Manan Island. Fiddleheads are tasty edible ostrich ferns, salted and prepared as a warm buttered vegetable or served cold in a salad. Hunt for and bake your clams along the coast. Provincial liquor outlets are open Monday to Saturday. The legal drinking age is 21.

TRANSPORTATION IN NEW BRUNSWICK The highways are first rate and it's relaxing to drive through the quiet countryside. The Trans Canada Hwy. (Route 2) is a major artery for vacationers. Good roads lead in the direction of Nova Scotia, Maine and Quebec and from there to Ontario and Western Canada. Ferries cross many main rivers at no cost to the passenger. Reservations aren't needed for the ferry operating frequently from Cape Tormentine to P.E.I. Boats link Saint John with Digby, Nova Scotia and vessels ply the route between Saint John and Campobello, Grand Manan and other islands. The section Ferry Services has additional details.

SHOPPING Good buys abound in New Brunswick. In St. Léonard, shop for hand woven clothing — scarves, ties, shirts, rugs. Gagetown is known for woven textiles, drapes, tweeds, scarves, afghans and woolens. Hooked rugs are found in many parts of the province. Indian produced wares sold in reservations include native crafts — baskets, woven goods and items in wood. See busy weavers and potters working on their creations in Fredericton's handicraft studios, open to visitors by arrangement. Edmunston is noted for wood carvings. Other specialties are maple syrup, miniature old fashioned sailing ships in bottles, model ships, ceramics, jewellery made of local stone, woolen and china imports from England. A provincial sales tax is imposed on goods purchased.

ACCOMMODATION Fredericton Howard Johnson's, Trans Canada Hwy. #2 at north end of Princess Margaret Bridge, (506) 472-0480, 150 rooms and suites, restaurant, swimming pool, sauna, whirlpool, lounge, billard tables, laundry service, colour TV. Lord Beaverbrook Hotel, 659 Queen St., (506) 455-3371, 210 rooms and suites, each has radio and colour TV, restaurant, bar, entertainment, indoor swimming pool, sauna, barber shop, laundry service, free parking, meeting and convention facilities. Wandlyn Motor Inn, 58 Prospect St., (506) 455-8937, 117 rooms, radio, colour TV, restaurant bar, outdoor swimming pool, beach, tennis courts, horseback riding, laundry service, free parking, meeting and convention rooms. **Campbellton** Howard Johnson's, Riverfront Dr. at Inter-Provincial Bridge to Quebec, (506) 753-5063, 150 rooms and suites, restaurant, near city center, shopping mall, colour TV, radio, lounge, bank, outdoor swimming pool, laundry service, free parking, family and group rates. **Edmunston** Howard Johnson's, 100 Rice St., (506) 739-7321, located in the city centre, close to shopping and tourist attractions, restaurant, indoor heated swimming pool, lounge, sauna, colour TV. Wandlyn Motor Inn, Trans Canada Hwy., (506) 735-5525, 86 rooms, radio and colour TV, restaurant, bar, outdoor swimming pool, water sports available, laundry service, free parking, meeting and convention facilities. **Moncton** Hotel Beausejour, 750 Main St., (506) 854-4344, 304 rooms and suites, air conditioned, downtown location, colour TV, swimming pool, specialty dining room, restaurant, coffee shop, lounge, rooftop night club and disco, room and laundry service, gift shop, barber and beauty shops. Howard Johnson's, Trans Canada Hwy. at Magnetic Hill, (506) 384-1050, 175 rooms and suites, restaurant, indoor heated swimming pool, sauna, hot tub, lounge, colour TV, coin laundry, golf course and horseback riding nearby. **Saint John** Hilton International Saint John, One Market Square, (506) 693-8484, spectacular harbourfront location, directly connected to the Saint John Trade and Convention Centre and the Market Square Complex, 196 rooms including 8 suites, restaurant, cocktail lounge, whirlpool, sauna and exercise room, nearby are beaches, golf, tennis, skating and skiing, parking, executive floor with private lounge, and concierge, 20 minutes from airport. Howard Johnson's, Chelsey Dr. at Main St., (506) 642-2622, 190 rooms and suites, near the Reversing

Falls in historic Saint John, airport limousine service, swimming pool, restaurant, lounge, sauna, colour TV. Holiday Inn, 350 Haymarket Sq., near downtown, King Square, New Brunswick Museum, (506) 657-3610, 128 rooms with radio and colour TV, restaurant, Squires Tap Lounge, bar, dancing, entertainment, outdoor swimming pool, sauna and whirlpool, private guest lounge, barber and beauty shops, games room, laundry service, free parking. Wandlyn Admiral Beatty Hotel, King Sq., (506) 652-1212, 198 rooms, colour TV, restaurant, bar, barber shop, laundry service, free parking, group and family rates.

MISCELLANEOUS

PROVINCIAL TOURIST BUREAU New Brunswick Department of Tourism, P.O. Box 12345, Fredericton, New Brunswick, E3B 5C3.

VISITOR INFORMATION CENTRES are located in Saint John, Fredericton, Edmundston, Campbellton, Woodstock, St. Stephen, Sussex, St. Leonard, Bathurst and Caraquet.

Unusual rock formation off the coast of New Brunswick

PERSPECTIVE

LOCATION The island is geographically closer to Europe than any other part of the North American continent: only 1,780 miles of the Atlantic Ocean separate Cape Spear, at the most easterly extension of the province, from Ireland. St. John's is located on a longitude more than 500 miles east of Bermuda. Labrador wilderness, in far northern latitudes, is close to Greenland.

AREA The island measures 41,004 square miles in area. Labrador on the mainland is 102,486 square miles in size. Total area: 143,490 square miles.

BACKGROUND The explorer John Cabot is credited with the discovery of Newfoundland in 1497, claimed on behalf of King Henry VII. The island became the first British colony in the New World. Self government (granted by England in 1855) was abandoned due to the great economic hardships experienced by the islanders arising from the 1930's depression. These difficulties convinced the government of the need to join the more prosperous mainland. A plebiscite held in 1948 approved by a narrow margin the decision to unite with Canada and in the following year Newfoundland became the 10th and newest province. Labrador has been a part of Newfoundland since the signing of the Treaty of Paris in 1763.

POPULATION Estimated at 600,000.

CAPITAL St. John's, the only urban centre of any importance in the province, is a city of 130,000. Corner Brook's population is about 25,500.

LANGUAGES English. French is spoken in St. George's Bay among the descendants of French settlers immigrating here from Nova Scotia.

TIME ZONE Both the island and Labrador observe Newfoundland Standard Time. Noon in St. John's is 10:30 a.m. in the Eastern Standard Time Zone.

WHEN TO VISIT St. John's, on the Atlantic Ocean coast, is milder than most inland cities in the winter and a bit cooler in the summer. The ideal time to travel here is July and August but sometimes September can be quite pleasant. In Goose Bay, Labrador, salmon fishing is excellent during the summer.

NEWFOUNDLAND AND LABRADOR

ST. JOHN'S is one of the oldest cities in the New World, but few of the older structures remain since St. John's has suffered from a series of fires during its history. The Colonial Building and Government House are representative of an earlier St. John's. The city's premier attraction is Signal Hill National Historic Park where Marconi received the first transatlantic wireless signal in 1901. The Basilica of St. John the Baptist on Harvey Rd. was erected in 1855. This cathedral is 243 feet long and 185 feet wide, capacious enough to hold as many as 2,000 worshippers at a time. The bell towers reach a height of 138 feet. The Quidi Vidi Battery, constructed in 1740 to guard the harbor, has been refurbished to its appearance of 1812. It's open daily during the summer. The Anglican Cathedral dates from 1816 and was restored in the Gothic style after its destruction by fire in 1892. The Chapter House (open daily at Gower and Church Hill) has a gold communion service, a gift of King William IV, uncle of Queen Victoria. Other local interests are Confederation Building, home of the provincial parliament, St. Thomas Church (1836) featuring an Hanoverian Coat of Arms (at Cavendish Square, open daily) and Bowring Park.

AVALON PENINSULA comprises the southeastern section of the province. It's interesting to take a voyage on one of the coastal steamers that regularly call on the fishing villages strung along the coast. This is one of two practical and interesting ways of seeing these settlements. (Modern roads also lead to these communities.) Alternatively, drive north of the capital to such places as Topsail and Cupid's on Conception Bay. **Cupid's**, established in 1610, is one of the oldest permanently settled communities in the province. You can circle around the top of Avalon from Conception Bay and return to the Trans Canada via the highway in Trinity Bay, where Heart's Content and Heart's Delight are located. Your return to St. John's is via the Trans Canada Highway. **Placentia** was used in the 1600's as a French base of military operations against English-held St. John's. Castle Hill, now a national historic park, features views of the partially restored fortification. The fishing community of Ferryland in the southeast was originally colonized (1662) for three years by George Calvert, later known as Lord Baltimore, before he left to establish the colony of Maryland.

NEWFOUNDLAND & LABRADOR

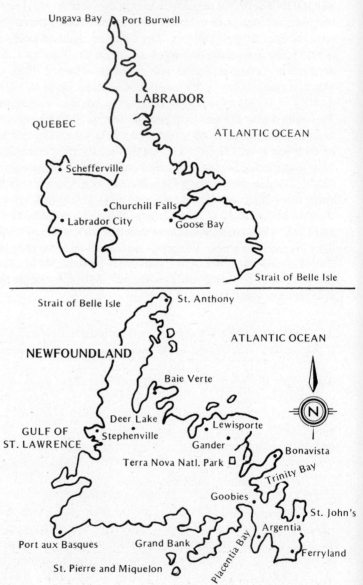

Ungava Bay · Port Burwell

LABRADOR

QUEBEC

ATLANTIC OCEAN

· Schefferville

· Churchill Falls

· Labrador City   · Goose Bay

Strait of Belle Isle

Strait of Belle Isle   · St. Anthony

NEWFOUNDLAND

ATLANTIC OCEAN

Baie Verte

Deer Lake

GULF OF
ST. LAWRENCE   · Stephenville   · Lewisporte

· Gander   Bonavista

Terra Nova Natl. Park □

Trinity Bay

Goobies ·

· St. John's

Argentia

Port aux Basques   Grand Bank   Placentia Bay   · Ferryland

St. Pierre and Miquelon

NORTH AND WEST NEWFOUNDLAND The Trans Canada Highway extends from Port aux Basques 565 miles through valleys, woodlands and hilly countryside to St. John's. There is an extensive network of picnic and campsites along the way. The entire region is known for trout and salmon fishing and big game hunting. **Corner Brook's** immense pulp and paper mill, said to be the largest in the world, is open to visitors on conducted tours. L'Anse-aux-Meadows is found in the far north of the island. Though only a few household articles have been unearthed, superficial excavations reveal the outlines of what are believed to be buildings of a 1000-year-old Viking settlement. The scanty remains are tangible proof that the Vikings were the first to colonize the New World. **Port au Choix** archeological site is south of and a few miles off the same route. An Indian burial ground dating back to the third millenium B.C. was unearthed on this spot. More superb hunting (moose) and fishing tempt the sportsman in this remote region. St. Anthony, due south of the Norse settlement, is the centre of the Grenfell Mission, established by Dr. Grenfell in 1892 to serve the medical needs of isolated communities in the north; the mission welcomes visitors. Terra Nova National Park is 153 square miles of recreation area overlooking Bonavista Bay.

LABRADOR wilderness region supports a few nodern towns, Hudson's Bay Company trading posts, fishing lodges, Indian and Eskimo villages. **Goose Bay**, accessible by plane or boat, assures anglers of excellent salmon fishing. Labrador City and Wabush are adjacent modern mining commmunities in western Labrador. A new community has been created since the completion of the Churchill Falls power project, which eliminated the majestic falls as such. The water has been channelled into huge tunnels to power the turbines. CN steamers departing from St. John's call on coastal communities on regularly scheduled summer services. Summer cruise boats sail by marvellous coastal scenery, fjords and pass several hundred islands on the way. Other trip specialties are sights of whales, seals, icebergs growing progressively bigger the farther north you sail and visits to Eskimo villages. You might imagine at times that you see icebergs and sailing vessels that aren't really there to see because of the tricks the northern sun plays on your eyes. There is a frequently operated air service scheduled from Eastern Canada to Labrador.

HISTORIC SITES, MUSEUMS AND ART GALLERIES St. John's The Colonial Building (1850) on Military Rd. served for a century as a previous home of the provincial legislature; presently it houses the provincial archives. Government House in the older part of town used to be the residence of colonial governors sent over from England to preside over Newfoundland's affairs. Confederation Building, Prince Philip Dr., contains a fine naval and military history museum. The fine Newfoundland Museum (Duckworth St.) houses interesting exhibits on the Beothuck Indian whose origins are a mystery, paintings of historical value and miscellaneous items. It's open weekdays and Sunday afternoons. Gander's Aviation Museum focusses on the pioneer days of flight. Port au Choix, the 4000-year-old Indian cemetery, is yet another historic site. Other museums are open at Grand Falls, Placentia, Heart's Content, Gander, Trinity and Bonavista.

MUSIC AND THE THEATRE St. John's Arts and Culture Centre is the centre of the province's artistic and cultural life. Plays and ballet productions are offered in the Centre. Symphony orchestra concerts are often given in many of the communities of this province.

HUNTING AND FISHING Newfoundland's and Labrador's wilderness regions support three varieties of big game — caribou, bear and moose; archery hunting for caribou and moose is allowed. Smaller game include rabbit, snipe, partridge, ptarmigan, wild duck and geese. Trout, salmon and tuna are found in the surrounding waters. Salmon also populate many rivers in Labrador; other species include Arctic char and northern pike. The province has been fished hundreds of years for cod. Information concerning current hunting and fishing regulations is obtainable from Newfoundland and Labrador Department of Tourism, Recreation and Culture, Tourist Services Division, P.O. Box 2016, St. John's, Newfoundland, A1C 5R8.

WINTER AND SUMMER SPORTS The normal range of winter sports include hockey, skating and snowmobiling. **Golf** courses are located in St. John's, Corner Brook and most other communities. Public tennis courts are in St. John's (Bowring Park) and Corner Brook. Eastport, Conception Bay, Terra Nova National Park, Sandy

Cove and the fishing village of Happy Adventure have fine beaches. Lakes in provincial recreation areas are good for swimming; both boating and horseback riding are allowed in provincial parks. Boating competitions are the highlight of St. John's Regatta, staged in early August. Spectator sports are baseball, hockey, soccer, harness racing and stock car races. Skiing facilities can be found at Marble Mountain near Corner Brook and the Smokye Mountains.

NATIONAL PARKS Signal Hill National Historic Park commands a panoramic view of St. John's harbor. Several fortresses were located here, the site of the final battle of the Seven Years War, fought between the victorious English and the French. See ruins of forts and the Cabot Tower, erected in 1897 in memory of the explorer's discovery of the province. Marconi received the first transatlantic wireless signal at this place in 1901. A visitor centre in the park is open all day. **Terra Nova National Park** is situated some 30 miles south from Gander, accessible by the Trans Canada Highway. Its 153-square-mile area features views of icebergs along the coast in springtime, a rugged coastline, animals, Arctic and other birds, camp grounds and cabins. Open May-October. **Gros Morne National Park** This new park is located on the island's west coast. The 750 square-mile area consists of lovely lakes, soaring peaks and wooded areas. **L'Anse-aux-Meadows National Historic Park** offers a visitor centre and guides during the summer. The sod buildings of the Norse settlers of long ago are re-created in the manner and with the materials used at the time.

FOOD AND DRINK Seafood is an ivevitable specialty of this maritime province. Cod — fried or baked cod tongues, fresh, fried or salted cod — are staples of the diet. Other fish varieties are Atlantic salmon, lobster, shrimp or clams. Local blueberries are delicious; partridge and squash berries are found nowhere else. Provincial liquor outlets open Monday to Saturday. The legal drinking age is 21.

TRANSPORTATION IN NEWFOUNDLAND There are more than 6,000 miles of adequate roads on the island. The Trans Canada Highway crosses the province. Buses drive directly from Port aux Basques to St. John's and the trip takes approximately 12 hours. Ferries are the chief means of getting to and around the province.

Car ferries link North Sydney, Nova Scotia to Port aux Basques and the longer voyage to Argentia (operated in the summer only) costs more but saves a long trip to the capital. Steamers frequently stop at outlying fishing villages, Labrador settlements and St. Pierre and Miquelon. Planes fly between provincial towns on a regular basis.

SHOPPING Handicraft studios turn out embroidered, woven and knitted goods, hooked mats and rugs. Other specialities are novelties in wood and a jewellery made of a local mineral, Labradorite. While many shops remain open from 9 to 5 or 6, retail outlets in the many new plazas stay open to 10 p.m. A provincial sales tax is imposed on goods purchased.

ACCOMMODATION St. John's The Battery, 100 Signal Hill Rd., (709) 626-0040, 103 rooms and suites, radio and colour TV, restaurant, bar, indoor swimming pool, sauna, laundry service, free parking, meeting rooms. Crossroads Motel, Trans Canada Hwy. Rts. 1 and 60, (709) 368-3191, 12 rooms, radio and colour TV, restaurant, bar, dancing, entertainment, free parking. Holiday Inn St. John's, (709) 722-0506, Portugal Cove Rd. at MacDonald Dr., downtown, 190 rooms, in-room movies, outdoor heated pool, dining room, restaurant, lounge, gift shop, weekend rates available, beauty salon, 24 hour room service, entertainment nightly. **Corner Brook** Hotel Corner Brook, Main St., (709) 634-8211, 45 rooms with radio and colour TV, restaurant, bar, dancing, free parking, meeting and convention facilities. Holiday Inn Corner Brook, (709) 634-5381, 48 West St., downtown, 103 rooms, 4 floors, parking, restaurant, lounge. **Gander** Holiday Inn, Caldwell St., (709) 256-3981, 64 rooms, each room has radio and colour TV, restaurant, bar, outdoor swimming pool, laundry service, babysitting, free parking. **Grand Falls** Caribou Motel, Trans Canada Hwy. (709) 489-5639, 20 rooms, kitchenettes available, radio and colour TV, restaurant, bar, entertainment, beach, golf, tennis, water sports, laundry service. **St. Anthony** Vinland Motel, (709) 454-8843, 31 rooms with phones, colour and cable TV, central location, dining room, lounge, free parking, trailer site, 20 minute drive from national park, all major credit cards, open all year. **Springdale** Pelley Inn, (709) 673-3931, off Trans Canada Highway, 24 rooms with colour TV and direct dial phone, 24 hour movie channel, free parking, open all year, major credit cards, lounge with wide screen TV. **Deer Lake** Deer Lake Motel, on Trans Canada Highway

(709) 635-2108, 54 rooms, 2 suites, all with colour cable TV and direct dial phones, dining room, coffee shop, free parking, main credit cards, car rental office, open year round. **Bonavista Bay** (Centreville) Beothuk Lodge, 6 rooms, double beds, 3 self contained with fridge, stove and TV, dining room, free parking, boat tours arranged. **Clarenville** Holiday Inn, on Trans Canada Highway, midway between Gander and St. John's, 64 rooms, lounge, dining room, outdoor heated swimming pool, patio deck bar, gift shop.

MISCELLANEOUS

PROVINCIAL TOURIST BUREAU Newfoundland and Labrador Department of Tourism, Recreation and Culture, Tourist Services Division, P.O. Box 2016, St. John's, Newfoundland, A1C 5R8

VISITOR INFORMATION CENTRES are open in St. John's, Port-aux-Basques and more than a dozen other locations throughout the island.

PERSPECTIVE

LOCATION The Northwest Territories, including the Arctic islands, comprise the roof of Canada, stretching from the Yukon border in the west to Baffin Island, 100 miles north of Labrador. The region's most northerly islands reach to within 500 miles of the North Pole. Yellowknife is accessible from Edmonton by car, bus, or airplane.

AREA The vast territories occupy an area of 1,253,438 square miles, about as large as the entire United States east of the Mississippi River.

BACKGROUND The first Europeans to visit the Arctic Islands were the Vikings, whose artifacts have been found on Ellesmere Island. The English explorer Martin Frobisher took possession of Baffin Island in 1577. Other explorers and fur traders followed, irresistibly drawn to the Far North in the hope of discovering the fabled and elusive Northwest Passage to China and the tremendous riches of the East. The Passage was discovered in 1845 by John Franklin. Control of the entire Northwest Territories was transferred over to the federal government by 1880, but the sparsely settled territories have yet to attain provincial status.

POPULATION About 45,000. The population density is extremely low: approximately one person every 37 square miles.

CAPITAL Yellowknife. The community has a population of 9,000 permanent residents.

LANGUAGES English. Many Eskimos have retained their original language. Indian dialects are also spoken.

TIME ZONES The immense N.W.T. spans five time zones — Pacific Standard, Mountain Standard, Central Standard, Eastern Standard and Atlantic Standard Time. Noon in Yellowknife is 2 p.m., Eastern Standard Time.

WHEN TO VISIT The summer season is short. The best time for a trip to the territories is from the middle of June to late August. Daytime temperatures are comfortable but evenings can get quite cold.

NORTHWEST TERRITORIES

MACKENZIE HIGHWAY TO YELLOWKNIFE The journey begins at **Grimshaw**, Alberta. The 300 mile stretch of gravel road to the Northwest Territories border passes through a sparsely inhabited section of Canada. Insect repellent will save grief at camping sites, conveniently spaced 50-75 miles apart. A frontier tourist information booth is open every day during the summer. Another camp site is located a short distance away. Alexandra Falls (near Enterprise) plunges from the Hay River into a gorge 109 feet below. A mile away is the 46-foot-high Louise Falls, a fine picnic spot. The road continues east from Enterprist (where you may buy gas) to Hay River, a mission, fishing community and trading post. An Indian village across the river may be of interest. Pine Point is another modern community of 1,800, the site of a lead and zinc mine. You may choose to go to Fort Smith, administrative centre of Wood Buffalo National Park, or continue on the route to Fort Providence. You cross the Mackenzie River on a free ferry a couple of miles before you get to Fort Providence, a town of 600. **Fort Rae** has a hospital, mission, R.C.M.P. and Hudson's Bay post and a gas station. You will find a few camping sites and hotels in this geologically interesting district.

YELLOWKNIFE is a modern city. The city basks under approximately 20 hours of daylight each day from mid June to early August. A number of gold mines operate in the locality and two of them, Giant Yellowknife Mine and Cominco's Con Mine, offer tours in the summer months. Great Slave Lake area invites the rockhound and the fisherman. In The Prince of Wales Northern Heritage Centre, an array of exhibits depict the territories' colourful history.

TRIPS FROM YELLOWKNIFE Fort Simpson is a Mackenzie River port of 1,000, inhabited by Indians, Mounties and fur traders. Charter planes take off from this point for Nahanni National Park where you will view mineral springs and the immense Victoria Falls. **Fort Wrigley** is a Slave Indian village of 175 and a Hudson's Bay post. The phenomenon of continuously burning coal beds, smoking for hundreds of years, can be observed a few miles north of Fort Norman. **Inuvik**, headquarters of the West Arctic, population 3,000, probably is the one northern settlement suitably constructed to the requirements of the north; the neat homes are built on immovable

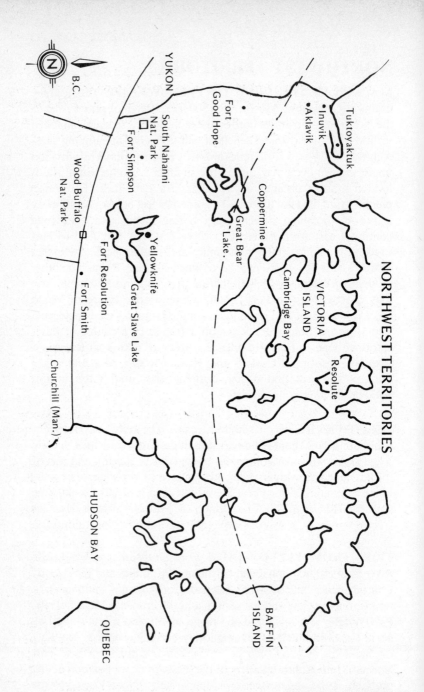

NORTHWEST TERRITORIES

YUKON

B.C.

Tuktoyaktuk

Inuvik
Aklavik

Fort
Good Hope

South Nahanni
Nat. Park

Fort Simpson

Wood Buffalo
Nat. Park

Coppermine

Great Bear
Lake

Fort Resolution

Yellowknife

Great Slave Lake

Fort Smith

Churchill (Man.)

Cambridge Bay

VICTORIA
ISLAND

Resolute

BAFFIN
ISLAND

HUDSON BAY

QUEBEC

piles. The town is a fur trapping and hunting centre, a base for petroleum exploration of the Beaufort Sea and a point of departure for boat and place trips to the Arctic Ocean. Aklavik and Arctic Red River are Eskimo and Indian communities respectively. **Tuktoyaktuk,** an Arctic port, is interesting for its pingoes — volcano shaped mounds that reach a height of 110 feet. They are composed of permafrost (permanently frozen ground). Summers are short, hence the permanently frozen terrain. Coppermine is an Eskimo village; Resolute and Cambridge Bay are other very isolated outposts in the Arctic Islands. Chartered planes will fly the intrepid sightseer 1,000 miles north to the top of the world. Frobisher Bay on Baffin Island is an outpost of 2,000 inhabitants, the administrative headquarters of the East Arctic.

BAFFIN ISLAND Iqaluit (Frobisher Bay) offers hotels, a small museum, hiking trails and the ruins of ancient Thule Inuit homes. Tuugaalik Outfitters specializes in white water rafting and sea kayaking trips, adventure trekking through Auyuittuq National Park, cross country ski tours (supported by dog sleds) in the spring, trips to historical sites and nature photography and whale watching tours. Nuna Kuuk Outfitters also offers the traveller the opportunity to explore the Arctic by operating wildlife safaris, day-long dog team excursions and even longer trips to the community of Lake Harbour and the floe edge. In addition, trips by dog sled are featured to Peale Point, an 11th century, Thule Inuit historical site. **Pond Inlet** A trip by boat or snowmobile can be taken to Bylot Island, a rugged land of glaciers and mountains and a sanctuary for a wide variety of bird life. Local outfitters can be hired for a trip by snowmobile to the floe edge, where narwhal, walruses, whales, seals and polar bears may be seen. Other things to do in and near town include hiking over the tundra, visiting ancient, archeological sites, fishing for char and viewing the wide range of local flora. A sport fishing camp is in operation ouside Pond Inlet. **Pangnirtung** is located at the main entrance of Auyuittuq National Park, 8,290 square miles of Arctic wilderness. The park and surrounding countryside hold a particular appeal for wilderness campers and hikers, fishermen, mountain climbers and nature photographers. The staff at the local lodge can arrange fishing trips and excursions into the park. The visitor centre will provide additional information on the park's attractions. Added places to visit on Baffin Island are Igloolik (museum, stone church and caribou hunting), and Cape Dorset (stone carvings, lithographs and limited edition prints on sale, Dewey Soper Bird Sanctuary). **Grise Fiord**, on Ellesmere Island, is the most northerly settlement in Canada. Of interest are Inuit historic sites, the opportunities for camping and hiking and the snowmobile trips you can take for viewing the Arctic animals roaming the countryside (best arranged in the spring). Kenn Borek Air schedules trips the year round to Grise Fiord from Resolute Bay and Pond Inlet. **First Air** operates to Frobisher Bay and many other communities on Baffin Island from Ottawa the year round.

HISTORIC SITES, MUSEUMS AND ART GALLERIES Yellowknife's Prince of Wales Northern Heritage Centre has exhibits on Inuit (Eskimo) life and art and on the region's early explorations and settlements. Open daily except Wednesdays and holidays. Displays in Father Ebner's Northern Life Museum in Fort Smith include an antique printing press. Open every day but Sunday from mid May to October.

MUSIC AND THE THEATRE Tea dances are a highlight of the Dene Celebrations held in July in Southern Mackenzie. Musical presentations and drum dancing are part of the Keewatin Regional Summer Festival, staged at Whale Cove in August.

HUNTING AND FISHING Black and grizzly bear, caribou, moose, polar bear weighing up to a ton, mountain goats, Stone and Dall sheep, wolves and white fox roam the vast Northwest Territories. Sportsmen must be accompanied by local guides for hunting the white Beluga whale, walrus and polar bears. Indian and Eskimo guides are also required for seal hunts by boat or dog sled. Beaver, mink and lynx are trapped by the Dene. Game birds include blue geese, ducks, ptarmigan and grouse. Fishing in the territories is stupendous: lake trout (up to 60 pounds) and grayling are commonplace in most parts of the territory. Other species caught in the region's waters are walleye, northern pike and Arctic char. Regulations for hunting and fishing are available from R.C.M.P. offices anywhere in the area or by writing to Travel Arctic, Government of the Northwest Territories, Yellowknife, N.W.T., X1A 2L9

WINTER AND SUMMER SPORTS Curling, a form of lawn bowling on ice, hockey, cross country skiing, snowmobiling and ice-skating are favorite pastimes. Yellowknife, Fort Smith and Pine

Point have golf courses. You may swim off the sandy beaches at Yellowknife's outskirts. Other recreational possibilities include horseback riding, hiking, boating, canoeing, and if you dare, swimming in the territories' numerous waterways during the short summer. Boats are available for hire.

NATIONAL PARKS Wood Buffalo National Park is part of Alberta and the Northwest Territories. Fort Smith in the N.W.T. is the park headquarters. A 17,300 square mile area of plains and forests, it supports herds of bison (buffalo), moose, elk and deer. The park is open all year. Nahanni National Park and Auyuittuq National park (on Baffin Island) are worth visiting. Points of interest of **Nahanni National Park** are Virginia Falls, campgrounds, waterways, the Kraus Hotsprings, wildlife (black bear, moose, Dall sheep), fishing for trout and hiking trails. **Auyuittuq National Park** in the Arctic wilderness offers mountain peaks, magnificent fjords, seals, whales and walrus, bird life, glaciers, hiking and camping.

FOOD AND DRINK Canning factories now produce smoked Arctic char and whitefish. Meals served at restaurants in the N.W.T. are often higher in price than in southern Canada. Licences are not required to purchase wine, liquor or beer, readily obtainable at territorial liquor stores in Yellowknife, Inuvik, Fort Smith and Hay River. Alcoholic beverages are served in hotels and lodges. The legal drinking age is 19. Some communities prohibit or ration liquor.

TRANSPORTATION IN THE NORTHWEST TERRITORIES Take the precaution of completely servicing your vehicle and bring along at least two spares, even a spare gas can, for the gravel road trip from Grimshaw to Yellowknife or from Dawson City (Yukon) to Inuvik via the newly opened Dempster Highway. Gas stations are infrequently spaced along the Mackenzie Highway. Cars are rented in Hay River and Yellowknife and taxis do operate as far north as Inuvik. The airplane is best suited to travel in the immense region. There are no passenger train services in the N.W.T.

Canadian Airlines has flights from Edmonton to communities in the N.W.T. You can also get to the N.W.T. from Ottawa. **City Express** features daily flights from Toronto to Ottawa non stop and the flight arrives in Ottawa in time for the connecting **First Air** service to the north. **First Air** travels from Ottawa to Iqaluit (Frobisher Bay) up to five times a week and the jet service takes about 3 hours. **First**

Air has an extensive network of services within the vast Northwest Territories. **First Air** flies from Iqaluit to numerous destinations within the N.W.T., including Pond Inlet, Igloolik, Yellowknife, Cape Dorset, Lake Harbour, Broughton Island, Pelly Bay, Cambridge Bay, Hall Beach, Coral Harbour, Lake Harbour, Pangnirtung, Clyde River and Nanisivik. **First Air** flies by jet from Iqaluit to Yellowknife via Rankin Inlet and the flight takes 3¾ hours. **First Air** also operates non stop from Nuuk, Greenland to Iqaluit throughout the year. **Kenn Borek** is an airline operating from Resolute, on Cornwallis Island, to Arctic Bay and Pond Inlet on Baffin Island on a regularly scheduled service once each week. Resolute is an air base that serves as a starting point for scientific and adventure trips to the High Arctic. **Kenn Borek** operates from Resolute to the northernmost community in Canada, Grise Fiord. **Kenn Borek Air** flies from Resolute to Grise Fiord, Ellesmere Island on a non stop service scheduled all year. **Kenn Borek Air** provides the only scheduled service available to Ellesmere Island from anywhere in Canada. **Calm Air** operates from Churchill, in northern Manitoba, to Coral Harbour, Chesterfield Inlet, Rankin Inlet, Whale Cove, Eskimo Point and Baker Lake in the Northwest Territories. **Calm Air** operates on a regularly scheduled service to Churchill from Thompson, Flin Flon, The Pas, Winnipeg and Lynn Lake. For instance, **Calm Air** travels from Thompson, where it is based, to Churchill on a non stop basis and from Churchill, **Calm Air** goes to Rankin Inlet, several times weekly.

SHOPPING Handicraft shops offer the popular Inuit soapstone carvings, ivory carvings, custom made parkas, Inuit prints on sealskin or paper and jewellery made of local stones. Other specialties are furs, handmade leather and fur garments, mukluks or footwear and snowshoes. It's quite in order to negotiate prices in person to person dealings with individual Eskimo artists. Goods are shipped south on request.

ACCOMMODATION Iqaluit (Frobisher Bay) The Navigator Inn, P.O. Box 185, close to the airport, (819) 979-6201, recently expanded, double rooms with private bath, TV and phone, clean and comfortable surroundings, licensed dining room, open daily for lunch and dinner, coffee shop open all day, friendly atmosphere, strongly recommended, local museum within walking distance, open all year, considered the best hotel in town. Kamotiq Inn nearby offers fireside dining and its specialties include smoked Arctic char, caribou steak and muktuk teriyaki. **Pangnirtung** Auyuittuq Lodge, offers clean and comfortable lodging, close to Arctic Circle, in operation for 15 years, has direct dial phones and all modern facilities, dining room, panoramic views of the fjord from the lodge, can arrange trips by boat to entrance of the national park and to Clearwater Fishing Lodge and Cumberland Sound. **Pond Inlet** Machmer Bread and Breakfast, on edge of the hamlet, family atmosphere, reasonable rates, one bedroom available, suitable for 1 or 2, home cooking, (819) 899-8825 or 889-8873. **Resolute Bay** Narwhal Inn, close to the air terminal. (819) 252-3968, 80 beds in 51 rooms, shared bathroom facilities, TV in many rooms, centrally heated, dining room with first rate food, TV lounge, games room, small library, direct dial phone to anywhere in the world, open all year, very relaxed and pleasant atmosphere, VISA credit card accepted, room rates include three meals a day plus self serve snack bar, transportation to and from airport, strongly recommended. International Explorer's Home, (819) 252-3875, accommodates 10 in 6 rooms, in village of Resolute Bay, airport transportation, guide services available, dining area, good food, friendly atmosphere. **Hall Beach** Hall Beach Eskimo Co-op Hotel, 17 beds in 5 rooms, centrally heated, three meals daily, showers, lounge, dining area, direct dial phone to anywhere in the world, manager provides information on hunting and fishing and other activities, open all year, VISA credit card. **Rankin Inlet** Siniktarvik Hotel, clean and comfortable rooms, dining room, meeting and conference facilities, phones, TV, open all year. **Grise Fiord** Small self contained cottage for two or more persons is available all year. The cottage is adjacent to the family home of the Pijamini family. Great views of the fiord and surrounding landscape from the cottage, which is well heated and spacious. The best place to stay in the village. Details available from Looty or Teepeelee Pijamini (819) 980-9048. **Yellowknife** The Explorer Hotel, 120 comfortable rooms, each room has colour TV, friendly service, cafeteria, dining lounge, cocktail lounge, fully equipped games room, open all year. **Arctic Bay** Enokseot Hotel, (819) 439-8911, accommodates 16 in 8 rooms, shared accommodation, shared bath, open all year, comfortable surroundings, three meals a day served and included in daily rate, can arrange taxi to Nanisivik, truck rentals.

PERSPECTIVE

LOCATION Nova Scotia, the easternmost province on the mainland, is almost completely surrounded by the sea. No part of the peninsula or Cape Breton Island is located more than 50 miles from the Atlantic Ocean.

AREA 20,402 square miles. Nova Scotia is the second smallest of the ten provinces.

BACKGROUND John Cabot landed in the name of the King of England on the northern coast of Cape Breton Island in 1497. Port Royal was the site of the oldest settlement in North America, founded by the Frenchman Samuel de Champlain in 1605. The region was traded off several times (a consequence of European wars) between the arch colonial rivals, England and France, until Britain took final possession of the mainland in 1713 and Cape Breton Island in 1758. Halifax was founded in 1749 by pioneers arriving from Britain. In the year 1867, the colony joined with New Brunswick, Ontario and Quebec to create Confederation, i.e. the political union of the former British colonies in the formation of a self governing Canada.

POPULATION Approximately 870,000.

CAPITAL Halifax numbers 280,000 inhabitants. Sydney currently has a population of 31,000. Yarmouth's population is close to 8,000.

LANGUAGES Predominantly English. The Gaelic language is heard if you venture into remote settlements and rural areas of Cape Breton Island.

TIME ZONE Atlantic Standard Time. When the clock reads noon in Halifax, it's 12:30 p.m. in St. John's, Newfoundland, 11 a.m. in Toronto and Montreal, 10 a.m. in Winnipeg, 9 a.m. in Calgary and Edmonton and 8 a.m. in Victoria and Vancouver.

WHEN TO VISIT The vacation season extending from June to September is the best time to travel here. Summer days are comfortably warm, if rainy, at times. Special events in the Maritime province during the month of July include Pictou's Lobster Festival and the famed Highland Games at Antigonish.

NOVA SCOTIA

HALIFAX, a port and major city of the Maritime provinces, offers much for the sightseer. Province House, completed in 1819, is Canada's oldest parliament building. This Georgian building features many portraits of the British royal family. It's located on Hollis Street and open 9-5 weekdays. The interesting St. Paul's, on Barrington Street, is the oldest Anglican church in the country (1750). Halifax Citadel National Historic Park contains the stone citadel constructed in 1828. This restored fort commands a panoramic view of the city and harbor. The Old Clock Tower below the citadel entrance was put up in 1803 and given to the city by the Duke of Kent, Queen Victoria's father. Point Pleasant Park, on the southern end of the peninsula, encloses within its 186 acres of wooded area, Martello Tower (National Historic Park), built in 1797 by the Duke of Kent. He was the colony's military commander at the time. Public Gardens at South Park Street and Sackville, established in 1753, is comprised of 18 acres of well-maintained flower gardens and tree-lined pathways. Other sights of interest are St. Matthew's Church, other churches, the campus of Dalhousie University, guided tours of the Volvo car assembly plant and several museums.

COASTAL TOURS FROM HALIFAX Artists and photographers flock to the attractive fishing village of **Peggy's Cove** that sits on massive rock. The popular holiday resort of **Chester**, overlooking Mahone Bay, offers boating, golfing, yachting competitions, excellent swimming and good hunting opportunities in the district. Oak Island, a few miles out, is allegedly the spot where Captain Kidd buried his treasure chests; excavations have revealed nothing more than wooden floorings from a sunken ship. Ferry service is scheduled to Tancook Island. **Lunenburg** fishing community was the home of the famous schooner Bluenose, winner of four international racing competitions. Historical places to visit are the Church of St. John's (1754), whose communion vessels were donated by George III and the Evangelical Communion Church, dating from 1777. The Fisheries Museum of the Atlantic is open for tours. Guided tours are offered on summer weekdays of a fish processing factory, Lunenburg Fish Products Company. Blue Rock is another attractive seaside village. **The Ovens Natural Park**, a dozen miles southwest of Lunenburg on Route 332, is so named because caves

HALIFAX

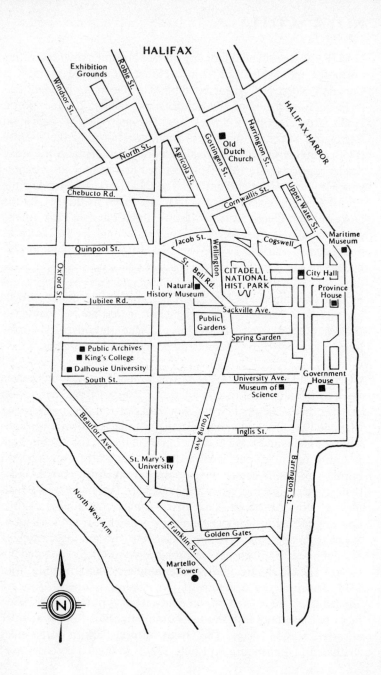

Bedroom in Louisbourg Fortress, Nova Scotia

were carved out of the cliffs by the surging sea. Gold was discovered here a century ago. **Bridgewater** holiday centre has the DesBriay Museum, featuring items from the district's pioneer and Indian era and other varied exhibits. Open 10-12, 2-5 and 7-9 every day, from the middle of June to Labour Day. The Dean Wile Carding Mill (1860), operated by the museum, still functions with its original machinery. **Liverpool** resort is popular for its excellent tuna fishing, hunting and fine beaches. Several colonial dwellings remain in the town, one of which is Simeon Perkin's Home (1766), which has been converted to a museum. Its interior may be seen from 9:30-5:30 p.m., mid May to mid October. Salmon and tuna fishing flourish in the vicinity. Shelburne contains an old wooden loyalist church and the Ross-Thompson House. The home, dating from 1754, contains period furniture, on view 9:30-5:30 p.m., May 15-October 15. McNutt's Island has picnic spots and an historic lighthouse. **Barrington** may be worth seeing for its Meeting House (1765), Canada's oldest nonconformist church, open 9-5 every day from the middle of June to the end of September. The other attraction in the community is the 19th century wool spinning mill that demonstrates all the stages of producing yarn from raw wool. You will note at a number of places along the coast, e.g. in the Peggy's Cove area, fine examples of the province's 500 lighthouses.

ANNAPOLIS VALLEY REGION Mount Uniacke, north of Halifax on Route 1, is undistinguished except for its Uniacke House. The home is maintained as an historic site on its 5,000 acre grounds. This fine specimen of a colonial mansion (1813) is open summer days. **Windsor's** interests include the Fort Edward blockhouse, built in 1750, and the Haliburton Memorial Museum. This was the home of the Canadian author Tom Haliburton (1796-1866) who wrote about the fictional character Sam Slick. The dwelling, surrounded by 25 acres of grounds, is furnished in the style of the period. Grand Pré National Park, site of an old Acadian Village (1675-1755), is famed for Evangeline's Well and the restored St. Charles' Church, a museum of pioneer Acadian life, open 10-5 every day and on summer evenings. Kentville's Agricultural Research Station receives visitors weekdays from 8 a.m. to 4:30 p.m. An Apple Blossom Festival in early June is highlighted by singing, dancing and parades. The Church of St. Mary's by Aylesford dates from 1791. Middleton's local church is nearly two centuries old.

Annapolis Royal is the site of one of the oldest settlements in North America (1605), predating Jamestown and Quebec by a few years. See the fort in Fort Anne National Historic Park and tour the replica of the original community established by Champlain in 1605 at Port Royal National Historic Park, eight miles west of Annapolis Royal on Highway 1A. Clementsport has good beaches, fishing and the two-century-old (1788) loyalist Church of St. Edward. Digby is a port and resort, affording from its heights a panoramic view of Annapolis Basin. **Yarmouth** Features of interest are the firefighting museum, the Yarmouth County museum of pioneer and marine life, and tours of the local textile plant.

HALIFAX TO CAPE BRETON ISLAND Carry on past Dartmouth in the direction of Truro. The Waverley Game Sanctuary, a nearby parkland, is dotted with several lakes, features small game animals and beaver in particular, abound. Shubenacadie Indian community is close to Wildlife Reserve. Its wooded 70 acres harbor deer, bobcat, rabbit and other animals. Truro's Victoria Park comprises a thousand acres of gardens, camp sites, pathways, woods and streams. Parrsboro is a fishing, hunting and swimming resort. The town could be interesting to the amateur geologist; rockhounds have uncovered amethysts and other precious stones on the beaches. **Southampton** is the location of the Chignecto Game Sanctuary, home to moose and beaver. Joggins, about 25 miles from Amherst, is noted for its ancient rock formations and fossils seen in the cliffs overlooking the bay. A short drive five miles south of Amherst off Highway 302 leads to the 600 acre Nappan Experimental Farm. Visitors are received 9-5, Monday to Friday. **Pugwash** attractions are afternoon tours of the salt mine and the Gathering of the Clans staged every first of July, with parades and aquatic sports. Tatamagouche has a small, local museum. The rebuilt Balmoral Mills (1860), one of Nova Scotia's water driven mills, is open 9:30-4:30, May to October. It is located a few miles south on Route 311. The interests of **Pictou** include swimming, boating, the 120-year-old Norway House, the Lobster Carnival in July and the Micmac Museum, a few miles east of town. Stellarton, a short distance from New Glasgow, features a mining museum. Antigonish is the site of the July Highland Games.

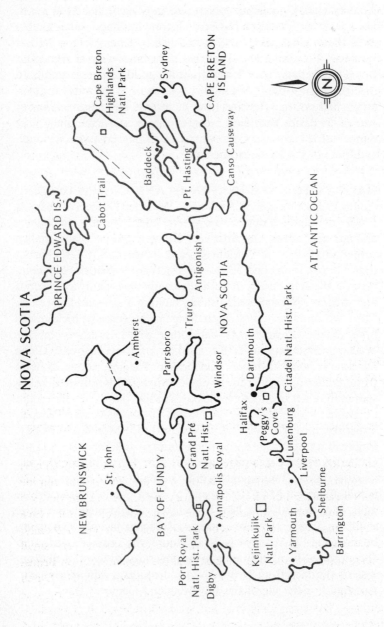

CAPE BRETON ISLAND, one of the beautifully scenic regions of Canada, is easily accessible by Canso causeway. **Cabot Trail** winds 180 miles over dramatically picturesque countryside, encircles the northern peninsula of the island and passes through Cape Breton Highlands National Park. Cheticamp, at the entrance to the park, has the interesting St. Peter's Church, good mackerel and cod fishing and the Acadian Museum. Cape Breton Highlands National Park is 370 square miles of splendid parkland and an animal sanctuary. Three miles east of Pleasant Bay fishing village, in a camping ground off the road, the "Lone Shieling", a copy of a Scottish shepherd's stone and thatched roof hut, invites a stop. Ingonish offers fishing, camping and yachting facilities. South Gut St. Ann's supports a Gaelic school teaching the Gaelic language, Scottish dancing and music. Visits can be arranged in July. The school museum and handicraft showroom are open 9-5:30, May to October and summer evenings. The Gaelic Mod held in August is highlighted by Highland Games and dances. **Baddeck**, a base of departure for the Cabot Trail, is popular for its Alexander Graham Bell Museum, housing exhibits on his life's work. Return to Port Hastings and continue via Highway 4 in the southeastern section of the island to Grand Anse, 25 miles away. Madame Island attracts sightseers for its numerous picturesque fishing villages. Outside of St. Peter's village stands the Nicholas Denys Museum, with an array of artifacts from the early 17th century. **Sydney**'s attractions are water sports, fishing and St. George's Anglican Church (1786) containing a chair from Nelson's ship "Victory". Cossitt House, built in 1787, is the oldest home in Sydney. Boats leave from the port of North Sydney for Newfoundland. Sydney Mines conducts an underground mine tour.

HISTORIC SITES, MUSEUMS AND ART GALLERIES Citadel National Historic Park in **Halifax** has a military and marine museum and the Centennial Art Gallery (Canadian art, on view 9-5 daily, plus summer evenings). The science section of the Nova Scotia museum, with displays on natural history, is open 9-9 daily, 9-5 weekends. St. Paul's Anglican church houses a very small museum (open 10-4, June-August) and the two churches on Brunswick Street, St. George's (1800, unusual design) and Old Dutch (Lutheran, 1757) with its colonial cemetery, are close by one another. **Dalhousie** University houses the provincial archives which include old documents, papers, prints and a library. Open 10-5 weekdays. Fort Anne Museum of History in the Fort Anne National Historic Park is concerned with the history of local communities. Displays in the Acadian Room (colonists' mid 18th century life), Garrison Room (military), Loyalist Room (late 1700's), Queen Anne Room (on the Queen) and the Port Royal Room (1605-1712 period) are open daily 10-5 (plus evenings during the summer). Uniacke House (1813) at Mount Uniacke is an interesting specimen of a colonial mansion. This historic site is open 9:30-5:30 every day, from mid May to mid October. Yarmouth's Firefighting Museum features antiquated equipment, on display 10-5 p.m., plus evenings in July and August (hours vary considerably at other times). The County Historical Society Museum and Research Library, containing models of ships, marine exhibits and a collection tracing Yarmouth's history, opens 9-5 weekdays. (In the summer the museum is also open Wednesday, Thursday and Friday evenings and Sunday afternoons.) Aylesford maintains a museum housing miscellaneous items on Canadian life, on view 9-5 daily. Glace Bay has a miners' museum that depicts the development of the coal mining industry. Open 10-6 daily, June to late September. Other museums are situated in Maitland, Bridgewater, Parrsboro, Wolfville, Dartmouth, Margaree Forks (salmon museum), Lunenburg and Liverpool.

MUSIC AND THE THEATRE The Atlantic Symphony Orchestra makes its home in Halifax, but it also travels throughout the province during the winter and spring seasons. Free evening band concerts are held weekly in Public Gardens. The highly regarded Neptune Theatre presents repertory productions in the summer season. The Gathering of the Clans Festival at Pugwash is highlighted by Highland dancing and pipe bands. South Gut St. Ann's Gaelic school offers a summer course of study in Gaelic songs, dancing and lessons in piping. Bagpipe music, parades, dances and contests are part of the Highland Games in Antigonish.

HUNTING AND FISHING Deer and bear are the main big game animals. Small game include fox, raccoon, mink, muskrat and rabbit. Upland game birds and waterfowl are Hungarian partridge, pheasant, Canada geese, woodcock, several species of duck and Wilson's snipe. Fresh and salt water fishing are exceptional and world records for tuna catches have been set here; a 1,496 pound tuna was landed off Cape Breton Island in 1979. Charter boats leave from Wedgeport and Yarmouth ports. Swordfish are mainly found in the waters off Cape Breton Island and pollock is found practically everywhere in the province. Other fish caught here include Atlantic salmon (up to 50 pounds), striped bass, brook, sea and lake trout. Details regarding current game and fishing laws are available from the Department of Tourism, Box 130, Halifax, Nova Scotia, B3J 2R5.

WINTER AND SUMMER SPORTS Kejimkujik National Park has facilities for snowshoeing, snowmobiling and cross country skiing. Ski facilities operate in Cape Smokey ski region by Cabot Trail. Golf is played at more than two dozen courses in Halifax, Windsor, Yarmouth, Lunenburg, Sydney, Ingonish, North Sydney, Bridgewater, Pugwash, Chester, Pictou (nine holes), Digby, Dartmouth, Kentville (nine holes) and at several places by the sea. Tennis courts are open to the public in Cape Breton Highlands National Park, Wolfeville, Bridgewater and at numerous seaside resorts. Swimming opportunities are numerous in a province where you are at all times within 35 miles of the sea. Swim in the coves and sandy beaches in the summer resorts of Chester and Digby, in provincial parks, Point Pleasant Park in Halifax, Truro's Victoria Park, Liverpool, Margaree Forks and Parrsboro. Boating and yachting flourish at provincial and national parks and coastal resorts. Trails lure the hiker in Kejimkujik and Cape Breton National Park, in the Chester region and at Point Pleasant Park in Halifax. Spectator sports include baseball, yacht races and harness racing at Sackville Downs in Halifax.

NATIONAL PARKS Cape Breton Highlands National Park comprises the northern side of Cape Breton Island and is enclosed by the 190 mile scenic Cabot Trail. The park's 367 square miles feature an indented, rugged coastline, wooded areas, wildlife, hiking trails, lovely valleys, summer sports, cabins and camp grounds. Most facilities are open from mid May to the middle of October. The Alexander Graham Bell National Historic Park is in Baddeck, 22 miles northwest of Sydney. The museum contains pictures, display models of his inventions and exhibits on the results of his ideas. Open 9-9 p.m., mid May to mid October. **Fortress of Louisbourg National Historic Park**. The federal government has undertaken a restoration of the fortress, once used by the French to defend their North American Empire. Some 45 buildings and ramparts are being reconstructed, complete with 18th century furnishings, antiques and artifacts. The 25-square-mile park is 25 miles east and south of Sydney, near Louisbourg. Open daily 10-5, May to October, July and August evenings. **Fort Anne National Historic Park** by Annapolis Royal features within its 36 acres the remains of the original fortress constructed by France, 1695-1708, and added to by England in the first half of the 18th century. The park museum traces the history of the district in a restored officer's quarters (1797), open 10-5, April-November and summer evenings. **Grand Pré National Historic Park** in Annapolis Valley, east of Kentville, contains an Acadian museum located not far from the community from which the Acadians (French-speaking Nova Scotians) were expelled (1755). **Kejimkujik National Park** Its 238 square mile area in southern Nova Scotia is highlighted by lakes, woodlands, wildlife, campgrounds, water sports and hiking. Open the year round. **York Redoubt National Historic Park** by Halifax dates from 1793. Britain built the fort for the defence of Halifax port. See the ruins of the Martello Tower and other works of military interest originating from the period, daily from June to the first week in September. **Port Royal National Historic Park** contains in its 20 acres a reconstruction of the first fortress put up by Champlain in 1604. The park is six miles from Annapolis Royal. Tourists are received from April-November.

FOOD AND DRINK Lobster is succulent (and relatively inexpensive) in this province and lobster you may wish to cook yourself is available from local pounds. Sample the freshly caught shrimp, salmon, swordfish from Cape Breton Island, and cod or halibut chowder. Other delights are Solomon Gundy or salt herring pickled with onions for about five days, tasty scallops from Digby and in Lunenburg, sausage served with sauerkraut. The Annapolis Valley is known for the quality of its apples. Local strawberries and cranberries are good. Provincial liquor outlets retail alcoholic beverages Monday to Saturday and drinks are served in Halifax bars until 12 p.m., in taverns to 2 a.m.. The legal drinking age is 19.

TRANSPORTATION IN NOVA SCOTIA The driving is enjoyable along unhurried highways and paved roads criss-cross all parts of the province. The Trans Canada Highway runs from Sydney through Amherst to Fredericton, New Brunswick. Car hire offices are located in Halifax. Rail tours of the Maritime provinces, departing from Montreal or Toronto, include major attractions of the province in their itineraries. VIA Rail Canada provides service to most sections of the province, to other parts of the country and ongoing connections to Maine. Sightseeing buses also operate from Montreal to Toronto. Bus lines link Halifax to Saint John, to New England and central and western Canada. Air service links Nova Scotia to P.E.I., St. Pierre and Miquelon, other provinces and many cities in the States. Canadian National ferries sail from North Sydney to Port aux Basques and Argentia in Newfoundland. Other boats sail between Yarmouth and Bar Harbor, Maine and Saint John, New Brunswick to Digby. For additional details see Ferry Services.

SHOPPING Shops across Nova Scotia specialize in Scottish clan tartans, tweeds and textiles. Wood carvings and knitted wear are sold in numerous small shops in Halifax and elsewhere in the province. Other specialties are glassware, model sailing ships, Eskimo art, hooked rugs from the handicraft studios of Cheticamp and antiques. There are good buys in textiles from mills open to tourists. Leading department stores are T. Eaton Company and Robert Simpson. Shops open 9 - 5 or 5:30, to 9 p.m. Thursday and Friday nights. There is a provincial sales tax.

ACCOMMODATION Halifax Halifax Sheraton, 1919 Upper Water St., (902) 421-1700, downtown on the waterfront, near historic section and Halifax Citadel, 356 rooms, restaurants, 2 lounges, entertainment, indoor pool, disabled facilities available, non smoking rooms available, mini bars in rooms, 9 shops, parking. Chateau Halifax, Scotia Square, (902) 425-6700, 305 rooms and suites, each room has a radio and colour TV, restaurant, bar, dancing, entertainment, indoor and outdoor swimming pools, sauna, laundry service, meeting and convention facilities. Holiday Inn Halifax Centre, (902) 423-1161, 1980 Robie St., 232 rooms, piano bar, indoor swimming pool, whirlpool, gift shop, coffee shop, dining room, special weekend rates, parking, sauna. Lord Nelson Hotel, Spring Garden and S. Park St., (902)

423- 6331, 200 rooms and suites, colour TV, restaurant, bar, barber and beauty shops, laundry service, babysitting, free parking. **Antigonish** Gael Motel, 41 James St., (902) 863-4212, 59 rooms, each room has radio and colour TV, restaurant, outdoor swimming pool. **Dartmouth** Holiday Inn Dartmouth, (902) 463-1100, 99 Wyse Rd., 119 rooms, with phone, TV and radio, restaurant, lounge, tavern, gift shop, cable TV, parking, near golf, tennis and skiing. **Digby** Mountain Gap Flag Inn, P.O. Box 40, Smith's Cove, (902) 245-2277, 112 rooms and housekeeping cottages, open June to October, located on tidal beach, licensed dining room, cocktail lounge, heated swimming pool, tennis courts, cribs provided free of charge. Admiral Digby Inn, Shore Rd., (902) 245-2531, 40 units, colour TV, restaurant, bar, indoor swimming pool, free parking. **Truro** Glengarry Flag Inn, 138 Willow St., (902) 895-5388, 47 rooms, dining room, lounge, outdoor heated swimming pool, meeting rooms, cribs provided free of charge. The Masstowner Motel, Trans Canada Hwy. 104, (902) 662-2500, 20 rooms, each room has a radio and colour TV, restaurant, free parking, meeting rooms. **Sydney** Wandlyn Motor Inn, 100 Kings Rd., (902) 539-3700, 71 rooms, radio and colour TV, restaurant, laundry service, free parking, meeting and convention facilities. Holiday Inn Sydney, (902) 539-6750, 480 Kings Rd. Hwy. near downtown, overlooks harbour, 20 miles to Louisbourg Fortress, 120 rooms, outdoor swimming pool, restaurant, quiet lounge, live entertainment. Vista Motel, 140 Kings Rd., (902) 539-6550, 50 rooms and suites, restaurant, radio, colour TV, free parking, meeting rooms. **Wolfville** Old Orchard Flag Inn, Exit 11, Hwy. 101, (902) 542-5751, 72 rooms, air conditioned, each room has colour TV and phone, licensed dining room and lounge, indoor swimming pool, tennis courts. Paramount Inn, 476 Main St., (902) 542-2237, 13 rooms, TV, restaurant, bar, dancing, entertainment.

MISCELLANEOUS

PROVINCIAL TOURIST BUREAU Nova Scotia Department of Tourism, P.O. Box 456, Halifax, Nova Scotia, B3J 2R5.

VISITOR INFORMATION CENTRES are located in Halifax, Yarmouth, Digby, Amherst and Port Hastings.

Casa Loma, Toronto

PERSPECTIVE

LOCATION Most of the province's boundary with the U.S. runs through the Great Lakes — Lakes Ontario, Huron, Erie and Superior. Southern Ontario extends to a latitude south of the California-Oregon border. Toronto is 350 miles west from Montreal, 2,800 miles east of Vancouver on the Pacific coast.

AREA 354,223 square miles, second in size to Quebec. Ontario contains an estimated 250,000 lakes.

BACKGROUND Ontario is one of the four original provinces which banded together to create the Canadian nation. The territory, a part of Quebec from 1774 to 1791, became a separate British colony, known as Upper Canada, following the sizeable immigration of United Empire Loyalists from the United States during the time of the American Revolution. Quebec and Ontario were again united in 1841 but the demonstrated inability of the French and English language groups to settle their differences resulted in the permanent formation of a separate province in the year of Confederation (1867).

POPULATION 8.750,000, or about a third of the country's population.

CAPITAL Toronto, population 2,700,000. Ottawa, the nation's capital, is a city of about 650,000. Hamilton has 350,000 inhabitants. The vacation centre of Niagara Falls has a population of close to 100,000.

LANGUAGES French is spoken in the eastern part of the predominantly English-language province.

TIME ZONES Ontario observes Central Standard Time in a wide western corridor and Eastern Standard Time where the main cities, including Toronto and Ottawa, are located.

WHEN TO VISIT The most enjoyable months for travellers in southern Ontario are May, June and September. July and August afternoons often reach in the 80's. Centres in the north, Thunder Bay for instance, are about seven to 10 degrees cooler in the summer than Toronto. Toronto's Canadian National Exhibition is staged from mid August to early September.

ONTARIO

TORONTO City Hall, completed in 1965 at a cost of some $40 million, has become the symbol of the city. Points of interest of the famous civic building are the chamber in which the Toronto City Council meets, a white dome enclosed by two towers and Nathan Phillips Square. Free tours of this impressive building are conducted every day. The Old City Hall (1899), home of the province's courts, still stands at the corner of Bay and Queen Streets. **Chinatown**, once confined to a small area just behind the new City Hall, has expanded considerably in size in recent years. **Casa Loma** is Canada's answer to the chateaux of Europe. This imposing 98-room castle was constructed from 1911-14 at a cost of $3 million. Highlights are tiled and mahogany stables, tunnels and secret passageways. The five acre site was ceded to the city by the original owner after he was no longer able to pay the taxes. It stands off Spadina Rd., just north of Davenport and is open daily. **Parliament Buildings** on Queen's Park, a complex of buildings north of University and College, are the home of the provincial legislature. The buildings were constructed between 1886-1893. The University of Toronto campus is close by. The 90 acre **Ontario Place**, built on artificial islands in Lake Ontario at the foot of the city, is cited as Toronto's answer to Montreal's Expo. Its numerous attractions include restaurants, beaches, a children's playground, a concert hall, theatres, shops, picnic and park areas. The season extends from mid May to mid September. The **Ontario Science Centre** is at 770 Don Mills Rd., south of Eglinton Ave. East. Open 10-6 p.m. daily, this highly regarded museum features hundreds of displays on the latest developments in technology. Visitors are encouraged to operate the various exhibits. The 3,100 seat **O'Keefe Centre** at Yonge and Front presents Broadway shows, ballet, jazz, opera, top singers and concerts. Top international guest artists appear regularly. **Fort York** is a pioneer fort situated on the original site of Toronto, at Fleet and Bathurst Streets by the Lakeshore. It dates from 1793, was invaded by the Americans in 1813 and has been restored to its early 19th century appearance. There are a number of original buildings made of log, brick and stone on the ground. Barrack guards stand on duty during the summertime. **The Royal Ontario Museum** at the corner of Bloor and Avenue Rd., is the country's finest museum. It houses displays on successive eras of history, Indian life, geology and a highly rated collection on Chinese civiliza-

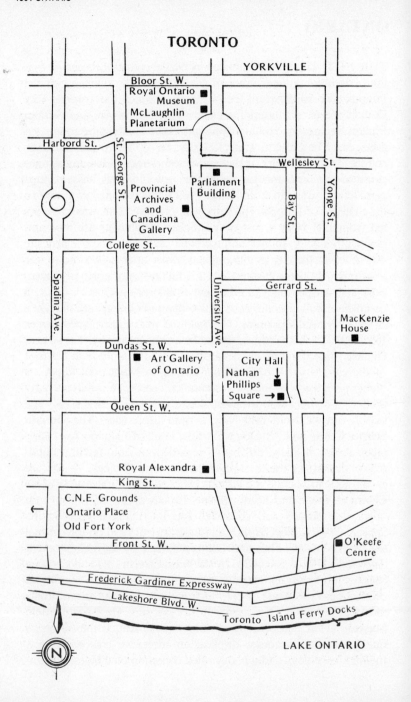

TORONTO

tion. Its neighbour, the fine **McLaughlin Planetarium** presents shows every day but Monday. The Canadiana Building, at 14 Queen's Park Cres. West, is noted for displays of Canadian furniture dating from the period of pioneer French and English Canada. The public is welcome 10-5, Monday to Saturday and Sunday afternoon. Mackenzie House (82 Bond St.), the renovated dwelling of the first mayor of Toronto and his home until 1861, displays furnishings of the period and an early printing press. Open 9:30-5 daily and Sunday afternoon. **Black Creek Pioneer Village** (at Steeles and Jane) is interesting. This open air museum represents 19th century Upper Canada (name of Ontario before 1867) rural community. Costumes of the time are worn by participating "members" of the community. Sights include a restored shoe repair shop, a general store, fire hall, printing office, blacksmith and harness shop, schoolhouse, flour mill and old dwellings. Open 10-6 July and August, and reduced hours at other times. The Hockey Hall of Fame in Exhibition Park (open 10:30-4:30) offers hockey trophies, momentoes of hockey all-stars and other exhibits recalling the development of Canada's national sport. The Sports Hall of Fame in the same building covers a wide range of sports from rowing to cycling. **Yorkville** district, consisting of Cumberland Street, Hazelton Avenue, Scollard Street and Yorkville Avenue, attracts out of town visitors because of its atmosphere, coffee-houses, boutiques and art galleries. Some two hundred gardens and parks are contained within the city's boundaries. Parks to visit include High Park enclosed by Bloor St., Parkside Dr., and the Queensway. Its 340 acres feature trails, picnic grounds, a zoo, snack bars, playgrounds, summer sports facilities and boat rentals. Edwards Gardens, at Leslie St. and Lawrence Ave. East, has picnic spots and rock gardens. Allan Botanical Gardens at Carlton and Sherbourne contains flower displays and James Garden (Edgehill Rd. in suburban Etobicoke) has rock gardens and pathways in its dozen acres. Riverdale Farm is located at Sumach and Winchester Streets. The outdoor fruit, vegetable and clothing stalls of Kensington Market (off Spadina Ave. and south of College) are spread over a small neighborhood. **Toronto Islands**, small islands in the harbor reached by ferry, offer swimming, picnic grounds, beaches, tennis and an amusement park for children. Ferries sail during the day from the docks at the foot of Bay Street. The **Canadian National Exhibition** lures hundreds of thousands of tourists a year from neighboring states and provinces for its midway,

O'Keefe Centre, Toronto

grandstand shows and exhibits. The world's biggest annual fair, staged from mid August to Labour Day, is open all day and evening and on Sunday afternoon and evening. Markham Village was converted from a rather drab neighborhood (at Bloor and Bathurst Streets) into a district of boutiques and art galleries. The Metro Toronto Conservation Authority operates a fine system of parks in Toronto's outskirts. **Harbourfront**, an 86 acre site located on Toronto's waterfront, offers 2 miles of lighted pedestrian paths, picnic tables and barbeques. The **CN Tower**, located at Front near Simcoe, is the tallest free standing structure in the world, attaining a height of 1,815 feet. A communications tower, it features glass walled elevators, indoor and outdoor observation platforms (the views of the southern Ontario countryside are excellent) and a revolving restaurant, the largest and highest in the world, seating 420 people. Boutiques and lounges are found at the base of the tower. The renovated **Art Gallery of Ontario** at Dundas and Beverley Streets contains a fine collection of contemporary art and sculpture. Added attractions in Toronto are Gibson House, Montgomery's Inn, St. Lawrence Hall, Toronto Eaton Centre, and the St. Lawrence Market. The highly regarded **Metropolitan Toronto Zoo** contains within its several hundred acres, a tremendous range of animals from around the world. The 3,800 animals can be viewed in habitats resembling their natural environments. The zoo is located at Highway 401 East at Meadowvale Road. **SkyDome**, in downtown Toronto, is the home of the Toronto Blue Jays of the American League. Canada's and indeed North America's, most impressive baseball stadium, it was completed in 1989 at the cost of several hundred million dollars.

CHILDREN'S TORONTO Attractions listed above that hold special interest for children are the Toronto Islands and Ontario Science Centre. Groups of schoolchildren come to see the Royal Ontario Museum. The McLaughlin Planetarium is an interesting midtown family attraction. Canadian National Exhibition and the Hockey Hall of Fame located on the Exhibition grounds, are dual kids' (and family) interests. Black Creek Pioneer Village is an excellent half day's outing, interesting for both adults and children alike. There are many parks within and on the outskirts of Toronto. Sights for kids in the Toronto region include the perennial favorite, Niagara Falls (featuring, in addition to the waterfalls, Marineland and Pyramid Place), old Fort George at Niagara-on-the-Lake and Fort Henry in Kingston. Canada's Wonderland, north of Toronto, is another fine family attraction in the province. Families go on weekend outings to Lake Simcoe or Muskoka.

EXCURSIONS FROM TORONTO East of Toronto near the town of **Whitby** visit Cullen Gardens and Miniature Village. Featured on the 50 acre site are dozens of miniature buildings (built on a scale of 1 to 12), trees, a pond, rose bushes, rides on a covered wagon and a train operating around the buildings. **Oshawa** is 30 miles east of Toronto. The local automobile museum (99 Simcoe St. S.) traces the development of passenger vehicles from 1771 to the present. An early Rolls Royce and turn of the century vehicles are among the automobiles exhibited 10-5, Monday-Saturday, Sunday 2-5, from late May to early October. The Pioneer Home Museum is a renovated early settler's (1830) dwelling, located at Courtice Rd. and Hwy. 401. It displays furniture of the period during the day from late in May to Labour Day. The Robinson House Museum is an 1846 family dwelling, open Tuesday to Sunday, 2-5 p.m., late May to early October. The National Stud Farm, a short distance north, is of interest for champion horses are bred here. Open 1-4 p.m., weekdays. Sharon's Temple is a 140-year-old house of worship of the Children of Peace Religious Society. Sightseers are received 11-5 p.m. from May to September. A half hour drive north of Toronto downtown on Highway 401 in the town of Vaughan is **Canada's Wonderland**, offering a 320 acre theme park with a man-made mountain, restaurants, boutiques, rides and games, street entertainers, the Medieval Pub, Canterbury Theatre, a waterfall, and Salt Water Circus. **Kleinburg**'s McMichael Canadian Collection of Art houses an extensive collection of works by the Group of Seven, a small group, who in the early 1900's created a distinctive school of Canadian art. Open 1-5:30, every day but Monday. The Toronto suburb of Oakville has two museums. The Post Office (1835-57) and the Thomas House Museum (1830) in Lakeside Park are open 2-5 Tuesday-Sunday, from mid May to October. **Burlington** The Joseph Brant Museum, home of the Mohawk Indian chief, Joseph Brant, exhibits Indian and pioneer relics, on view 10-5 p.m., daily all year. **Hamilton** is a steel manufacturing centre. The city's principal attraction is the 35 room Dundurn Castle, located at Dundurn Park on York Blvd. This restored mansion, completed 1832-35, was the home of Sir Allan McNab, a premier of the provinces of United Canada 1854-56; he bankrupted himself building this palatial residence. Open to the public 1-4 p.m. daily. Visiting hours are extended in the summer. The Royal Botanical Gardens' 2,000 acres consists of outstanding rock gardens, nature trails, and floral displays. Gage Park (Main Street) includes rose gardens within its 75 acres. Sam Lawrence Park on Hamilton Mountain has flower displays and a fine view of the city. The open air farmer's market at James and York operates 5 a.m.-6 p.m. on Tuesday, Thursday and Saturday. The Steel Company of Canada is on Wilcox St. near the harbour. You may take a conducted tour of steel making operations Tuesday-Friday, by appointment only.

SOUTHWESTERN ONTARIO An hour's drive from Toronto is African Lion Safari, a 500 acre park and home to tigers, rhinos, other animals and exotic birds. The wildlife area is located off Highway 8 at Rockton. **Guelph** is the birthplace of Colonel John McCrae, the Canadian poet whose work In Flanders Field was inspired during The Battle of Ypres in Belgium, 1915. The home is an historic site, exhibiting family belongings, 2-5 p.m., every day but Monday, mid-May to mid October. Many varieties of waterfowl live in the Kortright Waterfowl Park by Speed River, open daily from 10-5. Other local interests are the Gothic Church of our Lady of the Immaculate Conception, the 45-foot floral clock and the first wooden home (1828) in Guelph, both in Riverdale Park. **Kitchener** Woodside National Historic Park (528 Wellington St. N.) contains the childhood home of the former Liberal Prime Minister King, prime minister during much of the 1920's, 1930's and 1940's. Other attractions are the annual Oktoberfest festival held in the fall and the Saturday morning Farmer's Market operated near City Hall. Highlights of Doon Pioneer Village and Museum, a short distance southwest, are several pioneer dwellings — a church, general store and log cabin — open 10-5, May to October. It was in **Brantford** that Alexander Graham Bell made his first phone call. The Bell Homestead (a mile south) was his home; his inventions and first telephones are displayed here 10-6 every day but Monday. Items in Brant County Museum (Charlotte St.) describe Indian life and the life of early settlers. Regional interests are Glenhyrst Gardens Mansion (a mile north) with estate, garden and art gallery and St. Paul's Church, Her Majesty's Chapel of the Mohawks (3 miles southeast), the oldest Protestant church in the province, built 1785. Chiefswood, a few miles off, was the home of the Indian poetess Pauline Johnson. Open 10-5 p.m. daily from late

May to early September. The Six Nation's Pageant is staged by local Indians in August. **Simcoe**'s Eva-Brook-Donly Art Museum (109 Norfolk St. S.) exhibits miscellaneous items and paintings of pioneer life, on view 1-5 p.m., Wednesday to Sunday, the year round. Tours of the Imperial Tobacco Company in Delhi can be arranged. **St. Thomas** offers the Church of St. Thomas dating back to 1823. Elgin County Pioneer Museum, a short distance west of town, is a mid 19th century doctor's residence, open 10-5 weekdays, plus weekend afternoons. Closed Monday. **London** Eldon House at 481 Ridout St. N., the city's oldest home, contains furnishings of the 1830's, exhibited for public view 2-5 p.m. Opening hours are extended in the summer. Centennial Museum at 325 Queen's Ave. houses changing exhibits, on display 9-9 every day, Saturday to 5 p.m. and Sunday 2-5. Springbank Park comprises the six-acre Storybook Gardens, open 12-5 April to mid October and until 8 p.m. in the summer. Two local museums are the Indian Archeology Museum on the university campus and the Royal Canadian Regiment (military) Museum. Fanshawe Pioneer Village, five miles northwest, has log cabins and furnishings; Fanshawe Park features summer sports. **Stratford** is the home of the renowned annual Shakespeare Festival. **Dresden** Uncle Tom's Cabin was the dwelling of Rev. Henson, whose experiences in slavery inspired the author of the novel; his grave adjoins the museum. Open 10-6, every day, from May to the end of October. **Chatham** maintains the Chatham-Kent Museum of Indian and 19th century life and a Baptist church, dating from 1858. **Kingsville** is the site of Jack Miner's Bird Sanctuary, open weekdays from early in October to May. The best time to view the migrating birds is from late October to the end of November and late afternoons during the first half of April. Point Pelee National Park is east of here. **Windsor** Points of interest include free tours of Hiram Walker and Sons Distillery, the Art Gallery of Windsor, Hiram Walker Historical Museum and Windsor Raceway. Sombra village is of passing interest for its local museum on the township's history, open 2-5 p.m., daily, April to October.

NIAGARA FALLS There are numerous sightseeing supplements to the primary attraction, Niagara Falls. The world renowned falls measure close to 1,000 feet in width; the Canadian Horseshoe Falls cascade 176 feet and the American Falls drop 184 feet to the gorge below. The cataract is illuminated in the evening. Skylon Tower at

Skylon Park, Maple Leaf Village Tower and the Panasonic Observation Tower are ideal for viewing the falls. You can get a close up look of the falls from the cruise boat Maid-of-the-Mist departing regularly, May to October, from Princess Elizabeth Building at Centre St. The Whirlpool Aerocar provides another means of observing the falls. The cablecar on River Rd., a couple of miles from the falls, transports visitors 1,900 feet over the Niagara River, rapids and whirlpool. You will get yet another view of the whirlpool and gorge from the Great Gorge Elevator at River Rd., a short distance north of the falls, which descends to a vantage point for observing the nearby rapids. Other highlights in the Falls area are Marineland and Game Farm on Portage Rd. (roaming animals, dolphins, seals, open daily), Maple Leaf Village and Queen Victoria Park, illuminated in the evening. Table Rock House overlooks and provides an observation post for the Canadian Falls. **Pyramid Place** on Robertson Blvd., adjacent to the Skylon Tower, is an entertainment centre, presenting shows and attractions suitable for families. Pyramid Place features Kid's Place, where children can enjoy a wide variety of recreational activities. The entertainment complex also offers motion picture presentations shown on Canada's largest movie screen. There are several attractions worth noting on the American side of Niagara Falls. The Niagara Falls Aquarium on Whirlpool St. and Pine entertains with trained sea lions and porpoises, sharks, electric eels and exotic species of fish. The 280-foot-high Observation Tower at the foot of the American Falls commands spectacular views. Schoelkopf Geological Tower, overlooking the gorge, offers exhibits illustrating the geological development of the Niagara Falls region. Niagara Wax Museum at 333 Prospect St., presents life-like wax figures of prominent individuals. There are fine views of the falls from Power Vista, 5 miles north of Lewiston Rd. Also of interest here is the mural by Thomas Hart Benson on the discovery of the Falls, audio visual shows, a relief map and a diorama of the power station. Whirlpool State Park, 3½ miles north of the falls via the Robert Moses Parkway, is a fine vantage point for views of the rapids and whirlpool.

EXCURSIONS FROM NIAGARA FALLS Niagara-on-the-Lake is a dozen miles north of the Falls. The 175 year old Fort George is a rebuilt border defence post, active in the War of 1812. You can visit the original structures 9-6 daily, May 15-early September and 10-5 daily from early September until mid October. The fort is found by

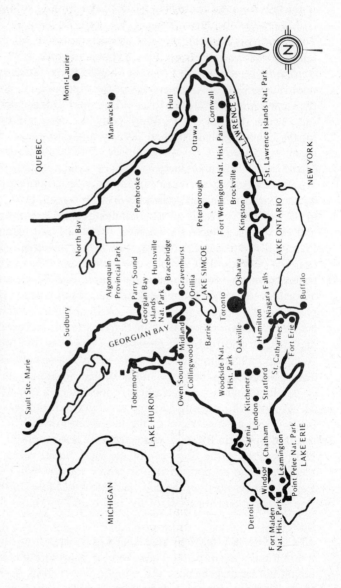

SOUTHERN ONTARIO

QUEBEC

Mont-Laurier

Maniwacki

Hull

Ottawa

Cornwall

Fort Wellington Nat. Hist. Park

ST. LAWRENCE R.

St. Lawrence Islands Nat. Park

Pembroke

Peterborough

Brockville

Kingston

NEW YORK

LAKE ONTARIO

North Bay

Algonquin Provincial Park

Parry Sound

Huntsville

Bracebridge

Gravenhurst

LAKE SIMCOE

Oshawa

Sudbury

Georgian Bay Islands Nat. Park

Orillia

Toronto

Niagara Falls

Buffalo

GEORGIAN BAY

Midland

Barrie

Hamilton

Sault Ste. Marie

Collingwood

Owen Sound

Woodside Nat. Hist. Park

Oakville

St. Catharines

Fort Erie

Tobermory

Kitchener

Stratford

LAKE HURON

Sarnia

London

Chatham

MICHIGAN

Windsor

Leamington

Point Pelee Nat. Park

LAKE ERIE

Detroit

Fort Malden Nat. Hist. Park

the Niagara Parkway on the south side of town. McFarland House (1800) is a museum depicting life in the first half of the last century. Open 11-5 Saturday to Wednesday from July to mid September and on weekends from May to September. Other town interests are St. Mark's Anglican and St. Andrew's Presbyterian colonial churches, a century-old restored pharmacy at King and Queen and the Niagara Historical Museum open 10-6 p.m., mid-May to mid-October. This town is the site of the popular summer Shaw Festival. **Queenston**, five miles north of the falls, lies at the foot of Queenston Heights, scene of a War of 1812 battle, commemorated in a monument to General Brock. Tour the Laura Secord Homestead, open 10-6 p.m. weekdays and until 7 on weekends from mid-May to mid-October. Fort Erie by the border preserves old Fort Erie, erected in 1764. View the drawbridge, cannon and items from the War of 1812 fought on Canadian soil between the Americans and the British. Open daily from 9:30-6 p.m., May to October. **St. Catharines** The main attractions include the September Grape and Wine Festival and the Royal Henley Regatta staged in August. Sights are the Mountain Mills Museum, a water powered mill (open noon-5 weekends, 1-5 Tuesday to Friday, from mid May to the end of August, and the St. Catharines Historical Museum (343 Merritt St.) with exhibits on local history, displayed 1-5 p.m.

EASTERN ONTARIO Bowmanville Two attractions worth visiting: the Pioneer Museum in Darlington Provincial Park, a log house erected in the 1830's (open Saturday 8-5, Sunday 12-5, late May-August), and the Bowmanville Museum (37 Silver St.) with displays of the 1850's. Open 9:30-5 Tuesday-Saturday plus Sunday afternoon, from late May to mid October, **Cobourg** The 30 acre Victoria Park overlooking Lake Ontario offers swimming and picnic grounds. Victoria Hall (1860) encloses a courthouse identical to the Old Bailey in London. Worth seeing is the refurbished opera house and the Barnum House Museum (1817). This Georgian home is five miles east on Hwy. 2, a half mile west of the village of Grafton. It has a fine display of pioneer furnishings, on view 1-5 p.m. Sundays from May to October, daily in July and August. Tours are conducted summer days (except for the second half of July) through Corbyville's Corby Distillery, 2 miles north of Belleville. **Belleville** maintains Hastings County Museum at 257 Bridge Street East, open 1-4:30 p.m., all year. Closed Monday. White Chapel, a pioneer

Methodist house of worship (1809), stands near Picton. **Kingston** Old Fort Henry was used in the War of 1812 and restored between 1832-35. This military history museum presents precision guards in old British uniform, the changing of the guard and drills. It has 125 rooms, open 9:30-5 every day from the middle of May to mid October, to 6:30 p.m. from mid June to Labor Day. The Royal Military College Museum located in Fort Frederick's Martello Tower, east of town on Highway 2, has a weapons collection. Open 10-6 every day, mid June to August. Queen's University Geological Museum houses rock and mineral specimens. The International Hockey Hall of Fame at York and Alfred Streets, traces the history of Canada's national game. Open 1-6 p.m., July and August, weekends from September to June. The Canadian Forces Communications and Electronics Museum is a mile east of the city on Highway 2. Open 1-4 daily, except Saturday. Bellevue House (1840), on Centre Street, was the home of Sir John A. MacDonald, Canada's first prime minister. The home's interior is open daily 10-5 p.m. The Murney Tower Museum in MacDonald Park is housed in the old stone Martello Tower completed in 1846. It depicts the military history of the region. Open 10-8 p.m., July and August, weekends late May and June. Kingston, Gananoque, Ivy Lea and Rockport are points of departure for cruises of the Thousand Islands. Upper Canada Village, six miles east of **Morrisburg,** reveals the way of life in a 19th century community. See the general store which dates from 1861, tavern (1863), church (1844), schoolteacher's house (1821), bakery, sawmill, a doctor's home, spinning mill and many other buildings. Open 9:30-5, mid May to mid October and to 6:30 p.m. in July and August. The Glengarry Pioneer Museum with its pioneer artifacts and the Nor'westers and Loyalist Museum are two of the main attractions in **Cornwall.** Along Water and Pitt Streets, several colonial buildings, including the court house (1795) and jail, can be seen.

OTTAWA The Parliament Buildings on Parliament Hill, completed between 1859-65, are the major sightseeing interest. The House of Commons and Senate assemble here. The summit of its Peace Tower commands a good city view. You may wander through the interior on your own or on conducted tours 9-9, Monday to Saturday, 9-5:30 on Sunday, July and August; from 9-5 in winter. The Changing of the Guard takes place on the front lawn of Parliament. Her Majesty's Canadian Guards perform at 10 a.m. daily during July and August, weather permitting. Laurier House at Laurier E. and Chapel was constructed in 1879. This was the home of two former Liberal Prime Ministers, Wilfred Laurier and William Lyon Mackenzie King. Open 10-5, Tuesday to Saturday plus Sunday afternoon, the year round. **Government House** (at Sussex by Rockcliffe Park) is the residence of the Governor General, Queen Elizabeth's representative in Canada. The estate has 90 acres of woods and gardens. The public is welcome when the Governor General is not in residence. Bytown Museum, on Wellington St., has Ottawa area historical exhibits, on view 10-5 every day except Sunday, mid May to October. The Museum of Canadian Scouting (at 1345 Base Line Rd.) is open 9-4 p.m. weekdays. City recreation areas are Rockcliffe Park, with picnic grounds; the Garden of the Provinces, west of Parliament; and Vincent Massey Park by the Rideau River. The Flower Garden and Arboretum and the 1,500-acre Central Experimental Farm are open every day. Make a weekday appointment to see money in the making at the Royal Canadian Mint, 320 Sussex Dr., by phoning 992-2348. The Royal Canadian Mounted Police Barracks on the east side of Rockcliffe Park receives visitors, 8:30-4:30 weekdays. The Sparks Street shopping mall is pleasant for just strolling. The National War Memorial, on Confederation Square, commemorates Canada's sacrifices in World War I. Local museums are the National Museum of Science and Technology, the National Library and National Archives, the National Gallery of Canada, the National Arts Centre and the National Museum of Man and the Natural Sciences. Boats cruise through the centre of the city on the Rideau Canal during the summer season.

EXCURSIONS FROM OTTAWA Renfrew The McDougall Mill Museum, a grist mill constructed in 1856, houses pioneer farm equipment and items used by local settlers. Champlain Storyland, several miles away, holds particular appeal for children. Hiking trails, picnic spots, an animal museum and about 100 nursery book characters in an outdoor setting are contained within the 45-acre site. It's open 10-sunset from mid May to Labour Day, weekends to mid October. Bonnechère Caves, five miles southeast of Eganville by Routes 41 and 513, have a network of passageways which can be explored, 10-5, May to October. Champlain Trail Museum stands on the outskirts of **Pembroke**. Highlights are a century old dwelling and school (1838), exhibits on early settlements and other buildings. Open 11-8 p.m., July to the first week in September, 2-8, May 24 to the end of June.

DOWNTOWN OTTAWA

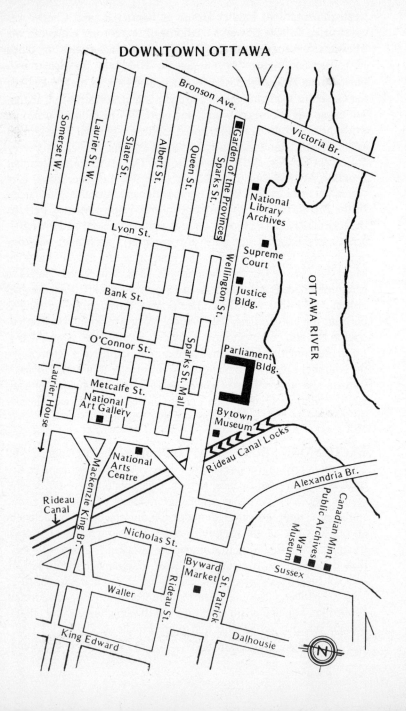

Stonehill Animal Farm, six miles east and north of town, features a variety of birds and animals, on view 9-7 p.m., from late May to the first week in October. **Arnprior's** local museum, tracing the history of the region, is open late May to September, 1:30-4:30 every day (but Monday) and on Sunday from 2-4 p.m. **Almonte** has the renovated Mill of Kintail (1831) with exhibits on pioneer life, as well as the works of world known sculptor Tait McKenzie. Open 10-6 Wednesday to Monday, May to October. Bon Echo Provincial Park, 20 miles north of Kaladar, is noted for Bon Echo Rock (at Mazinaw Lake) with ancient Indian paintings. The park has picnicking, fishing, swimming and camping facilities.

NORTH FROM TORONTO Several vacation areas north of Toronto are popular with Ontario residents and out-of-province visitors. Southampton's Bruce County museum deals with the early settlement of the district, showing household items and pioneer farm equipment. **Owen Sound** The County of Grey and Owen Sound Museum at 975 6th St. East specializes in pioneer and Indian life. Two log cabins on the site may be toured 9-5 daily and Sunday afternoon, July and August and Tuesday-Sunday afternoons other months. Other local attractions are the Tom Thomson Memorial Art Gallery for Canadian art, summer sports and camping in the surrounding countryside. **Collingwood** is a shipbuilding town, a port and a summer and winter sports centre. The local shipbuilding and pioneer museum, south of the shipyards, remains open 9:30-5:30 daily from late June to early September, weekends in late May, June and September. Other regional interests include winter-time skiing at Blue Mountain and tours of the Blue Mountain Pottery Shop near town. The Scenic Caves and Caverns to the west are open every day May-October (weather permitting). **Wasaga Beach** The 50-acre Ontario Zoological Park provides the habitat for roaming animals and birds of many countries. Other attractions: fine swimming, sports and the Nancy Island Historic Site, housing displays on pioneer Great Lake Ships and the ruins of the 1812 warship "Nancy". Open 10-6 p.m., late May to early September. Highlights of **Penetanguishene** are the St. James-on-the-Lines Church in continuous use since 1836, the Historic Naval and Military Establishment, a reconstructed British naval outpost, established on the Great Lakes for the defence of Canada after the War of 1812 (open daily 10-6 p.m., late May to early September) and the town museum exhibiting a 1903 Oldsmobile.

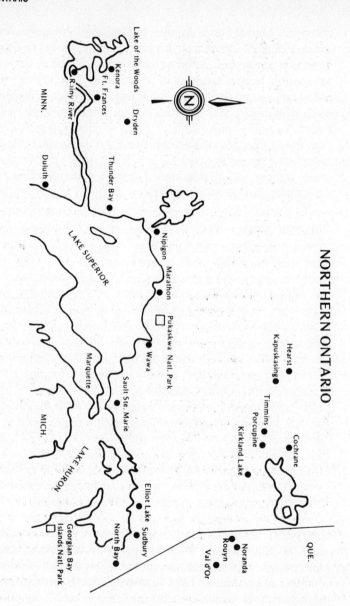

NORTHERN ONTARIO

Open 12-5 every day, July to the beginning of September and weekends in June. **Midland** is popular with many tourists, principally because of the Sainte-Marie-Among-the-Hurons pioneer community rebuilt on the eastern outskirts of town. This three acre former French Jesuit mission (1639-49) is interesting for its blacksmith shop, a museum, carpenter and shoemaker shops, longhouses and other buildings. It is open 10-6, late May to the first week in September, 10-5 until mid October. The Martyrs Shrine is dedicated to Jesuit missionaries slain by Indians. Little Lake Park houses Huronia Museum with pioneer and Iroquois Indian exhibits (on view 9:30-5:30 p.m. and Sunday afternoons) and the interesting Huron Indian Village. A sweat bath, fish drying racks, a longhouse, pottery shop and witch doctor's home recreate Indian life of the 1600's. **Orillia**'s Couchiching Beach Park is noted for its Monument to Champlain, a famed explorer of the early 1600's. The home of the humorist Stephen Leacock on Old Brewery Bay is open in the summer. The three interests of **Gravenhurst** are boat cruises on Lake Muskoka, tours of the 19th century steamboat anchored in Muskoka Bay and the home of Norman Bethune. **Bracebridge** Children delight in the 18-acre Santa's Village, featuring storybook figures, rides on miniature trains, various other rides and a paddle wheel river boat. Open 9-6 mid June to the first week in September, weekends in early June and September. Winter and summer sports are king in **Huntsville**. Chairlifts (six miles east) operate to Peninsula Peak for skiers. The several early settler's dwellings in the Muskoka Pioneer Village are open 10-5 from mid June to the middle of September and weekend afternoons until Thanksgiving. **Algonquin Park** is rewarding for campers. This 2,900 square mile provincial park features canoeing, fishing and is a game preserve as well. **Parry Sound** is noted for fishing, hunting and summer sports.

THE NORTH Northern Ontario is sparsely populated and would be even less settled were it not for its towns built after the discovery of precious metals. Vacation interests of **North Bay** include good fishing, hunting and cruises on Lake Nipissing. Tour the nearby Quints Museum where the well-known (in the 1930's) Dionne quintuplets were born. Open 10-5, late May to early October, 9-6 in July and August. The Northern Ontario Trapper's Museum on Highway 11, along the route from North Bay to Temagami, has exhibits on fur trapping and the pioneer era and a natural history collection. Open

8-8 p.m. daily from late in June to the beginning of September. Temagami Provincial Forest encompasses an area of 5,800 square miles. **Cobalt** The Cobalt Mining Museum has a collection of ore and silver displays and other exhibits, on view 9-5, June to the end of September (and on Sunday afternoon). The museum is located by the post office on Silver Street. **Haileybury** is noted for old homes built by early silver millionaires. Almost one quarter of Canada's gold is mined in **Kirkland Lake**. The Museum of Northern History on Duncan Ave. deals with the district's early history. Open 9-5 Monday to Saturday and Sunday afternoon, mid June to the middle of September, weekdays other months. The paper mill in **Iroquois Falls** offers conducted tours. The gold mining centre of **Timmins** operates tours of its gold mine summer weekdays. Excellent hunting and fishing draw sportsmen to the surrounding area. **Porcupine** features yet another small local history museum. **Sault Ste. Marie** You may view the Soo Locks (connecting Lakes Superior and Huron) in operation or take one of the daily cruises through the locks. A local sight is the Ermatinger House. This fur trader's dwelling, completed from 1814-20, is one of the oldest homes in the region. The restored interior may be toured 10-8 every day and Sunday afternoon, from the end of May to the end of September. Two highlights are Algoma Central Railway day long excursions through the Agawa Canyon wilderness area and the 60-acre Bellevue Park, complete with gardens and roaming animals. The Canoe Lock of 1798 that carried canoes past the rapids of St. Mary River has been restored as an historic site. The Bruce Mines Museum, housing items on the community's development, opens 9-9 p.m. July to August. Elliot Lake has a nuclear and mining museum open all day long, June to the first week in September. Tours of the uranium mine can be arranged every day. Blind River's Timber Village Museum describes the history of early settlements, open 2-5 p.m. and 7-9 p.m. late May to the first week in September. **Sudbury** The 21-acre Centennial Numismatic Park and its enormous replicas of Canadian coins is a major interest in this nickel and copper mining city. Inco Metals Company conducts tours May to early September, Monday to Saturday from 9-2:30 p.m.; children under 12 aren't allowed on the tour for safety reasons. Falconbridge Nickel Mines, 12 miles northeast, arranges summertime visits. Children under 12 aren't permitted to take this tour. Advance arrangements for inspecting the mines are necessary. **Manitoulin Island**, separating Lake Huron from Georgian Bay, is the largest fresh water island in the world. Interests of the 1,000-square-mile island include Indian reservations, and fine hunting and fishing. Local attractions are found in Manitowaning with its pioneer museum, Gore Bay Museum and Little Current-Howland Centennial Museum. Eighteen tribes from six Indian nations meet in Wikwemikong for the August Pow Wow and dances. The island is accessible by boat from Tobermory or by taking Route 68 to Little Current.

NORTH TO MANITOBA Train excursions are scheduled from Cochrane to Moosonee near James Bay; there are few roads that lead that far north. Deer and moose hunting flourish in **Kapuskasing**. The local railway museum, showing exhibits on railways from the turn of the century, is open 10-4, plus Sunday afternoons, June to the beginning of September. **Thunder Bay** (the former twin cities of Port Arthur and Fort William) is a large northern centre, population 100,000. Tours of the local pulp and paper mill are available. The 140-acre Centennial Park has a logging museum, a reconstruction of a 1910 period lumber camp with bunkhouses and cookhouse, picnic grounds, restaurant and animals which children may feed. Open all year. Boat cruises provide vacationers with a panoramic view of the harbor and the eight-mile-long, 1,000-foot-high rock formation called Sleeping Giant. Highlights of Chippewa Park, six miles south, are camp sites, swimming, boating and a miniature railroad. Open all day, mid May to September, A chairlift in the vicinity ascends Mount McKay. Kakabeka Falls (16 miles west of Thunder Bay on Highway 17) are 225 feet wide and 128 feet high. Kakabeka Falls Provincial Park has camping, swimming and picnic facilities. Atikokan's interest is the Centennial Museum and its rebuilt lumber train. **Fort Frances** region is fine for hunting and fishing and Ojibway Indians from the local reservation are available as guides. The Boise-Cascade Pulp and Paper Company operates conducted tours on summer weekdays. **Kenora**'s two interests are daily two-hour cruises of Lake of the Woods and a museum in Memorial Park. This houses relics of Indian and pioneer days, on view 9-5 every day and on Sunday afternoons. Both Dryden and Kenora offer guided tours of paper mills.

HISTORIC SITES, MUSEUMS AND ART GALLERIES The following are representative of the great number of historic sites and museums within Ontario's borders. **Toronto** St. Lawrence Hall (at 157 King St. East) is a restored building dating from 1850. The restored structure is noted for its Great Hall with an interesting chandelier. High Park's Colborne Lodge, dating from 1836, has Canadian art and original 19th century furnishings on display. Open 9:30-5 daily plus Sunday afternoon, all year. The Upper Canada Marine Museum (1841) in Exhibition Park describes the history of Great Lakes shipping. Open 9:30-5 and Sunday afternoon. Cornell House (built 1850) displays contemporary furnishings 12:30-5:30 p.m. weekends and holidays; the house in in Thomson Memorial Park, Brimley Rd. and Lawrence Ave. Scadding cabin in the Canadian National Exhibition grounds is an 18th century one room log cabin, the oldest home in the city, open 2-9, Thursday to Monday, July-August. The Art Gallery of Ontario (317 Dundas W. at Beverley) shows works by European masters as well as Canadian paintings. Also ιo ɒe seen are works by the sculptor Henry Moore. Open from 11-5:30 p.m. every day, Wednesday and Thursday to 9 p.m. **Ottawa** The National Museum of Science and Technology at Russell Rd. and St. Laurent Blvd., houses early inventions and displays on modern technology. Open 9-9 (closed Monday) from September 15 to May 15. The National Aeronautical Collection at Rockcliffe Airfield consists of nearly 100 aircraft tracing the development of flight. Open 9-9 daily, June-August (and closed Monday other months). The National Gallery at Slater and Elgin has an impressive Canadian collection. European masters and French Impressionists are also represented. Open 10-6, Tuesday to Saturday and on Sunday afternoon. The National Library and Public Archives on Wellington St. houses documents, manuscripts, paintings and maps outlining the nation's history. Open 9-5 weekdays. The National Museum of Man and the Natural Sciences at Metcalfe and McLeod Street centres on natural history and the Canadian Indian and Eskimo. The museum is open 10-6; closed Mondays, September to March. Exhibits in the Canadian War Museum (330 Sussex Dr.) trace the nation's military history from its origins to the 20th century. The Medal Room's fine collection of medals is on view 9-5 daily, throughout the year. **Niagara Falls** Tussaud's Wax Museum representations portray many of the world's famous people. The Niagara Falls Museum at Rainbow Bridge has a collection of Egyptian mummies. Oak Hall, the home of the late Sir Harry Oakes, the mining millionaire, is on Portage Rd. south. The Antique Car Museum, 1871 Falls Ave., features classic automobiles of presidents, kings and politicians. Ripley's Believe It or Not Museum features varied displays associated with the life and career of Ripley. **Peterborough** Century Village (several miles east on Route 7) is highlighted by several restored pioneer buildings, open 2-5 p.m. on weekend, in May, June and September-October, 1:30-5 daily in July and August.

HUNTING AND FISHING The forests of northern Ontario harbor moose and bear, the south, bear and deer. Small game include fox, rabbit, raccoon and squirrel. Upland game birds and waterfowl include pheasant, ptarmigan, partridge, woodcock, grouse, Wilson's snipe, quail and several varieties of geese. The main species of fish caught in the province's half million lakes and rivers include lake trout, walleye, largemouth bass, speckled trout, northern pike, whitefish, muskies and perch. Fishing is excellent in remote lakes of the northland. Current angling and hunting regulations may be obtained by writing to the Ministry of Natural Resources, Outdoor Recreation, 99 Wellesley St. West, Toronto, Ontario.

WINTER AND SUMMER SPORTS The range of winter sports includes hockey, ice racing and ice fishing, snowmobiling, skating, curling and sleighing. Ski facilities are located at North Bay, Sault-Ste Marie and Thunder Bay. Ski resorts closer to Toronto are found at Collingwood, Huntsville, Bracebridge, Orangeville and Barrie. The Toronto Maple Leafs professional National Hockey League team plays out its winter schedule at Maple Leaf Gardens. Golf courses, open to the public, are located throughout the province including Toronto, London, Hamilton, Point Pelee National Park, Stratford, Niagara Falls, the Muskoka Lakes region, North Bay, Parry Sound, Ottawa and Fort Frances. Tennis enthusiasts have a choice of courts in Toronto, the Muskoka resort region and in the parks operated by many municipalities. There are endless opportunities for safe swimming in a province containing approximately 250,000 lakes. You may swim in publicly maintained swimming pools of many communities, the Muskoka resort district, at over 100 provincial parks and at Point Pelee National park. Pleasure boats cruise along the Rideau Canal. Waterways in the north — Quetico Provincial Park, Killarney Provincial Park and Algonquin Park — are particularly tempting for canoeists. Hiking opportunities are unrivalled on the 430-mile long Bruce Trail. The trail follows the Niagara Escarpment which begins in Queenston and extends via

Hamilton, Georgetown, Collingwood and Owen Sound to Tobermory, Bruce Peninsula. The season of the Toronto Argonauts, Ottawa Rough Riders or Hamilton Tiger Cats, members of the professional Canadian Football League, continues from August to the late fall. The Toronto Blue Jays major league baseball team plays out its season at Exhibition Park. Toronto also has a professional soccer team (the Toronto Blizzard). Other spectator sports are horse racing at Woodbine (just outside of Toronto), and Greenwood and auto races at Mosport Track near Bowmanville.

NATIONAL PARKS Point Pelee National Park extends into Lake Erie, a few miles south of Leamington. The 4,500 acre park offers picnic grounds, water sports, a beach area, a forest, hiking, canoeing and birdwatching for migrating birds. **Georgian Bay Islands National Park** is comprised of 45 geologically interesting islands in Georgian Bay, at Honey Harbour, Tobermory and other places. Birds and wildlife abound. Flowerpot Island is unusual for its rock pillars. The park's total area is 5.4 square miles. **Fort George National Park** in Niagara-on-the-Lake originates from 1797-1807. This was the main British colonial defence post until the American invasion in 1813. Several of the military structures have been restored, open May-October. **Fort Malden National Historic Park** is at Amherstburg, 18 miles south of Windsor. The fort was constructed by Britain from 1797 - 99 and used in the War of 1812. Two museums are open 10 - 5 (and in the early evening) during June, July and August. **Queenston Heights National Historic Park** is not far from Niagara-on-the-Lake. This was a battlefield, scene of an important American defeat in the War of 1812. **Bellevue House**, the refurbished residence of Sir John A. MacDonald, Centre St., Kingston has been turned into an historic site. **Fort Wellington National Historic Park** is in Prescott by the St. Lawrence River. The stone fort was prepared for the War of 1812. See the blockhouse (1839) fortified by five-foot thick walls, the museum, an arms display, munitions room and other interests. Open daily, May-October. **St. Lawrence Islands National Park** is comprised of 17 wooded islands and numerous islets in the Thousand Islands area. The park's 255 acres boast such features as boating and camping facilities, lovely scenery, bathing and fishing.

MUSIC AND THE THEATRE Roy Thomson Hall is the home of the Toronto Symphony Orchestra and the Toronto Mendelssohn Choir.

Roy Thomson Hall also offers a complete range of musical offerings, from jazz to light rock to classical productions. The National Ballet and Canadian Opera Company both perform in the **O'Keefe Centre** several times a year. Major legitimate theatres are the **Royal Alexandra** on King W. and the **St. Lawrence Centre for the Performing Arts.** The city supports many other small theatres including the Tarragon Theatre (30 Bridgman Ave.), Limelight Dinner Theatre (2026 Yonge St.), Alumnae Theatre (70 Berkeley St.), Toronto Free Theatre (20 Berkeley St.), Bathurst St. Theatre (736 Bathurst St.), Adelaide Court Theatre (57 Adelaide St. E.), The Second City (110 Lombard St.), Club 21 (21 Yorkville Ave.), and Garbo's Bistro (429 Queen St. E.). Recommended dinner theatres are: Harper's (38 Lombard St.), His Majesty's Feast (1926 Lakeshore Blvd. W.), Teller's Cage Dinner Theatre (Commerce Court South), Limelight Dinner Theatre (2026 Yonge St.), and Variety Dinner Theatre (2335 Yonge St.). The Grandstand Show of the Canadian National Exhibition presents top American and Canadian entertainers. Summer evening concerts are offered in Hamilton's Gage Park. **The Stratford Festival** in Stratford continues for about 20 weeks every summer. Plays by Shakespeare, Molière, Isben and others are presented. Performances are given Monday to Saturday and matinees on Wednesday, Friday and Saturday. The highly popular **Shaw Festival** at Niagara-on-the-Lake presents drama by the Irish playwright from May to October. Niagara-on-the-Lake's three theatres, the Festival, the Court House and the Royal George, feature as well, a diverse selection of productions including works by Agatha Christie, Noel Coward, George Gershwin and Ben Travers. Ottawa's National Arts Centre features a 2,500-seat opera house and a 900-seat theatre, where international guest artists appear.

FOOD AND DRINK Toronto has gained an enviable reputation for the variety and quality of its restaurants. Specialty restaurants abound and you could eat at a different one practically every day of the year. Take your choice of Italian, Chinese, Mexican, Swiss, Ethiopian, Thai, Austrian, French, Kosher, Hungarian, Spanish, German, Japanese, Polynesian and Indian cuisine. Reservations are advisable at top restaurants Friday and Saturday evenings. Better known restaurants in Toronto include **Winston's, Southern Accent, Pantalone Restaurant, La Bussola Ristorante, Baretta's Bistro, Le Fave, Seashell Seafood Restaurant, Old House on Church St., J.S.**

Shane's, Scaramouche, Nekah, Bistro 990, Beaujolais, La Grenouille, Barberian's and Mastro's. Licensing hours in Toronto (Monday to Saturday) are noon to 1 a.m. Drinks are served on Sunday, noon to 10 p.m. Liquor is sold at Liquor Control Board outlets, beer from Brewer Retail stores. The legal drinking age is 19.

TRANSPORTATION IN ONTARIO The road network is generally quite adequate. Superhighways give the motorist fast direct connectons from Windsor to the Quebec border and beyond to Montreal. Gravel roads in the extreme north are adequate. Car rental offices are located in main tourist centres and at airports. **VIA Rail Canada** schedules train service to most communities within the province and there are regular departures for transcontinental trains from Toronto to Vancouver. Frequent runs are offered by **VIA** between Montreal and Quebec and Toronto and Ottawa and Toronto. The Ontario Northland Transportation Commission operates trains through north eastern Ontario. Rail service leads from North Bay to the principal northern communities of Cobalt, Haileybury, New Liskeard, Timmins, Cochrane and Moosonee. Algoma Central Railway offers special one day Agawa Canyon wilderness train trips that originate in Sault Ste. Marie and continue to Agawa Canyon in the otherwise inaccessible north. These trips run daily from June to mid October. Sightseeing buses run tours of northern Ontario, in combination with trains, as far north as Thunder Bay. Buses operate every day between Toronto and Niagara Falls and Ottawa. Buses are also scheduled from Toronto to Detroit, Buffalo, New York City and other American and Canadian centres. City buses provide dependable service to midnight in Ottawa, to the early hours of the morning in Toronto. Sightseeing buses tour both cities. Toronto's subway system runs east - west along Bloor St., north - south along Yonge St., and via a parallel route on University Ave. A newer subway route, the Spadina line, takes passengers to the northwest end of the city. Some streetcars remain in operation all night. It's legal for motorists in Ontario to make a right turn on a red light after having come to a complete stop. It's also important to note that motorists are required to yield the way to pedestrians crossing streets at designated crosswalks. Motorist and passengers must wear seatbelts. Almost any place in the province is accessible by airplane; planes may also be chartered to remote fishing and hunting regions. City-run ferries sail between downtown Toronto and islands in the harbour.

Air Canada and **Canadian Airlines** fly to major centres in Ontario from elsewhere in Canada, the United States and western Europe. Regional and commuter airlines supplement their services, among them **Air Ontario, First Air, City Express** and **Skycraft Air. Air Canada** operates from Los Angeles, New York and Cleveland non stop to Toronto. **Canadian Airlines** travels from Vancouver to Toronto non stop daily. **Air Canada** also flies to Montreal and Toronto from London and Paris. **Air Ontario** travels from Toronto to numerous points in northern Ontario, including Kenora, Elliot Lake, Thunder Bay, Sault Ste. Marie, Marathon, Cochrane, Dryden and Kapuskasing. **Air Ontario** provides service to Toronto from Winnipeg. **Air Ontario** also operates from several cities in the United States, including Minneapolis to Thunder Bay and Hartford, Detroit and Dayton, Ohio to Toronto.

First Air operates to Ottawa from Boston daily and the non stop flight takes about 1¼ hours. **First Air** travels to Ottawa from Montreal twice daily and the non stop service takes 35 minutes. **First Air** also goes to Ottawa from Goose Bay, Labrador and Frobisher Bay, N.W.T. **Skycraft Air,** based in Oshawa, departs from Oshawa for both Windsor and Ottawa three times a day on weekdays and once daily on Sundays. **Skycraft Air's** service to both centres is offered non stop. The **Skycraft Air** flight between Oshawa and Ottawa takes about one hour. **Skycraft Air** also flies from Detroit and Montreal to Oshawa. **City Express** operates non stop from Toronto Island Airport to Ottawa numerous times each day throughout the year. **City Express** also goes from Montreal to Toronto on a frequently scheduled service and on the non stop service, the flying time is about 1¼ hours. **City Express** operates to Toronto from Newark - New York non stop several times a day. **City Express** has a service from Windsor to the Ontario capital that is scheduled the year round. **Tempus Air** operates from Hamilton to Kenora and Minneapolis.

Pan American Airways flies to New York from major cities in Europe, the Caribbean and Latin America. **Pan Am** flies from London, Paris, Rome, Madrid, Geneva, Zurich, Stockholm, Brussels, Nice, Amsterdam, Milan, Frankfurt, Helsinki, Oslo and other major European cities to New York and from there **Air Canada** operates to Toronto. **Pan Am** flies to New York from Buenos Aires, Rio de Janeiro, Caracas and other Latin American centres. **Pan Am** also operates from London to Detroit, a service convenient for visitors heading to southwestern Ontario. **Pan Am Express** flies from New York to Buffalo non stop several times a day, a service convenient for visitors bound for southern Ontario. **Finnair** operates from Helsinki to Toronto non stop. **Finnair** also travels from Singapore, Bangkok and other centres in the Orient to Toronto, with a change of plane required in Helsinki. **Scandinavian Airlines (SAS)** operates to Toronto from Copenhagen, Oslo and Stockholm. **SAS** now travels from Copenhagen to Toronto non stop on regularly scheduled service throughout the year. **Royal Jordanian Airlines** operates twice weekly service from Amman to Montreal and from there **City Express** flies to Toronto.

SHOPPING Provincial specials include maple syrup, cheeses, Eskimo soapstone carvings, Eskimo prints, antiques, wines and furs. Eaton's, Simpson's and the Bay, three leading department stores with several branches in Toronto and suburbs, stock a wide variety of quality merchandise, Irish linens, English crystal and chinaware, men's and women's clothing and souvenirs. **The Eaton Centre** downtown at Yonge and Dundas is one of the most impressive shopping complexes in the country. Fine shops are concentrated at Toronto's Yorkdale Shopping Centre at Dufferin and Highway 401 (120 shops), on Bloor Street between Yonge and Avenue Rd. (furs, jewellery, china, antiques, clothing, furniture), Sherway Gardens at the junction of Queen Elizabeth Highway and Highway 27 and Fairview Mall at Don Mills and Sheppard East. The **Yorkville** area, just north of Bloor Street between Avenue Rd. and Yonge St. boasts many fine shops. Toronto downtown stores open from 9 - 6 p.m., to 9 p.m. on Thursday and Friday nights. A provincial sales tax is imposed on goods purchased.

Tilley Endurables is a company based in Toronto, Canada, manufacturing smart looking, high quality clothing made specifically with the sportsman and traveller in mind. Tilley's apparel meets a genuine need of the outdoorsman and others whose vacation plans include time spent boating, sailing, bicycling, fishing, hiking and golfing. The first clothing item produced by Alex Tilley, the firm's founder, is appropriately named the Tilley Hat, now acknowledged as the world's finest outdoor hat. The hat, made in four styles, has been praised for its ingenuity and workmanship. It ties on, won't shrink, repels rain and floats.

The enthusiastic acceptance of his first creation encouraged him to follow up on his success with other travel-related clothing items that include pants and shorts, safari and bush jackets, vests of many pockets, gentleman's vests, Bomber Jackets, sweaters, Mephisto shoes, a complete line of cotton clothing for men and women, windbreakers, shirts, skirts and culottes, many with secret pockets suitable for passports. The clothing is comfortable and tough enough to stand up to the roughest conditions. The apparel is so durable, in fact, that Tilley guarantees to replace, free of charge, a worn out pair of endurables within a five year period. The hats are sold with a lifetime guarantee.

The line of clothing is sold at shops across North America. Tilley Endurables are located at 900 Don Mills Road, Don Mills, Ontario, (416) 444-4465, and in downtown Toronto at 207 Queen's Quay West, (416) 865-9910, 158 Rue Laurier W. in Montreal, (514) 272-7791, 1537 West Broadway Ave. in Vancouver, (604) 732-4287, 31 Lakeshore Rd. W. in Oakville, (416) 338-3248, 118 Needham St. in Boston, (617) 964-0917 and 520 East Hyman in Aspen, Colorado, (303) 925-8220. Mail orders are accepted from Tilley's 33 page catalogue. The phone number to call in Canada is 1-800-387-0110. In the United States the phone number is 1-800-338-2797.

ACCOMMODATION Kenora *Minaki Lodge* (807) 224-4000, a beautiful resort 30 miles north of Kenora, 120 rooms, beautiful setting, located on edge of a lake, all water sports, water skiing, wind surfing, canoeing, swimming pool, fishing with guide available (at extra charge), volleyball, jogging, bicycles, badminton, dining room, library lounge, major credit cards, parking, golf, tennis and other sports facilities, open May to early October. **St. Catharines** *Holiday Inn* at 2 North Service Rd. (416) 934-2561, not far from Niagara Falls, Niagara on the Lake and Welland Canal, 140 rooms with TV and air conditioning, indoor leisure and fitness centre, outdoor swimming pool, restaurant and wine bar, parking, major credit cards. **Sudbury** *Holiday Inn* at Ste. Anne Rd. and Notre Dame Ave., (705) 675-1123, off Hwy. 17, 146 rooms, dining room, coffee shop, indoor swimming pool, gift shop, in-room movies, near fishing and hunting. **Toronto** *Inter Continental Hotel,* 220 Bloor St. West, (call 1-800-327-0200 for reservations), part of a first class chain of hotels operated in North America and internationally, centrally located near Yorkville shopping district, the fine shops on Bloor St. W., the Royal Ontario Museum and Planetarium, near Queen's Park, convenient to Bloor Street and Yonge Street subway lines, 218 air conditioned rooms, colour TV in rooms with movie channel and mini bar, excellent restaurant, tea lounge, courtyard for outdoor dining, 24 hour room service, laundry and valet service, concierge, health club with swimming pool, sauna and massage room, major credit cards. *Toronto Harbour Castle Westin,* 1 Harbour Square (416) 869-1600, 974 rooms, overlooking the lake, convenient to downtown business section, complimentary shuttle service to shopping areas, 3 lounges, indoor parking, revolving rooftop restaurant plus 3 other restaurants, including Chateauneuf 5 star award-winning restaurant, gift shops, indoor heated swimming pool, health facilities, steam room, sauna, squash courts, non smoking floors available. *Sutton Place Hotel,* 955 Bay St., (416) 924-9221, 208 rooms, 72 suites, air conditioned, colour TV, mini bar and phone in each room, indoor swimming pool, fitness centre, sauna, sun deck, 24 hour room service, 2 restaurants, Sans Souci restaurant specializes in haute cuisine, piano lobby bar, indoor parking, gift shops, barber shop, indoor parking, major credit cards accepted, one of the finest hotels in Toronto, well recommended. *Holiday Inn Toronto Downtown,* 89 Chestnut Street, (416) 977-0707, neighbouring the new City Hall, 715 rooms, colour TV, phones, in-house movies, close to major shops and sightseeing attractions, minutes walk from Chinatown, indoor parking, 2 main restaurants, including a revolving restaurant, 2 lounges, live entertainment featured, indoor and outdoor pools, sauna, games room. *Hotel Radisson Toronto Don Valley* at 1250 Eglinton Ave. E., (416) 449-4111, close to the Don Valley Parkway, ten minutes from downtown Toronto, 354 rooms, air conditioned, colour TV, restaurants, lobby bar has evening piano entertainment, Ravine Club features indoor pool, weight room and aerobics, Plaza Club floor has king sized rooms for the business traveller, hotel is not far from Ontario Science Centre, Metro Toronto Zoo, museums, shops and entertainment, major credit cards accepted. *Four Seasons Hotel,* 21 Avenue Rd., (416) 964-0411, in Yorkville shopping district, near Royal Ontario Museum, 379 rooms and suites, with air conditioning, colour TV, mini bar, indoor and outdoor pool, fitness room with whirlpool and sauna, massage, lounge, lobby bar, gift shop, 24 hour room service, informal cafe, award winning Truffles Dining Room, major credit cards accepted, one of the best hotels in the city. *Inn on the Park,* at Leslie and Eglinton Ave. E., (416) 444-2561, 568 rooms and suites, with air conditioning, colour TV, desk, mini bar, indoor and outdoor swimming pools, health club with indoor track, exercise bikes and an indoor pool, sauna, tennis club, squash and racquetball next door, formal dining lounge, informal restaurant, piano bar, lounge, free parking, major credit cards, 24 hour room service, gift shops, close to Don Valley Parkway. *Sheraton Centre Hotel*, 123 Queen St. W., (416) 361-1000, in the centre of town opposite City Hall, 1398 rooms, 79 suites, 4 restaurants and lounges, parking, indoor and outdoor heated pools, sauna, whirlpool, hot tub and exercise room, many specialty shops, large landscaped garden, disabled facilities available, no smoking rooms, attached to underground city of shops and close to the famous Eaton Centre. *Windsor Arms*, (416) 979-2341, 22 St. Thomas St., near shops at Bloor and Bay, elegant hotel, has 81 rooms and suites, rooms have high ceilings, furnished with European and Canadian antiques, Three Small Rooms restaurant consists of three restaurants, The Restaurant, The Gull and The Wine Cellar, Courtyard Cafe is a contemporary version of a European cafe, Twenty-two piano bar offers light lunches, open all year, highly recommended. *Prince Hotel*, 900 York Mills Rd., accessible from Hwy. 401, (416) 444-2511, 404 rooms with air conditioning and colour TV, sports complex with tennis courts, fitness room, indoor and outdoor swimming pool, five restaurants, coffee shop, formal dining, lounge, free parking, 24 hour room service, major credit cards, shops on premises, friendly service, tours to sightseeing attractions can be arranged. *Sheraton Toronto East Hotel*, 2035 Kennedy Rd., convenient access off Hwy. 401, (416) 299-1500, 386 rooms, air conditioned, colour TV, indoor swimming pool, squash courts, mini putting green, sauna, whirlpool, fitness room, games room, 2 restaurants including informal restaurant, free parking, major credit cards accepted, piano lounge in the main lobby, gift shop, squash courts, 24 hour room service. *Hotel Admiral*, 249 Queens Quay West, (416) 364-5444, on edge of Lake Ontario, 158 rooms with colour TV, air conditioning, radio and mini bar, whirlpool, squash courts, outdoor swimming pool, Commodore Dining Room, informal restaurant, piano lounge, 2 ballrooms, underground parking, programmes of entertainment, credit cards accepted included Amex, Visa, EnRoute, Mastercard and Diner's Club, close to new baseball stadium and Union Station, free shuttle bus service to Union Station or the downtown area, shops on ground floor of hotel, travel agency. *Toronto Airport Hilton International*, 5875 Airport Rd., (416) 677-9900, 259 guest rooms and 154 mini suites, minutes from the airport, all rooms have colour TV, radio, telephone, mini bar and in house movies, 2 restaurants, cocktail lounge, disco, year round swimming pool, gift shops, barber shop, free transportation to and from airport, major credit cards, fitness centre, free parking. *Hotel Hilton International Toronto*, 145 Richmond St. W., at University Ave., (416) 869-3456, 600 rooms with colour TV, mini bar, phone, downtown location, terrace dining in garden setting, Trader Vic's restaurant with international cuisine for lunch and dinner, nightly entertainment, lounge, indoor and outdoor swimming pools, health club, close to downtown sightseeing attractions, including the City Hall, underground parking. *The Guild Inn*, 201 Guildwood Pkwy, (416) 261-3331, 95 rooms including 5 suites, located at the Scarborough Bluffs on Lake Ontario, newly renovated, most have two double beds, all have balconies, situated in 90 acres of parkland and gardens, 26 acres of them are manicured lawns with statues, dining room, outdoor terrace dining in the summer, outdoor heated pool, tennis court, games room, major credit cards, open all year, convenient access to downtown Toronto and close to the Metro Zoo. **Niagara Falls** *Sheraton Hotel* (Buffalo Airport), 2040 Walden Ave., (716) 681-2400, not far from the Falls, 300 rooms, 12 suites, courtesy car to airport, restaurant, lounge, pool, saunas, exercise room, disabled facilities, no smoking rooms available, parking, major credit cards. **Niagara-on-the-Lake** *Prince of Wales Hotel*, (416) 468-3246 or 1-800-263-2452, 1 ½ hours south of Toronto, recommended place to stay when attending the Shaw Festival, 104 rooms, air conditioned, dining room, full range of amenities, several golf courses nearby, floodlit tennis court, trips can be arranged to Niagara Falls and wineries, bar, sunroom, exercise room, health club, heated indoor swimming pool, saunas, whirlpool, built 1864, retains charm of its Victorian origins. **Ottawa** *Hotel Radisson Ottawa Centre*, 100 Kent St., (613) 238-1122, close to Parliament Bldgs., within walking distance of other tourist attractions, museums and shops, 504 rooms, air conditioned, mini bar, colour TV, indoor swimming pool, sauna, exercise room, billiards room, indoor parking, lounges, revolving rooftop restaurant, Cafe Toulouse, major credit cards accepted. *Four Seasons Hotel*, 166 Albert St., near Parliament Bldgs., (613) 238-1500, 222 rooms, 17 floors, rooms with colour TV, radio, mini bar, formal dining called Carlton Restaurant, serves fine French cuisine, sidewalk cafe for lunch and dinner, two cocktail lounges, valet parking available adjacent to hotel, health club open daily, exercise bikes, indoor swimming pool, sauna, whirlpool. *Westin Hotel*, 11 Colonel By Drive, (613) 560-7000, located in heart of shopping area, near Parliament Hill and National Arts Centre, 475 rooms with colour TV, 3 restaurants, 2 bars, poolside snacks, 24 hour room service, indoor pool with terrace, 3 squash courts, exercise club, underground parking, gift shop, in room movies. *Holiday Inn Market Square* at 350 Dalhousie Street in heart of Byward Market, (613) 236-0201, 160 rooms with colour TV, close to many restaurants, Parliament, museums, gift shop, outdoor pool, parking, piano lounge. **Windsor Hilton International**, 277 Riverside Dr. W., (519) 973-5555, 304 rooms and suites, overlooks Detroit River, near shops, 2 restaurants, cocktail lounge, indoor pool, whirlpool, sauna, exercise room, major credit cards accepted.

ONTARIO RESORTS *Hart Lodge,* located near village of Minden in the Haliburton Highlands, phone (705) 286-1738 or toll free 1-800-461-7699, 120 miles from Toronto, recreational facilities include swimming pool, tennis, whirlpool, shuffleboard, badminton, volleyball, nearby golf courses, 48 rooms, suites and cottages, ski trails, 350 acres of woods, two lakes, poolside barbeques, licensed dining room, new indoor whirlpool, sauna and exercise area, water sports include water skiing, swimming, canoeing and boating, Visa and Master Card credit cards accepted. *Fern Resort,* R.R. No. 5, Orillia, (416) 364-4069 or (705) 325-2256, within convenient driving distance of Toronto, 103 rooms and lakefront cottages, with fireplaces, telephone and colour TV, located on Lake Couchiching, children's play village, trampoline house, hot tub, Gazebo Bar overlooks the lake, 2 outdoor swimming pools, 1 indoor pool, sauna, whirlpool, 5 flood-lit tennis courts, par 3, 5 hole golf course, cross country equipment rentals and ski trails, skating rink, water skiing, dining room, entertainment lounge. *Wig A Mog Inn,* Haliburton, (416) 861-1358, a lovely and highly recommended family resort located on Lake Kashaga, rooms, chalets and cottages, chalets have fireplaces, poolside suites, open year round, fine dining, satellite TV, billiard room, indoor swimming pool, sauna and whirlpool, 3 tennis courts, outdoor barbecues, golf course nearby, cross country ski trails, ice skating on lake, snowmobile trails and equipment rentals. *Delawana Inn,* (705) 756-2424 or (416) 869-0244, located on Georgian Bay in a beautiful setting 3 hours from Toronto, clean, comfortable rooms with TV, boating facilities, outdoor swimming pool, racquetball, sauna, children's programmes in summer, tennis courts, friendly service, nightly entertainment, air conditioned, lounge, open from late May to October. *Clevelands House,* Minett Post Office, Muskoka, largest privately owned resort in Ontario, (416) 364-3945, cottages, suites and cabins, over 100 rooms, 9 hole golf course, 16 tennis courts, swimming pool, children's pool and playground, 2 hot tubs, boating and recreational facilities, badminton courts, nightly entertainment, children's programmes, dining room, bar, lounge, major credit cards accepted, open mid May to mid October. *The Briars Inn,* P.O. Box 100, Jackson's Point, Ontario L0E 1L0 (416) 364-5937, 90 rooms in summer, 70 rooms in winter, dining room, indoor swimming pool, whirlpool, sauna, cross country skiing, ice skating, ice fishing in area, 18 hole golf course, 3 tennis courts, 2 outdoor heated pools, lake swimming, one hour north of Toronto, open all year. *Sandy Lane Resort,* near Minden, open all year, 1-800-461-1422 or (705) 489-2020, family operated resort, spacious grounds overlook Halls Lake, individual chalets with fireplaces and colour TV, sandy beach, boating, water sports, hot tub, tennis and golf nearby, horseback riding, ice fishing, skiing and snowmobiling in winter, equipment rentals, *Loralea Lodge,* with dining room and similar facilities, is next door. *Cedar Grove Lodge,* 10 miles east of Huntsville on Peninsula Lake, 1-800-461-4269 or (705) 789-4036, an attractive property located 2½ hours from Toronto, comfortable log cottages with open fireplaces, home-cooked meals, features water skiing, boating, boat rentals, hot tub and tennis, games room, near golfing, winter activities offered are cross country skiing, snow shoeing, snowmobiling, downhill skiing and ice skating on lake. *Tally Ho Inn,* Huntsville, 1-800-461-4232 or (705) 635-2281, on Peninsula Lake, open all year, 2½ hours from Toronto, rooms or cottages, most with fireplaces, colour TV and satellite TV, winter sports include downhill and cross country skiing, has own ski area, also whirlpool, sauna, ping pong, billiard table, indoor and outdoor shuffleboard, boat rentals, tennis courts, dining room, golf nearby. *Island Lodge,* a lovely property located on two islands north of Manitoulin Island at foot of La Cloche Mts., 1-800-461-1119 or (705) 285-4343, boat service to lodge, secluded cottages, offer modern comforts in a wilderness setting, cottages range from 1 to 6 bedrooms, features fishing, swimming and boating, hiking trails, 5½ hour drive from Toronto, delightful atmosphere and highly recommended, open from June to mid September. *Locarno Resort,* R. R. #2, Haliburton, (705) 457-2012, intimate resort only 2½ hours north of Toronto, in the highlands of Haliburton, TV, air conditioning, some fireplace chalets, indoor swimming pool, sauna, whirlpool, cocktail lounge, dining room, tennis, golf, water sports include canoeing and water skiing, also features many miles of wooded trails ideal for hiking. *Birch Cliff Lodge,* R. R. #2, Bancroft, 1-800-267-6303 or (613) 332-3316, well maintained cottages and rooms in relaxing setting, natural sandy beach, features badminton, table tennis, extensive playground, horseshoes and pedal boats, water sports facilities are available, also good fishing for pickerel, bass and muskie, three hours from Toronto, a family resort open May to October, recommended for friendly atmosphere and personalized service. *Viamede Resort Hotel,* on Stoney Lake, 120 miles from Toronto, 1-800-461-1946 or (705) 654-3344, rooms and cottages, tennis, snack bar, colour TV in lounge, shuffleboard, swimming, sandy beach, dining room with excellent meals served, fishing is good for bass and pickerel, major credit cards are accepted, open the year round, weekends only in the winter, special weekly rates in the summer, winter activities are cross country skiing, hayrides, snowmobiling, skating on the lake, snowshoeing, games in the main lodge. *Prudhomme Landing,* (416) 562-4101, located at Vineland in Niagara Peninsula, an hour's drive from Toronto, 120 rooms with direct dial phones, cable TV, indoor swimming pool, whirlpool, billiards, tennis, conference rooms, major credit cards accepted, free parking, open the year round, water sports facilities. *Bonnie View Inn,* 1-800-461-0347 or (705) 457-2350, near Haliburton, a fine property located just 2½ hours north of Toronto, open all year, rooms, cottages and hotel suites, friendly service, full range of recreational activities, supervised children's programme in the summer, water sports, windsurfing, canoeing, water skiing, golfing nearby, winter activities include ice skating, snowmobiling and cross country skiing, alpine skiing nearby, dining room, hot tub, sauna, lounge has a bar, fireplace and piano. *Tyrolean Village Resort,* at Blue Mountain, near the town of Collingwood, a 2 hour drive northwest of Toronto, (416) 690-0841 or (705) 445-1467, rustic casual atmosphere in 26 Swiss style chalets ranging from 4-10 bedrooms each, all have a sauna, fireplace, full kitchen and sundeck, kitchen has utensils, features 10 tennis courts, swimming pool, children's play area, volleyball, private beach area, close to ski facilities in winter, 3-18 hole golf courses within 7 kilometres, water sports in Georgian Bay in the summer, weekend rates all year. *Severn Lodge,* P.O. Box 250, Port Severn LOK 1S0, 1½ hours from Toronto, 1-800-461-5817 or (705) 756-2722, a fine property with 45 rooms and suites, some units have jacuzzis, main building dates back from 1800's and is not refurbished, heated outdoor swimming pool, solar heated, tennis, volleyball, shuffleboard, water sports, hiking trails on property, horse back riding and golf nearby, gift shop, licensed dining room, patio bar, children's programmes, Master Card or Visa, management operates evening cruises on fine, antique boat, open May-October, sightseeing attractions in area. *Red Umbrella Inn,* 1-800-461-0316, a 2½ hour drive north of Toronto near the town of Minden, located on Twelve Mile Lake, rooms and cottages, some with fireplaces, outdoor swimming pool, open most of the year, features games room, dining room, water sports, boating, family social programme, children's programme, TV lounge, winter activities available include ice fishing, snowmobiling and cross country skiing, many sights to visit and things to do in the nearby area, major credit cards are accepted, fully licensed. *North Ridge Inn,* 1-800-461-5551 or (705) 384-5373, located off Hwy.11, just south of Sundridge, 3 hours north of Toronto, beautiful rooms and chalets with fireplace, VCR and stereo TV, tennis, whirlpool, indoor pool, major trails, cross country skiing, children's programme in the summer, volleyball, sailing, swimming, water skiing, horse drawn sleigh rides in winter, skating, snow shoeing, snowmobiling, safaris, ice fishing, live entertainment on weekends, saunas and outdoor hot tubs, sugar bush tours in the spring, golf and horseback riding nearby, major credit cards, open all year except November and April, highly recommended. *Lumina Resort,* R.R. #1, Dwight, Ontario near Huntsville, 1-800-461-4371 or (705) 635-2991, open first week in June through to Thanksgiving, a large property, the largest cottage resort in Lake of Bays area, modern main lodge, dining room, features rooms and chalet cottages, family resort offers children's supervised programme in the summer, sandy beach, tennis, outdoor swimming pool, marina, water skiing, boat rentals, athletic and social programme, in operation some 70 years, Visa credit card, well recommended. *Ox Bow Lodge*, located near Huntsville, 1-800-461-4302 or (705) 635-2514, resort overlooks a lake, log cabins by the water have 1-3 bedrooms along with fireplaces, motel units also available, dining room in main lodge, TV in lounge, hot tub, water sports facilities on the lake include boating, games room, spacious grounds, scenic area, family-oriented in the summer, horseshoes, badminton, winter activities include cross country skiing, snowmobiling, snowshoeing and ice skating, major credit cards, open all year.

RESTAURANTS Toronto Barberian's Steak House Tavern, in an historic building centrally located at 7 Elm St. (597-0335, 597-0225), close to the Eaton Centre, luncheon served on weekdays, from noon to 2:30 p.m., dinner only on Saturday and Sunday from 5 p.m., steak the specialty, also choice aged beef cuts and rack of lamb, also features seafood, famous for 25 years for excellent meals and service, after theatre menu, reservations recommended, major credit cards are accepted, fully licensed, one of the finest restaurants in Toronto, most highly recommended. **La Grenouille,** 2387 Yonge St. (481-3093), just north of Eglinton subway stop, newly and beautifully refurbished, well known for mussels marinières, specialties include frog's legs, filet de boeuf with bearnaise sauce, salmon with creamy cucumber sauce, and fish soup, a special is served for dinner daily, open from 12 - 2:30 p.m. for lunch, Monday - Friday, menu is changed for lunch daily, dinners from 5:30 - 10:30 p.m. Monday - Thursday, on Friday and Saturday the kitchen closes at 11:00 p.m., closed Sundays, credit cards accepted are Amex, Visa and Master Card, also fully licensed, excellent service and French cuisine. **Mastro's Restaurant,** 890 Wilson Ave. W., (636-8194), serves authentic Italian cuisine, home made pastas, green ravioli with either a tomato or cream sauce, rigatoni a la vodka, cannelloni, veal piccata, filetto farcito, filet mignon amalfitana, fully licensed, bar, famous wine cellar, strolling musicians on weekend, open 12 noon - 11 p.m. Monday to Thursday, 12 noon - midnight on Friday, 4 - 1 a.m. on Saturday, 4 - 10 p.m. on Sunday, all credit cards, close to 25 years in operation, highly regarded restaurant, reservations suggested. **Katz's Deli and Corned Beef Emporium,** in beautiful new location at 3300 Dufferin St. (782-1111), situated close to Yorkdale Shopping Centre and Hwy. 401, one of the finest delis in North America, family-operated business for 20 years, specialties include corned beef, pastrami, roast beef, smoked meat and hot dogs, self service, almost everything made on premises from the finest quality ingredients, open from 8:30 a.m. to 10 p.m. Monday - Saturday, free parking, major credit cards accepted. **Swirler's Restaurant,** 2450 Sheppard Ave. E., (493-4001), fine dining, specialties include Alaskan King Crab legs, rack of lamb, variety of steak, chicken and pasta dishes, also businessman's luncheon specials, interesting selection of desserts, bar on premises, non smoking section, dancing and disc jockey nightly, free parking, credit cards accepted are American Express, Visa and Master Card, open 11 a.m. to 1 a.m. Monday to Saturday and occasional Sundays. **An Evening**

at La Cage Restaurant, 279 Yonge St., 2nd floor, (416) 364-5200, dinner theatre with a definite difference, North America's finest celebrity impersonators perform 90 minutes of non stop laughter, high energy production numbers presented Tuesday - Sunday, prix fixe menu, starts at $25 per person which includes the show, choice of three entrees, third smash year of operation, all major credit cards, fully licensed, nearby parking, also offers Sunday brunches, reservations are recommended. **Southern Accent Restaurant,** 595 Markham St., (416) 536-3211, not far from the Royal Ontario Museum and Yorkville district, Cajun and Creole cooking is at its best in this highly acclaimed restaurant in the heart of Mirvish Village, specialties include voodoo pasta with crawfish, bronzed catfish, jambalaya, squid and shrimp, Cajun martinis, special cognacs and eau de vie are served at the uniquely shaped 40's bar, performances of live zydeco music on Thursday, open from 5:30 p.m. every night, tapas after 11 p.m., credit cards accepted are Amex, Visa and Master Card. **Miffy's,** 954 Brimorton Drive, Scarborough, (416) 431-3000, your atypical Chinese dining room, genuine Szechuan and Cantonese dishes freshly prepared, specialties include potsticker, hot and sour soup, variety of chicken wings, noodle dishes, Szechuan orange beef, breaded chicken balls with honey garlic sauce, also miffin and gelato fresco lichee ice cream for dessert, relaxed and unassuming atmosphere, one of best Chinese restaurants in Scarborough, short drive by car from Metro Toronto Zoo, fully licensed, free parking, all major credit cards including JCB. **La Bussola Restaurant** on 3434 Bathurst (789-4444) serves Italian specialties in a most congenial atmosphere. Entrees include New York sirloin steak, veal sorentino (veal with eggplant, mozzarella cheese and tomato in a sherry wine sauce), chicken bussola and home made pasta such as trenette casalinga (green noodles with basil, tomato and parmesan cheese). Fresh fish is available daily. There is an extensive wine list and domestic and imported beers are available. A pasta special served Tuesday to Thursday evenings is recommended. Fully licensed. Major credit cards. Parking available. La Bussola offers a most satisfactory dining experience and is strongly recommended. **Seashell Seafood Restaurant** at 5197 Yonge St. (225-1895) is, as the name states, a specialty restaurant devoted to serving a wide variety of fresh fish and seafood. Among the suggested appetizers are clam chowder, steamed fresh mussels, escargots, oyster stew and lobster bisque. Recommended entrees include jumbo shrimps meuniere, rainbow trout, halibut steak, grilled or poached fresh salmon or Arctic charbroiled scampis, fresh water whitefish and grilled fresh filet of haddock. Major credit cards accepted. Beer and wine served. Open daily from 11-10 p.m. and Sundays 4-10 p.m. A fresh fish counter, with a wide choice of take out food, is on the premises. Seashell prepares seafood just right for the fish lover in me and you. **J. S. Shane's** at 286 Eglinton Ave. W. (489-3998) is noted for its continental cuisine and, in the nearly two years of its operation, has established a reputation for the quality of the food served. The bar and bistro accommodate guests who are interested in both a bar service and a dining room cuisine. Specialties of the house, changed seasonally, include fresh fish catch of the day, such as East Coast salmon, Alberta beef cuts and many fashionable European and tropical side dishes. Prices for a complete meal are continually held from $8.95 to $15.95. On weekends, Shane's provides a full breakfast-brunch from $3.95 to $7.95. Shane's, open for lunch and dinner daily, is a fine midtown restaurant. **Old House on Church St.** in central Toronto at 582 Church (925-5316) serves French classical and southern Mediterranean cuisine. The restaurant's specialties include black tiger shrimps, boneless breast of roast duck with cassis and prune sauce, New York pepper steak, blue Marlin and swordfish (when available) and pork tenderloin Wellington wrapped in a blanket of puff pastry. Various fresh pastas for lunch. Special salads, such as a California salad, are available. There is a patio, where you can dine, weather permitting, from May to September. Lunch is served from Wednesday to Saturday and dinner is served daily. Brunch is served on Sunday from 11:30-3 p.m. Major credit cards accepted. Fully licensed. One of your best downtown restaurants. **Carolyn's Restaurant** is on 1566 Avenue Rd. (789-5363), a short drive south of Hwy. 401. Carolyn's has, after only slightly more than one year of operation, quickly gained a loyal following among local residents and a clientele coming from beyond the city proper. That speaks well of the restaurant. The strength of the menu is in its home made, freshly prepared Italian specialties and that means everything from antipasta and pastas to veal and seafood. There is also an extensive list of red and white wines available. The atmosphere is cozy, the surroundings attractive, and the service, attentive. Major credit cards are accepted. Parking available nearby. Open for lunch Tuesday-Friday and dinner 5-11 every day of the week. **Poor William's Fine Food Restaurant** at 507 Parliament St. (924-7572) is a place to eat well, and at the same time, feel at home. Poor William's serves a standard lunch menu and salads come at no extra charge. For dinner, fresh fish, fresh pasta and a selection of grilled fare featured, as well as the regular light menu. Open for lunch and dinner daily. Sunday brunch, from 12-4 p.m. offers buttermilk pancakes, blueberry pancakes, Rocky Mountain French toast and crepes. Homemade desserts include strawberry rhubarb sour cream pie, blueberry crumble pie and a real Key West lime pie. Fully licensed. Visa, Master Card and Amex. Parking available nearby. This is the sort of place I always like to discover, one offering good food at reasonable prices. There is also an uptown location at 2721 Yonge St. (487-3934). **PANTALONE RESTAURANT** at 3032 Bathurst St. (781-6322) has been in the same location for the past eleven years. Italian food, of course, is the specialty and dishes served include fettucine Bolshoi, fusilli primavera, rigatoni cucina nuova, linguine vongole, calamari alla marinara and filet of sole. Fish is served fresh daily. The chef will prepare small portions for children, upon request. Free parking on the premises. Major credit cards. Open for lunch Tuesday-Friday, dinner from Tuesday-Sunday. Reservations are recommended for dining on the weekend. Pantalone is regarded as a good Italian restaurant and I concur in that judgement.

MISCELLANEOUS

PROVINCIAL TOURIST BUREAU Ontario Travel, 900 Bay St., Queen's Park, Toronto, Ontario M7A 2E5

VISITOR INFORMATION CENTRES are open in Niagara Falls, Windsor (2), Ottawa, Sarnia, Toronto, Sault Ste. Marie, Barrie, Cornwall and Fort Frances all year. Offices in Fort Erie, Hawkesbury, Hill Island, Kenora, Lancaster, Pigeon River, Prescott, Rainy River and St. Catharines are open from mid May to mid September.

Toronto's City Hall and Nathan Phillips Square.

PERSPECTIVE

LOCATION Prince Edward Island, across the Northumberland Strait from Nova Scotia and New Brunswick, is completely surrounded by the waters of the Atlantic. Charlottetown is conveniently accessible from the mainland of Canada by plane, boat and train.

AREA P.E.I. is only 2,186 square miles in size, the smallest of the ten provinces.

BACKGROUND The island, claimed by the explorer Jacques Cartier in 1534, remained a French colonial posession until 1764. Prince Edward Island was joined politically to its neighbouring colony, Nova Scotia, for a brief period. The island was the setting of the Conference of 1864, at which time delegates from P.E.I., Nova Scotia and New Brunswick met to discuss the proposed union of the three Maritime provinces. Proposal to establish Canada's independence from Britain were also considered, yet the islanders declined the original offer of membership in Confederation. P.E.I.'s government reconsidered and asked to be admitted as the seventh province of Canada in 1873.

POPULATION The population is about 120,000, least among the provinces.

CAPITAL Charlottetown, population 18,000. Summerside has close to 8,600 inhabitants.

LANGUAGE English. French is spoken in some places.

TIME ZONE Atlantic Standard Time. When the clock reads noon in Charlottetown, it's 11 in the morning in the Eastern Standard Time Zone (i.e. Toronto-Montreal-New York), 10 a.m. Central Standard Time (Chicago-Winnipeg), 9 a.m. Mountain Standard Time (Denver-Calgary), and 8 a.m. Pacific Standard Time (Vancouver-Los Angeles).

WHEN TO VISIT June, July and August are the most pleasant months for a vacation. The ocean waters off the northern shore are surprisingly warm (thanks to the Gulf Stream), averaging temperatures of 70-72 degrees in the summer.

PRINCE EDWARD ISLAND

CHARLOTTETOWN Province House should be interesting to anyone familiar with Canadian history. The home of the provincial government, it houses Confederation Room where delegates met in 1864 to consider unification of the British colonies. Government House, a colonial building completed 1835, was the official residence of the lieutenant-governor. The Confederation Centre of the Arts has an art gallery, library, restaurant and a modern theatre. St. Paul's Anglican church (1895) off Queen Square, is the island's oldest Anglican church dating back to 1747. Other attractions are Victoria Park, site of Fort Edward, the interesting St. Dunstan's Basilica, the Charlottetown Festival and Provincial Exhibition and Old Home Week Fair held in August.

TRIPS EAST FROM CHARLOTTETOWN Highway 2 leads to St. Andrew's via Tracadie, one of the island's pioneer communities (1721). Souris is noted for fine swimming and good fishing. Boats sail from Souris for the Magdalen Islands (part of Quebec). Other good beaches are strung along the coastal route through St. Peter's, to East Point and beyond. Excursions south lead to Murray Harbour, through Montague. Montague's interests are the Garden of the Gulf Museum and the neighbouring Moore's Bird Sanctuary, with varieties of geese and ducks; it's best to visit in September and October. Fantasyland Provincial Park near Murray River is a family playground offering children's attractions, boating and swimming, June to September. Highlights of the 1,400 acre Brudenell Resort and Provincial Park are golfing, camping, horseback riding, picnic grounds, lodging, swimming, lawn bowling, canoeing and volleyball.

TRIPS WEST OF CHARLOTTETOWN Cavendish The summer resort is popular for Green Gables, the farmhouse featured in Anne of Green Gables, written by Lucy Maud Montgomery; the home is on the west side of Prince Edward Island National Park. Wildlife Park and Santa's Woods, located a short distance from North Rustico, consists of a lake, nature trails, picnic grounds and houses a variety of birds and animals. At Marineland Aquarium at Stanley Bridge, varied fish species can be seen every day from mid June to mid September. **Burlington**'s main interests are the Woodleigh Replicas, open all day every day, late May to October.

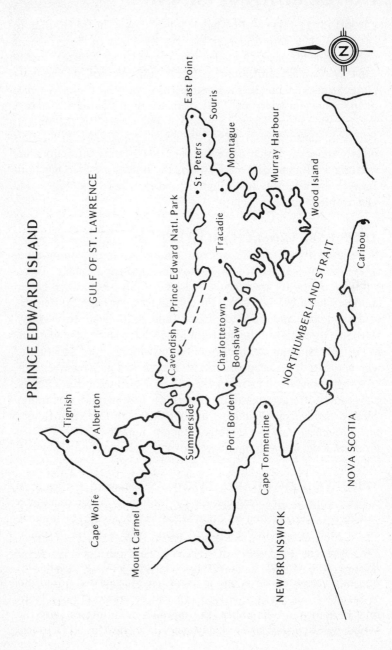

PRINCE EDWARD ISLAND

GULF OF ST. LAWRENCE

East Point

Souris

Montague

Murray Harbour

St. Peters

Wood Island

Tracadie

Prince Edward Natl. Park

NORTHUMBERLAND STRAIT

Caribou

Cavendish

Charlottetown

Bonshaw

Summerside

Port Borden

Tignish

Alberton

Cape Tormentine

NOVA SCOTIA

Cape Wolfe

Mount Carmel

NEW BRUNSWICK

See stone models of historical buildings — Glamis Castle, Penn Manor House, birthplace of Shakespeare, Tower of London and several other buildings — illuminated by night. Southwest of the capital are Fort Amherst, the Micmac Indian Village, Fairyland, which is a children's playground and Bonshaw 500 with go-kart racing.

WESTERN P.E.I. Summerside provides canoeing facilities, horse racing, golf and in July, the week-long Lobster Carnival. The Acadian Museum at Miscouche displays artifacts of the early French settlers of the province. Mount Carmel's 18th century "Village des Pionniers Acadiens" (Acadian Pioneer Village) consists of several buildings such as cabins, school and church, giving the visitor a glimpse into the way of life of a typical period settlement. Bideford is famed for its oyster research station and Port Hill is the site of Green Park Historic Park with its shipbuilding museum. In Kildare, a miniature passenger carrying railway set amidst rural surroundings, operates daily.

HISTORIC SITES, MUSEUMS AND ART GALLERIES. Elmira Station, a restored railway museum, tells the story of an earlier period of railroading. Green Park Historic Park recreates the shipbuilding era of the 19th century with several points of interest, including a carpenter's and blacksmith's shop. The Basin Head Fisheries Museum pays tribute to the dominant role played by the fishing industry in P.E.I. by depicting the history of fishing in the province. Orwell Corner, a fine reconstruction of a rural pioneer community, contains barns, a church, school, farmhouse, post office and blacksmith's shop. In Summerside visit the Eptek Centre which houses a national exhibition centre and the P.E.I. Sports Hall of Fame. Province House in Charlottetown dates from 1847. Confederation Room houses the original furniture used by delegates to the Confederation Conference of 1864. Discussions were held at this time on the proposal to unite the Canadian colonies. Open 9-8 p.m., July-September, 9-5 other months. Confederation Centre of the Arts has a collection of works by the Canadian artist Robert Harris. The **Micmac Indian Village** near Rocky Point, 15 miles west and south of Charlottetown, is a reconstructed 16th century village containing wigwams, a museum, canoes and artifacts. Open 9:30-5:30 daily, June-September, plus evenings in July and August. Car Life Museum, not far from Bonshaw, displays antique cars and farm implements. Open 10-6 p.m., daily, mid May to October, plus evenings in July and August. The House of International Dolls with costumed dolls from many nations is open 9-8 p.m. Monday to Saturday and Sunday afternoons in the summer. Strathgartney Homestead Museum is a farm whose furnishings of the mid 19th century may be viewed 10-6 p.m., daily, June to September. Montague's Garden of the Gulf Museum has miscellaneous articles of pioneer life on the island, on view 9:30-5 p.m., late June to the second week in September. The Acadian Museum of P.E.I., located at Miscouche, a few miles west of Summerside, houses exhibits on early Acadian settlements. Open weekdays 10-6 p.m., Sundays 1-6 p.m., July and August.

MUSIC AND THE THEATRE The summer Charlottetown Festival, held at Confederation Centre of the Arts Theatre, presents Anne of Green Gables in its annual program of musicals. Jazz performances are offered evenings on occasion in the Confederation Centre.

HUNTING AND FISHING Small game includes muskrat, rabbit, beaver and raccoon; game birds are partridge, geese, grouse, black duck and woodcock. The main fish species yielded are rainbow, brook and speckled trout and salmon. Salmon fishing is good in P.E.I.'s rivers. Tuna fishing is becoming increasingly popular and record catches have been recorded; a 1,235 pounder was landed off North Lake a few years ago. The best catches are being made in the early fall. Information on current fishing and hunting laws is available from the Fish and Wildlife Division, Department of the Environment, P.O. Box 2000, Charlottetown, P.E.I.

WINTER AND SUMMER SPORTS Winter pastimes are curling, skating and cross country skiing. Summer vacationers have a choice of golfing in Charlottetown, Summerside, Cavendish, Rustico, Mill River, Brudenell and the P.E.I. National Park. Public tennis courts are found in P.E.I. National Park, in the Summerside area and in Charlottetown's Victoria Park. Boating is popular at Summerside and Charlottetown as well as in the numerous bays along the coast and on inland rivers. Visitors are welcome at the provincial yachting clubs. The water temperature off P.E.I. National Park averages 70 degrees in the summer. Most provincial parks, as well as many coves and bays through the island are good for swimming. There are hiking trails at several of the island's parks. A popular spectator sport in Charlottetown and Summerside is summer harness racing.

NATIONAL PARKS Prince Edward Island National Park features 25 miles of beaches along the north coast, golfing, fishing in lakes and off the coast, picnic grounds and shelters, camp sites and a varied terrain. Park headquarters are at Dalvay, three miles from Tracadie. **Fort Amherst National Park** is situated opposite Charlottetown harbor, at Rocky Point. The French fortress Port La Joie was built in 1720; the British invaded in 1758 and established the site as Fort Amherst. View the remains of this fort 9-5 p.m. mid May to October. In July and August the historic site stays open to 8 p.m.

FOOD AND DRINK Prince Edward Island has delicious oysters from Malpeque Bay, prepared raw, deep fried or cooked in butter. Other seafood specialties are clams, mackerel and blue mussels. Lobster is served boiled, broiled, steamed, hot or cold. You might want to dig for clams on the numerous beaches and have a clambake. Lobster suppers are a highlight of the Lobster Carnival held in Summerside each July. Places to eat in the capital are Vito's and Minnie's. Provincial liquor outlets are open Monday to Saturday. The legal drinking age is 21.

TRANSPORTATION IN PRINCE EDWARD ISLAND Driving is relaxing on uncrowded paved roads that connect all the main sections of the island. The Trans Canada Highway extends through the central section of the island. Car rental offices are located in the capital and Summerside. Via Rail Canada links eastern Canada with the island by train-bus service via Moncton, N.B., and Amherst, N.S. Car ferries are scheduled frequently between Cape Tormentine, N.B. and Borden. Other ferries sail between Caribou, N.S. and Woods Island, P.E.I.

SHOPPING The variety of shopping specials include woolen imports, Irish glassware and English china. Other items on sale are locally made handicrafts such as pottery, hooked rugs and mats, sweaters and woodwork. There are about 35 craft shops operating in different parts of the province. Shops in the capital remain open 9-5 or 6 and some malls from 10-10 p.m. A provincial sales tax is imposed on goods purchased.

ACCOMMODATION **Charlottetown** Kirkwood Motor Hotel, 455 University Ave., (902) 892-4206, 70 rooms and suites, restaurant, bar, indoor swimming pool, laundry service, colour TV, free parking, meeting and convention facilities. Wandlyn Motor Inn, North River Rd., (902) 892-1201, 75 rooms, radio and colour TV, restaurant, bar, beach, outdoor swimming pool, laundry service, free parking. McLauchlan's Motel, 238 Grafton St., (902) 892-2461, 86 rooms and suites, indoor swimming pool, water sports, sauna, barber and beauty shops. **Cavendish** Cavendish Motel, Rts. 6 and 13, (902) 892-8645, 27 rooms, kitchenettes available, restaurant, bar, dancing, entertainment, outdoor swimming pool, free parking, babysitting service, colour TV. **Cornwall** Sunny King Motel, P.O. Box 159, (902) 657-2209, 38 rooms and suites, TV, restaurant, bar, outdoor swimming pool, beach, horseback riding, laundry service, free parking. **Summerside** Garden of the Gulf Quality Inn, 612 Water St., (902) 436-2295, 52 rooms and suites, restaurant, bar, dancing, entertainment, outdoor swimming pool, beach, golf course nearby, radio and TV, free parking, babysitting. The Linkletter Motel, 311 Market St., (902) 436-2157, 55 rooms, restaurant, bar, radio and colour TV, free parking, meeting rooms.

MISCELLANEOUS

PROVINCIAL TOURIST BUREAU Prince Edward Island Tourist Information Centre, P.O. Box 940, Charlottetown, P.E.I. C1A 7M5

TOURIST INFORMATION CENTRES are open during the summer months at Alberton, Borden, Brackley, Cavendish, Kings Byway Interpretive Centre in Poole's Corner, Souris, Stanhope, Summerside and Wood Islands.

North America's oldest wooden chapel (1647), Tadoussac, Quebec

PERSPECTIVE

LOCATION The St. Lawrence River flows through southern Quebec from Gaspe Peninsula past the port of Montreal. While Quebec province extends to a latitude almost as far south as Boston, the extensive wilderness of Ungava Peninsula reaches as far north as Hudson Strait.

AREA Quebec, 524,253 square miles in area, ranks as Canada's largest province.

BACKGROUND The explorer Jacques Cartier landed in Gaspe Peninsula in 1534. Quebec City was founded by Samuel de Champlain in 1608, soon to be the capital of New France, i.e. the French held possessions in North America. Their rule in the province ended with defeat at the hands of the British in the Battle of Quebec in 1759. Subsequently, Britain passed the Quebec Act guaranteeing the French speaking majority rights of religion, language and customs and in 1867 Quebec was persuaded by the colonies of Nova Scotia, New Brunswick and Ontario to unite with them in establishing the Dominion of Canada.

POPULATION Estimated at 6,390,000, second only to its neighbour, Ontario.

CAPITAL Quebec City, population 560,000. Montreal has 2,820,000 inhabitants. Trois Rivieres has a population of 51,200.

LANGUAGES While the first language of Quebec is French, many urban dwellers are bilingual.

TIME ZONES The immense province spans two time zones. Montreal and Quebec City observe Eastern Standard Time. Gaspe Peninsula in the east is located in the Atlantic Standard Time Zone. Noon in Gaspe is 11 a.m. Eastern Standard Time.

WHEN TO VISIT Montreal is comfortably warm from late May through to the middle of September, although July and August do get humid at times. Skiing in Laurentian resorts and Quebec City's famous annual Winter Carnival are outstanding features of the winter season.

QUEBEC

MONTREAL is the world's second largest French speaking city. **Man and His World,** a less spectacular version of Expo '67, is one of the foremost attractions in Montreal. Many of the original buildings left intact, once again represent foreigh countries. Other highlights are numerous exhibits, restaurants and La Ronde amusement park. They remain open from June to the first week in September and are accessible by subway. **Place Ville Marie** at 777 Dorchester W., erected at a cost of $100,000,000, is dominated by the 45-storey Royal Bank of Canada building. Shops, movie houses, cocktail lounges and restaurants operate beneath the plaza. Place des Arts is situated on St. Catherine St. at St. Urbain. This impressive complex houses a 3,000-seat concert hall, two theatres and several shops. Place Victoria, between Vitre and St. James Streets, also houses numerous shops and restaurants and the Montreal Stock Exchange, open for guided tours 10 to 5:30 p.m. The church of **Notre-Dame-de-Montreal** by Place d'Armes, constructed 1823-28, is 260 feet long and 135 feet wide and holds up to 7,000 people. It is noted for its interesting stained glass windows and wood carvings. The church museum, open daily from 9-4:30 (except Sunday morning), displays religious objects donated by French monarchs, books and other articles. The nearby Sulpician Seminary dates from 1685. The Roman Catholic Cathedral Queen Mary of the World (1870) is on Dorchester Ave. The interior is 330 feet long and 150 feet wide. A golden 19-foot-high cross surmounts the 250-foot-high dome. The church of Notre Dame de Bonsecours was built on the site of the original wooden church, erected in 1658. The stone church (1771) was dedicated to sailors visiting the port of Montreal. A small doll museum adjoins the church. St. Joseph's Oratory is a shrine on the slope of Mont Royal (Mount Royal). The huge church holds up to 10,000 worshippers at a time and over a million pilgrims a year visit here. The crypt church can contain another 1,000 people. Christ Church Anglican (Gothic) Cathedral was constructed in 1859. Its interior is 210 feet in length and 100 feet in width. St. Patrick's Church at Dorchester and Saint Alexander dates from 1847. Mont Royal Park on the summit of Mont Royal has 500 acres of parkland with restaurants, winter sports and picnic sites. Lafontaine Park's 110 acres offer boating, picnic grounds, a children's zoo, a puppet and outdoor children's theatre and miniature train rides.

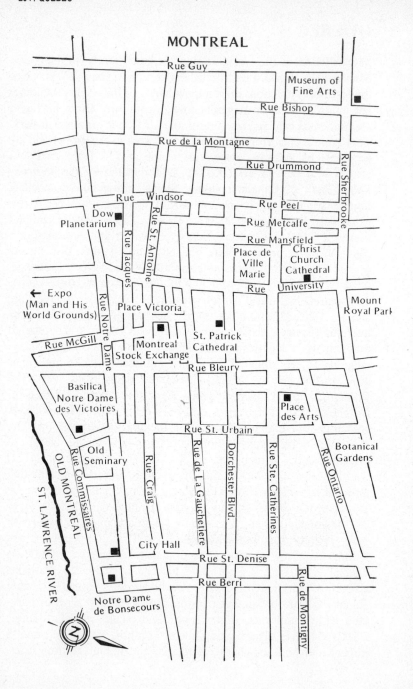

Antique shop in Three Rivers, Quebec

Maisonneuve Park in eastern Montreal consists of 550 acres of gardens, lakes, a golf course, a sports centre and the botanical gardens with 20,000 plant varieties from around the world. **Old Montreal** (the old quarter of Ville Marie), in which the original settlement was founded)1642), has been classified as an historic site. A walking tour is recommended along Bonsecours, St. Paul and Notre Dame Streets. See the Sulpician Seminary and Place d'Armes, which is the oldest square in the city. Other interests are Place Royale and Place Jacques-Cartier, Château de Ramezay, plaques denoting sites of historical interest, old churches, shops and a few old homes. Maison de Calvet, at 401 Bonsecours, was constructed in 1725; another old dwelling (open afternoons) is at number 418. Ste.-Hélène Island in the St. Lawrence River has an historic fort, now a military museum and a theatre. Maison St. Gabriel, at 2146 Favard, occupied by the Nuns of the Congregation of Notre Dame, is one of the oldest homes in Montreal. It dates from 1668. Museum goers should find McGill University, founded 1821, worthwhile for its Redpath Museum of Natural History. Dow Planetarium (1000 St. Jacques St.) presents daily shows on the stars. The St. Lawrence Seaway lookout (Belvédère Observatory), on top of the Seaway Authority Building by Victoria Bridge, commands a view of the Canadian-American operated Seaway. Other city interests are Belmont Park, a children's amusement centre, and a number of local museums.

EXCURSIONS FROM MONTREAL St.-Jérôme, in the Laurentians north of Montreal, has an active ski program in the winter and offers golf, swimming and tennis during the summer. The Village de Séraphin in **Ste.-Adèle** is a 60 acre restoration of a late 19th century village (open May to mid October). Ste.-Adèle is also known for its cantilever structure over Chemin du Sauvage which is unique in North America. **Ste.-Agathe-des-Monts** provides winter and summer sports. St.-Faustin's Fish Hatchery is open daily in the summer and on weekdays in the winter. St.-Jean, 20 miles south of Montreal, is notable for its Museum of the Haut-Richelieu region. **Granby** Local interests include several parks, the art centre, the Automobile Museum, picnic spots and a zoological garden at 303 Bourget. It is open 10-5 daily, from May to mid October. St.-George Anglican church contains medieval baptismal fonts dating from the 12th century. Golfing, fishing, camping and skiing are vacation pursuits in the Magog holiday area. See the Abbey of St.-Benoît-du-Lac situated 12 miles south of Magog. The attractions of **Sherbrooke** are the Gardens at Victoria Park (swimming facilities), the Township Festival (end of May, early June) and the St.-Michel Cathedral on Marquette Street. Visit Beauvoir (four miles north) for the Shrine of the Sacred Heart. Sightseers are permitted to inspect asbestos mining operations at open pits in the town of Asbestos, south of Montreal. Tours operate at 1:30 p.m. on weekdays. Thetford Mines, site of another huge asbestos mining complex, provides visitors with the opportunity to view open air pit mining. **Chambly** (about 20 miles east of Montreal) is noted for Chambly National Historic Park and Chambly Village. This neighbouring community is a collection of original 18th and 19th century buildings, furnished in the style of the period.

SOUTHWESTERN QUEBEC Hull is across the border from Ottawa. Gatineau Park's 75,000 acres have forests, lakes, camping grounds, small game, beaches, fishing and skiing. Visit the summer home of former Liberal Prime Minister King, open afternoons. There is good canoeing in the region's waterways. Hunting and fishing are excellent and guides from the Algonquin Indian reservation are available for fishing trips. La Vérendrye Reserve north of Mont Laurier encloses 5,000 square miles of lakes. Features of the parkland include fishing, camping, picnic grounds, canoeing and an animal and bird sanctuary. Val d'Or operates seasonal tours of local mines. Rouyn-Noranda gold mines and copper smelter are open to tourists on weekdays.

MONTREAL TO QUEBEC CITY Longueuil, on the south shore of the St. Lawrence River, commands a good view of Montreal. Two old dwellings in the town are the Maison de la Fabrique (1834) and the Maison des Oeuvres (1815). **Boucherville** Historic buildings are the church (1801) housing baptismal records from 1668 and the home of François-Pierre Boucher, constructed in 1672. Varennes and Verchères (old windmills) feature other structures dating from an earlier period of Quebec history. Sights in **Contrecoeur** include old homes, its church and a couple of historic mills. **Sorel** maintains Christ Church, dating from 1841, the Château des Gouverneurs, used as the summer residence by several Governors General of Canada. It is also known for its shipbuilding yards and the Gibelote (fish soup) Festival in July. Baieville's Maison Belcourt is typical of the houses found in the Montreal region. Pierreville village offers duck hunting; on the neighboring Odanak reserve, Indian residents cure fish and weave baskets. Nicolet has several historic dwellings: Lemay House, erected in 1794 and Maison Proulx (1792). Note that the architectural styles begin to change after you leave Nicolet; home construction in this area is more typical of the province. **Lotbinière** This holiday resort contains a typical church (1818), the Maison Pagé in the centre of the village, Maison de Vandal (1817) and the Moulin du Domaine (1799, an old windmill). An excursion from Montreal via the north side of the St. Lawrence River leads to Repentiguy whose stone church dates back to 1725. The old town in **Trois-Rivières** (Three Rivers) is noted for architecture originating from the 1600's and 1700's. Take a walking tour of the historic section past Tonnancour Manor, completed in 1696; Ursuline convent with its art displays (1701) on Rue des Ursulines; Maison des Gannes (1756) at Rue St.-Francois-Xavier and Rue des Ursulines; St. James Church, built between 1693 to 1700 and rebuilt in 1754; Place d'Armes, an old market square originating from 1651. The cathedral has beautiful stained glass windows. Cap-de-la-Madeleine on the other side of the Saint-Maurice River is noted for its Most Holy Rosary Shrine, since 1883, one of Canada's three most important Catholic places of pilgrimmage. The other two are Saint-Anne de Beaupré near Quebec City and Montreal's St. Joseph's Oratory. Tens of thousands of pilgrims assemble at this shrine every year. The original chapel, erected in 1694, was converted to a field-stone church in 1714. The Basilica, Canada's national shrine to Mary, holds 2,000 people. Candlelight processions are held nightly, May to October. The St.-Maurice Ironworks (1737-1883), seven miles north of Trois-Rivières, is open to the public from June to October.

QUEBEC CITY is the continent's only walled city. The primary sightseeing interest is the Citadel, a fort comprised of 25 buildings, completed by the British between 1819-1832. Citadel attractions are a museum, officer's quarters, and the panoramic views offered of the St. Lawrence River below and the surrounding region. The Royal 22nd Regiment enacts the Changing of the Guards (if weather permits, at 10 a.m.) and Beating the Retreat at 7:00 p.m. (from early June to Labour Day; Churchill, Roosevelt and King met here during their W.W. II Quebec Conference. Battlefield Park (235 acres) west of the citadel features monuments (of Wolfe, Montcalm and Joan of

Arc). The Plains of Abraham was the scene of the conflict between armies of Wolfe (England) and Montcalm (France). Victory by England in 1759 led to the expulsion of France from the continent. The **Parliament Buildings**, erected (1886) in the French Renaissance style, house works of art, bronze sculptures of pioneer settlers, murals and paintings. A walking tour of historic Quebec could begin from Château Frontenac Hotel (1892). Ursuline Convent, noted as the continent's first girl's school, contains wood carvings, ivory crucifixes, a votive lamp burning steadily since 1717 and paintings. Montcalm is buried under the chapel; the convent museum (closed for renovation) collection includes old books, engravings, Montcalm's skull and relics. Rue Donnacona emerges into St. Anne Street, site of the Anglican cathedral of Holy Trinity, dating from 1804. The Basilica of Notre Dame, with origins from 1647, has fine paintings and articles from the French period (New France). Quebec Seminary's chapel (1663) houses the remains of Bishop Laval, Quebec's first bishop, marble statues of pioneer settlers and wooden sculptures. Bishop Laval founded the seminary and trained priests and missionaries. The French language Laval University (1852) springs from the seminary. Hôtel-Dieu-du-Précieux-Sang (1637) founded over three centuries ago, is one of the oldest hospitals on the continent. The Champlain Stairs (Break-Neck stairs) lead to the Place Royale. The small restored church of Notre-Dame-des-Victoires (Our Lady of Victories, 1688), features an interesting altar shaped like an old fort, paintings and several wood carvings. Most of the buildings have been restored and made into art galleries and craft stores. The aquarium in Quebec Bridge Park has 75 species of tropical and freshwater fish, including alligators and turtles. Open daily. The **Winter Carnival** staged two weeks before Shrove Tuesday is highlighted by hockey competitions, parades and a curling bonspiel. Make hotel reservations for this event months in advance through the Carnival Lodging Committee. Boats cruise on the St. Lawrence in the summer. The Provincial Zoological Gardens feature birds and animals from North America and other parts of the world. Open 10-5 every day (and summer evenings). The gardens are located by Orsainville, ten miles north. Other local sighseeing interests are the artist's quarter by Place d'Armes and Montmorency Park. The restored Jesuit home in suburban Sillery is one of Canada's oldest surviving buildings, dating back to 1637. It's open weekdays in the summer (Tuesday to Sunday in the winter) at 2320 Chemin de Foulons.

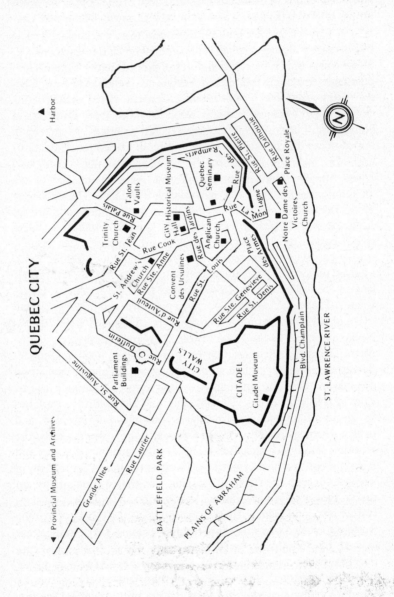

QUEBEC CITY

CHILDREN'S MONTREAL AND QUEBEC Man and His World exerts a powerful appeal on children. La Ronde amusement park, fascinating exhibits and restaurants can occupy a family for an entire day. For a touch of Europe to stir the imagination of parents and teenagers, visit the immense church of Notre-Dame-de-Montreal, the Mary Queen of the World Cathedral, St. Joseph's Oratory and old Montreal. Quebec City resembles a French provincial town. Laurentian resorts north of Montreal offer vacation pursuits for the entire family — fishing, swimming, golf and tennis. Children find the aquarium in Quebec Bridge Park — with alligators and turtles featured — most interesting. The Wax Museum offers reduced admission prices for children. Old Quebec has no parallel for historical interest in North America — fascinating for adults and youngsters alike.

EXCURSIONS FROM QUEBEC CITY Montmorency Falls is seven miles east on the north shore of the St. Lawrence. Kent House (La Maison Montmorency) was the residence of the Duke of Kent 1791-4, father of Queen Victoria. Several of the communities in the district were founded in the 1600's. The **Ile d'Orléans** in the St. Lawrence is accessible by a bridge from near Montmorency. If you visit the island, you'll see rural churches, pioneer farmhouses, homes and the Manoir Mauvide-Genest (1735), open summer days and evenings. A Quebec 19th century way of life has been preserved in this locality. **Ste. Anne de Beaupré**, 15 miles from Quebec, is the setting of a famed shrine drawing over a million visitors per year. The first church was completed in 1658, the year a miraculour cure was reported. The magnificent Basilica of Ste. Anne is 370 feet long and 210 feet wide. A museum of wax figures describing Ste. Anne's life adjoins the Basilica. The reconstructed Commemorative Shrine (1878) stands on the grounds of the original wooden chapel. Santa Scala Chapel is accessible by holy steps climbed on one's knees; the Way of the Cross is close by. The Cyclorama is a 360-foot-long painting of the Holy Land. The relatively isolated Baie-Saint-Paul, opposite the little island of Ile-aux-Coudres, is another part of Quebec that has maintained a former way of life. Les Eboulements and La Malbaie communities preserve interesting old dwellings. Either detour northeast to Port Alfred (on the Saguenay River) or continue on the route for Tadoussac. Interests of **Port Alfred** are the lovely St.-Alexis Church (1863) and the Notre-Dame-de-la-Baie Shrine.

Chicoutimi The Arthur Villeneuve House with its primitive art collection, the local cathedral, camping and swim marathons in the summer season, constitute the appeal of this city. Laurentide Park offers mountains, forests, camp sites and over a thousand lakes in its 4,000 square mile expanse. Jonquière (formerly Arvida) conducts free bilingual tours past the Aluminum Company of Canada smelter. St.-Félicien by Lake Saint-Jean has a Zoological Park, noted for a variety of animals and birds. **Tadoussac** The restored Chauvin home is said to originate from 1599, one of the first dwellings built by a French settler; the community's wooden chapel dates from 1747. **Ilets-Jérémie** has a renovated mission chapel. Ferries sail from Godbout to Matane. Sept-Iles offers a rebuilt three-century-old trading post, camping and beaches. **Lévis,** south of Quebec City, features the Notre-Dame-de-la-Victoire Church, an Eskimo art museum and pioneer dwellings. Sights in **Saint-Marie-de-Beauce** are an interesting church (1856), the home of Cardinal Taschereau, Canada's first cardinal, the Maison Lacroix (1793), the oldest and only stone house of the Beauce region, the shrine of Ste.-Anne and industrial visits of the Vachon bakeries. This area is also well known for its maple sugar bushes (early spring).

GASPE PENINSULA Gaspé was first sighted by Europeans in 1534. A couple of days could be spent on the peninsula, a 9,500 square mile region, distinct from the rest of Quebec. Varied activities of Rivière-du-Loup holiday centre include camping, golfing, visits to late 19th centur churches, swimming, boating and concerts. **Rimouski** is within reach of good hunting preserves. Gaspé Provincial Park is a sanctuary for wood caribou and is also noted for fishing and mountain climbing. Ferries sail from Souris (Prince Edward Island) to the Magdalen Islands 175 miles away; the 12 islands (only 7 are inhabited) have excellent swimming. **Percé** fishing village and resort is noted for its scenic beauties. Percé Rock, a rock formation 280 feet high, 1,600 feet long and 390 feet wide, contains hundreds of thousands of fossils. Pathways ascend to the top of Mont Blanc and Mont Sainte-Anne, both commanding good views of the surrounding countryside. **Bonaventure Island** is a sanctuary for many thousands of sea birds, including the herring gull, penguin, gannet and cormorant. Boats sail to the island from Percé. Grande-Rivière has a biological research station and aquarium. **Restigouche** Local interests are the Shrine of Ste. Anne de Restigouche, a des-

destination for pilgrims since 1740, the local monastery museum, and the remains of shipwrecked (1760) vessels: the Machault and the Bienfaisant. Fishing flourishes in the Matapédia region.

HISTORIC SITES, MUSEUMS AND ART GALLERIES

Montreal Château de Ramezay on Rue Notre-Dame and Saint-Claude was constructed as a baronial residence in 1705, to be converted into a history museum in 1929. Its contents are portraits of early settlers, old maps, prints, Indian relics, documents and furniture. Open every day but Monday (and Sunday morning) from 10-4:30 p.m. The Montreal Museum of Fine Arts collections include medieval tapestries, glass, wood carvings, furniture, classical and Canadian art and exhibits on Indian life, displayed Tuesday-Sunday (11 to 5). The museum is located at 1379 Sherbrooke W. The Museum of Contemporary Art (closed Monday), at Man and His World, Cité du Havre has changing exhibits on modern art. McGill University's Redpath Museum is noted for a fine collection of geological and zoological exhibits. The 18th century fort on Ste.-Hélènes Island has been converted to a military museum. The fort is open 10-5 daily, mid June to the first week in September. The Canadian Historical Museum, 3715 Queen Mary Rd., houses wax figures portraying events of ancient Rome and early Quebec. **Quebec City** Conducted tours are scheduled through the Citadel museum. A walking tour of old Quebec takes in a number of historic buildings and sites. The Provincial Museum in Battlefield Park has a display of Quebec art (traditional and contemporary) and crafts. Open daily 9 to 5, plus Thursday nights. Laval University, in the old city, houses an extensive library, a geology and natural history museum and Canadian and European art. The restored Maison Fargues (92 Rue Saint-Pierre) is a lovely specimen of an 18th century dwelling. Kent House (at 25 St.-Louis) is one of the city's oldest residences. Maison Maillou at 17 St.-Louis is another example of a renovated 200-year-old home. The Wax Museum at Ste.-Anne and Rue du Trésor is open May to November. Dow's Brewery still uses the original vaults of Quebec's first brewery. It was built in 1675 (at 15 St. Nicholas.) Musée du Fort, 10 St.-Anne, has a diorama of the six seiges of Quebec outlining the city's military history.

MUSIC AND THE THEATRE

Montreal's Place des Arts and Quebec's Grand-Théâtre offer recitals, concerts, drama and top

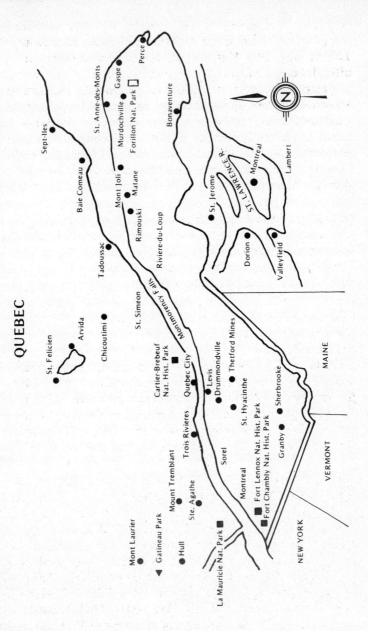

QUEBEC

St. Felicien

Arvida

Chicoutimi

Sept-Iles

Baie Comeau

Tadoussac

St. Simeon

St. Anne-des-Monts

Murdochville

Gaspe

Perce

Forillon Nat. Park

Bonaventure

Mont Joli

Matane

Rimouski

Riviere-du-Loup

Monmorency Falls

Cartier-Brebeuf
Nat. Hist. Park

Quebec City

Levis

Drummondville

Thetford Mines

St. Hyacinthe

Sherbrooke

Granby

Fort Lennox Nat. Hist. Park

Fort Chambly Nat. Hist. Park

Montreal

Sorel

Trois Rivieres

Ste. Agathe

Mount Tremblant

Gatineau Park

Hull

Mont Laurier

La Mauricie Nat. Park

St. Jerome

Montreal

Lambert

ST. LAWRENCE R.

Dorion

Valleyfield

MAINE

VERMONT

NEW YORK

entertainers throughout the year. French language dramas are performed in Montreal at the Théâtre du Nouveau Monde and the Théâtre du Rideau Vert. English language productions are also offered. For information on current plays consult local newspapers and magazines. Open air concerts are presented in the summer at Maisonneuve Park and an open air puppet theatre is featured at Lafontaine Park. Summer stock is produced at a few Laurentian resorts and in the Townships; open air concerts are given in Gatineau Park. Concerts and drama are highlights of Magog's Jeunesse Musicale du Canada Village, a summer music camp. International guest artists appear.

HUNTING AND FISHING Hunters and anglers are welcome at the many hunting preserves and fishing waters leased to private clubs and outfitters; outfitters accommodate, equip and guide sportsmen. At Quebec's forested and highland areas you find white-tail deer, bear, bull moose and beyond the 50th parallel, caribou. Small game animals are fox, snowshoe hare, bobcat, wolf and coyote. Ptarmigan, grouse, snipe, woodcock and partridge may also be hunted. The province's hundreds of thousands of rivers and lakes yield striped and black bass, whitefish, rainbow and speckled trout, sturgeon, pickerel, northern pike and perch. Atlantic salmon populate many rivers and streams in the Gaspé Peninsula. Fishing is first rate in Mont Tremblant, Laurentides and La Vérandrye parks. Recent hunging and angling regulations are obtainable from the Ministère du Loisir, de la chasse et de la pêche, Direction des Communications, P.O. Box 22,000, Quebec, Quebec, G1K 7Z2.

WINTER AND SUMMER SPORTS Skiing is excellent throughout the province. You may enjoy both alpine and cross country skiing in the Laurentians, the Outaouais (north of Hull), the Eastern Townships and the Quebec City area. The Montreal Canadiens, members of the professional National Hockey League, perform during the winter season at Montreal Forum. Other participatory winter sports are curling, skating and snowmobiling. Public golf courses are open at Magog, Montreal (several links), Quebec City, Trois-Rivières, Rivière-du-Loup, Sherbrooke, Hull, Noranda and other locations. Tennis is a feature of Maisonneuve Park and several Laurentian resorts. The province's many tens of thousands of rivers and lakes, Maisonneuve Park, beaches in Magdalen Islands, resorts in the Gaspé Peninsula and Magog provide innumerable opportunities for safe swimming. Enjoy boating in Mont-Tremblant or Gatineau Parks. You can mountain climb by Percé, hike in Montreal's Mont Royal Park and Quebec's Mont Ste.-Anne Park or ride in Mont Royal Park and at resorts in the Laurentian area. Children's pony rides are an attraction of Granby's Zoological Garden. Spectator sports include harness racing at Montreal's Richelieu Park and Blue Bonnets Raceway, wrestling, boxing, major league baseball (Montreal Expos) and football. The Montreal Alouettes are members of the professional Canadian Football League. Both the baseball and football teams play at the Olympic Stadium.

NATIONAL PARKS Fort Chambly National Historia Park is 18 miles south and east of Montreal. The original fort was built in 1665, destroyed by a fire and restored in stone, 1709-11. It was occupied by France at the time of the Indian and French War, then held by the British and Americans successively. Fort remains and the museum may be viewed daily, 10-6. **Fort Lennox National Historic Park** is located at Ile-aux-Noix, 10 miles south of St. Jean. The fort was originally constructed by France in 1759, then captured and destroyed by the English 1776-80. The fort was in action during the War of 1812. Open daily 10-5, May-October. **Sir Wilfred Laurier's Birthplace** at St.-Lin des Laurentides has been converted to an historic site. **Coteau-du-Lac National Historic Park** is the site of a British fort, built in 1812, and the oldest canal constructed on the St. Lawrence River. It is located by Route 20 east from Montreal. **La Mauricie National Park**, accessible by Highway 138, is situated between Quebec and Montreal. The park's features are wooded areas and many small lakes. There are only a few roads. **Forillon National Park** is being developed at Forillon Peninsula, on the Gaspé Peninsula. Currently there are camp sites in the park.

FOOD AND DRINK French cuisine is the specialty in Montreal, gourmet capital of Canada. Traditional French-Canadian dishes are ragoût de boulettes, spiced pork, meatballs in gravy, cretons du Quebec or cold pork paté with bread, tourtière, which is pork pie. Other provincial specialties are onion soup, pea soup, pig's cheeks, tails and feet, delicious local cheeses, maple sugar, maple syrup and sugar pie prepared with maple sugar. Oka cheese made by the Trappist Monks of Oka (near Montreal) is world famous. Restaurants in Montreal specialize in serving Chinese, Kosher, French, Polynesian, Indian, German, Italian and Spanish food. Well known restaurants in Montreal are Ruby Foo's (Chinese), L'Escargot, Gibby's, La Marée, Le St. Amable, Le Vieux Saint Gabriel (French-Canadian cuisine), La Richolette, Geronimo's, La Pergola (Italian), Les Filles du Roy, Le Caveau and Katsura (Japanese). Recommended places to eat in Quebec City include Chalet Suisse, Le Continental, and Café d'Europe. Beer, wine and cider are available from grocery stores, liquor from provincial outlets. The legal drinking age is 18.

TRANSPORTATION IN QUEBEC The road network is quite adequate in the heavily populated south. There are numerous car rental offices in Montreal, Quebec and other centres. In contrast to Ontario, motorists cannot make a right turn on a red light, even after having made a complete stop. Highway signs are written in French; for a description of the most important signs see the section Canadian Road Signs. Buses operate on sightseeing tours of Montreal; there is good bus service to other points in the province. From Toronto, New York and Montreal, sightseeing excursions by bus, of a few days to a few weeks duration, take in the Gaspé Peninsula, Montreal and/or Quebec or Quebec - New England. Scheduled bus service connects Montreal to Toronto, New York and to other parts of North America. Montreal's modern Metro (subway) operates past midnight. Horse drawn carriages or calèches are a relaxing way to see Quebec and Montreal, Cruise ships ply the St. Lawrence and Saguenay Rivers and ferries cross the St. Lawrence between a number of municipalities along the river. Boats sail to the Magdalen Islands.

Canadian Airlines travels to Montreal from major cities across Canada. **Air Canada** also travels to Montreal and Quebec City from major Canadian centres, among them Vancouver, Winnipeg, Edmonton, Toronto and Ottawa. **Air Canada** operates from Vancouver to Montreal every day of the week non stop. **Air Canada** also goes to Montreal from Halifax and Winnipeg daily. **Pan American Airways** operates from major centres in Europe, the Caribbean and Latin America to New York and from there **Air Canada** flies to Montreal. For instance **Pan Am** operates to New York from London, Paris, Brussels, Amsterdam, Rome, Madrid, Rio de Janeiro, Caracas and Buenos Aires on a frequently scheduled service.

City Express operates to Montreal from Ottawa several days of the week and on the non stop service the flying time is about 30 minutes. **City Express** travels from Toronto Island Airport to Montreal several times daily throughout the year. On the non stop **City Express** flights between the two cities, the flying time is around 1 ½ hours. The **City Express** service is especially convenient for anyone travelling to Montreal from Toronto's downtown area. A free shuttle service is provided by **City Express** from the Royal York Hotel to the airport on Toronto Island. The Royal York Hotel itself is conveniently accessible by subway from many parts of Toronto. Toronto Island Airport is a preferable alternative to the increasingly congested and overcrowded Lester Pearson Airport. As well, the **City Express** flight is a generally less expensive and more efficient method of travelling between the downtown areas of the two cities and the frequency of service is an added reason for taking **City Express** to Montreal. **Skycraft Air** operates between Oshawa and Montreal non stop the year round. **Skycraft Air,** based in Oshawa, travels to Montreal on a frequently scheduled service. **Skycraft** offers a particularly convenient service to Montreal for passengers departing from the north and northeast parts of Toronto. **First Air** travels from Ottawa to Montreal (Mirabel Airport) non stop twice daily and the flying time is 35 minutes. **Air Ontario** travels from London, Ontario to Montreal, via Ottawa, on a regularly scheduled basis. **VIA Rail** schedules train service to the main provincial centres from major cities across Canada, including Toronto, Edmonton, Ottawa and Winnipeg. **VIA Rail's** efficiently run service between Toronto and Montreal is scheduled on a frequent daily basis. **VIA Rail's** service between Ottawa and Montreal is also offered daily. **VIA** provides a regularly scheduled year round rail link between Montreal and major cities in western and eastern Canada, including Halifax, Winnipeg, Vancouver, Calgary and Edmonton.

SHOPPING Many downtown shops are open 9:30-5:30 or 6, to 9 on Thursday and Friday evening. Two leading department stores, Eaton's and Simpson's, both stock imported china and woolens from England. French perfumes, men's and women's clothing. Glassware, furs and linens are good buys. Other provincial specialties are hooked rugs, wood carvings, Canadian art, ceramics, French and Canadian antiques, Eskimo prints and sculptures, enamelware, textiles, jewellery and leatherwork. A provincial sales tax is imposed on goods purchased.

ACCOMMODATION Quebec City *Hilton International Quebec*, 3 Place Quebec, (418) 647-2411, 563 rooms and suites, centrally located, each room has colour TV and refrigerator/bar, rooftop disco, French cuisine, seafood restaurant, family restaurant, swimming pool, connected to shopping complex. *Holiday Inn Downtown*, (418) 647-2611, 395 Rue de la Couronne near historic section, 232 rooms, in room movies, gift shop, parking, indoor pool, lounge, dining room next to shopping mall, close to Mall and bus terminal, night clubs, fitness centre. *Hotel Le Chateaubriand*, 3225 Hochelaga St., Ste. Foy, (418) 653-4901, 342 air conditioned rooms, not far from downtown, near shops and Old Quebec, free parking, outdoor swimming pool, room service, no smoking floor. **Montreal** *Ritz-Carlton*, centrally located on 1228 Sherbrooke St. West, (514) 842-4212, 240 rooms and suites, air conditioned, mini bar, colour TV, 3 minute walk from downtown, elegant dining room, pleasant atmosphere, Le Maritime restaurant featuring seafood, cocktail lounge, coffee shop, piano bars, room and laundry service, car rentals, babysitting, major credit cards, parking, one of top rated hotels in Canada. *Holiday Inn*, Longueuil, 999 de Serigny (514) 670-3030, 208 rooms, lounge, bar, gift shop, piano bar, indoor swimming pool, dining room, direct access by subway to downtown, Olympic Stadium, and Man and His World. *Holiday Inn*, Pointe Claire, (514) 697-7110, 6700 Trans Canada Highway, 301 rooms, air conditioning, lounge, indoor swimming pool, French cuisine, fitness area, sauna, dining room, coffee shop, piano bar, squash courts, major credit cards. *Le Grand Hotel*, 777 University St., (514) 879-1370, 737 rooms plus 40 suites, located in the business centre, minutes from Old Montreal, gourmet dining room, revolving rooftop restaurant and lounges, spectacular atrium lobby, underground connection to theatres and shops, coffee shop, swimming pool, health club, boutiques. *Bonaventure Hilton*, 1 Place Bonaventure, (514) 878-2332, 394 rooms, indoor access to shops, train station and subway, 2 restaurants, lobby bar, entertainment lounge, pool-bar, 24 hour room service, year round outdoor heated pool, health clubs, garden. *Four Seasons*, at 1050 Sherbrooke West, (514) 284-1110, close to shops and boutiques, 300 rooms and suites, with mini bar, TV, and clock radio, fine dining at Le Restaurant, more informal dining at Le Café, piano bar, discotheque, multilingual concierge, 24 hour room service, complimentary nightly shoe shine, twice daily maid service, complete fitness centre, year round outdoor pool, sauna, whirlpool, massage. *Aeroport Hilton Interna-*

tional, 12505 Cote de Liesse, (514) 631-2411, 485 rooms, mini bars, 20 minutes from downtown, dining room, coffee house, free parking, cocktail lounge with entertainment and dancing, disco, year-round swimming pool, bar by the pool, health club, sauna, massage and whirlpool, 24 hour room service, in-house movies, free transportation to and from Dorval airport. *Le Centre Sheraton Hotel and Towers*, 1201 Boulevard Rene Levesque Ouest, (514) 878-2000, 131 rooms and suites, 84 non smoking rooms, private lounge serving breakfast, many extras in the rooms, disabled facilities available, major credit cards accepted. *Le Centre Sheraton*, 1201 Boulevard Rene Levesque Ouest, (514) 878-2000, downtown, 824 rooms, 3 restaurants, 4 lounges, indoor heated swimming pook, pets, health clubs, sauna, whirlpool, indoor parking, shopping arcade, major credit cards accepted, disabled facilities available. *Sheraton Laval*, 2440 Autoroute des Laurentides, (514) 687-2440, 246 rooms, 11 suites, coffee shop, restaurant, lounge, entertainment, disco club, indoor heated pool, pets, disabled facilities, major credit cards accepted, non smoking rooms available. *Holiday Inn Downtown*, 420 Sherbrooke St. W., (514) 842-6111, centrally located, within walking distance of shopping areas, museums, and Place des Arts, has 483 rooms, completely renovated, colour TV, new Cafe - Restaurant with Continental cuisine, indoor swimming pool, whirlpool, saunas, indoor parking available, gift shop, beautiful lobby, major credit cards accepted. *Holiday Inn Le Seville*, 4545 Cote Vertu W., Exit 62 Trans Canada Hwy., (514) 332-2720, not far from Dorval Airport, 91 rooms, with colour TV, restaurant and lounge, outdoor swimming pool, free parking facilities available, fine dining at Le Seville Restaurant. *Holiday Inn Richelieu City Centre*, 505 Sherbrooke St. East, (514) 842-8581, centrally located not far from Olympic Stadium, Greyhound bus terminal 2 blocks away, 320 rooms on 23 floors, no smoking rooms available, mini bars available, free indoor parking facilities, indoor swimming pool, lounge, live entertainment features, sauna, Cardinal Richelieu Restaurant, major credit cards accepted. *Holiday Inn Seigneurie*, (514) 731-7751, at 7300 Cote de Liesse, free transportation to nearby Dorval Airport, 198 rooms, with colour TV, outdoor heated swimming pool, no smoking rooms available, movie channels by satellite, golf range across the street, weekend golf packages, lounge, free parking available, major credit cards. *Meridien Hotel*, (514) 285-1450, 4 Complex Desjardins, a fine property located in the heart of Desjardins area, centrally located near shops and subway, 601 rooms with colour TV, radio, in house video movies, mini bar, hair dryers and ice dispensers, 2 restaurants including one for fine dining, Le Cafe Fleuri for breakfast, lunch and dinner, Le Club for gourmet dining, recreational facilities in health club, indoor swimming pool, terrace, sauna, whirlpool, snack bar, piano bar, drug store, shops, baby sitting, car rental, newstand, parking available, major credit cards. **Orford** *Sheraton Orford*, a resort at 2387 Chemin du Parc, Autoroute 10, Exit 118, (819) 847-4747, 117 rooms in a resort location, 80 miles from airport in Montreal, by lake, provincial park and ski centre, rooms have TV, coffee shop, restaurant, lounge, entertainment, outdoor heated pool, tennis, golf, health clubs, disabled facilities, parking. **Sherbrooke** *Le Baron Motel*, 3200 King St. West, (819) 567-3941, 126 rooms and suites, air conditioned, radio and colour TV in every room, restaurant, dancing, bar, entertainment, outdoor swimming pool, laundry service, free parking, babysitting.

QUEBEC RESORTS Gray Rocks Inn, 75 miles north of Montreal near St. Jovite, full service resort, 205 guest rooms, year round sports facilities, health and fitness centre includes an indoor swimming pool, whirlpools, saunas and exercise room, 18 hole golf course, 22 tennis courts, horseback riding, beach area, water sports, 9 hole putting green and lawn bowling.

MISCELLANEOUS

PROVINCIAL TOURIST BUREAU Tourism Quebec, P.O. Box 22,000, Quebec City, Quebec G1K 7Z2.

VISITOR INFORMATION CENTRES are open the year round in Montreal, Quebec City, Notre Dame du Portage, Mirabel and St. Pierre de Veronne. Other communities maintain offices during the summer.

One of Canada's most historic homes, Sillery, Quebec

Side view of Legislative Building, Regina, Saskatchewan

PERSPECTIVE

LOCATION Saskatchewan, in the heart of Canada's wheat belt, is landlocked between its prairie neighbours, Alberta and Manitoba. The province extends more than 750 miles north from the states of Montana and North Dakota to the border with the Northwest Territories. Regina is 480 miles east from Calgary. Saskatoon is 1,850 miles west of the capital, Ottawa.

AREA 220,122 square miles, of which 31,700 square miles are fresh water.

BACKGROUND The year 1794 marked the beginning of European settlement. The huge profits to be gained from the fur trade stimulated exploration and colonization of the little populated region during the 19th century. The territory, a part of the enormous domain administered by the fur-trading Hudson's Bay Company, was sold in 1869 to the newly formed federal government and made a part of the Northwest Territories. In 1905 the territorial districts of Assiniboia, Athabaska and Saskatchewan were combined to become a province of the Dominion of Canada.

POPULATION Approximately 1,000,000.

CAPITAL Regina. Its population is around 165,000. Saskatoon is a city of nearly 150,000. Moose Jaw currently has a population of 33,000 inhabitants.

LANGUAGES While there are several bilingual towns, English is spoken everywhere.

TIME ZONES Most of the province (except for a narrow southeastern corridor observing Central Standard Time) is located in the Mountain Standard Time Zone. Noon in Regina is 2 p.m. Eastern Standard Time.

WHEN TO VISIT The summer months offer excellent camping, boating, fishing and swimming in over 100,000 clean lakes. Duck hunting opportunities during the fall season are first rate. In February, Prince Albert and other northern communities stage their annual winter festivals.

SASKATCHEWAN

REGINA The Legislative Buildings, surrounded by 160 acres of gardens and grounds, were built of marble and stone in the Renaissance style (1908-1912). Both the legislative chamber and the library are open to tourists. Recruits are trained for the national police force at the Royal Canadian Mounted Police Barracks. The R.C.M.P. also act as police in all provinces but Ontario and Quebec. Attractions include the museum, the barrack's chapel (1882) and police recruits on ceremonial parades. Waterfowl Park in Wascana centre provides a sanctuary for ducks, Canadian geese and swans. The centre also has picnic grounds, boating and sports facilities. Other city attractions are the August Buffalo Days, the Museum of Natural History and the Diefenbaker Homestead, home of one of Canada's Prime Ministers.

EXCURSIONS FROM REGINA The Ipsco Wildlife Area, three miles north, is noted for animals of the province, buffalo, antelope, birds and a steam locomotive dating from 1918. The prairie town of Weyburn offers access to fishing and camping sites. The Soo Line Historical Museum displays a collection of rocks and articles from the Indian and pioneer era of the province. **Estevan** is eight miles north of North Dakota. The local sightseeing interests are the museum in Woodlawn Regional Park, an Indian and pioneer museum and Boundary Dam, which can be toured by appointment. Moose Mountain Provincial Park harbors wildlife and also features golf, boating, horseback riding, hiking, tennis, fishing, swimming and camping. A Cree and Ojibway Indian Reservation is located near Carlyle. Moosomin vacation pursuits are summer sports, hunting and a visit to the local museum; the town pioneer opera house was never used for a performance. Yorkton's big attraction is the Western Development Museum (at the airport), displaying antique farm equipment, gas, steam and oil driven tractors and old cars. Open all year. Kamsack is a few miles southwest of Duck Mountain Park. The towns and villages near Kamsak reflect the Ukrainian settlers influence through the local architecture. Last Mountain Lake, 50 miles north of Regina, is a bird sanctuary, a place to see the whooping crane on migrations north and south.

SOUTHWEST SASKATCHEWAN Touring interests in **Moose Jaw** are Crescent Park with swimming and tennis and the Wild Animals

Park (south of the city) housing a Kiddie's Zoo. Buffalo Pound Provincial Park, 10 miles north, is a summer and winter holiday region. **Gravelbourg** is noted for its cathedral which displays a number of religious works of art. **Swift Current** maintains a museum of pioneer history. Frontier Days — with a rodeo, fair and parades — is staged in early July. Hunting and fishing flourish in the surrounding district. Animals roam the wooded hills of Cypress Hills Provincial Park, 20 miles south of Maple Creek; it has a golf course, camping, hiking, fishing, tennis, swimming and picnic grounds. The park should be interesting to the geologist. **Maple Creek** is noted for an Old Timer Museum, showing fossils, rocks and pioneer articles, the restored Fort Walsh used by the R.C.M.P. for breeding horses and the Prairie Museum. Fort Walsh was originally erected to introduce police control when Chief Sitting Bull and his tribe moved here after the Battle of the Little Big Horn (1874). Colonies of prairie dogs roam Frenchman Creek Valley, south of Val Marie (80 miles south of Swift Current). View large herds of antelope in fields off the Trans Canada Highway, in Maple Creek vicinity.

SASKATOON AND THE NORTH The Forestry Farm Animal Park and Bird Park west on 33rd St. features foreign and domestic animals, birds, children's pony rides and picnic spots. The Pioneer Days event held for two weeks every July re-enacts the early history of the city with parades. Other possible interests are the Mendel Art Gallery and Conservatory, a combined theatre and art gallery. The local branch of the Western Development Museum stands at 2610 Lorne Ave. South. **North Battlefield** was one of the first settlements of the west. The Western Development Museum and Pioneer Village is a restored community of the pioneer era. The Imhoff studio, five miles west of St. Walburg, exhibits portraits of European royalty, presidents and religious leaders. **Lloydminster** features another Imhoff art collection in the Barr Colony Museum. Camping and picnic areas are found in Weaver Park. The museum in Duck Lake houses Indian relics and articles of pioneer days. **Prince Albert** is a point of departure for fishing and hunting trips to the north. Local attractions are the Lund Wildlife Exhibit housing numerous varieties of Canadian animals and birds and Little Red River Park, offering picnic grounds and skiing. An old log church and schoolhouse are maintained in Bryant Park. Lac la Ronge, 110 miles north.

Southern Saskatchewan countryside

SASKATCHEWAN

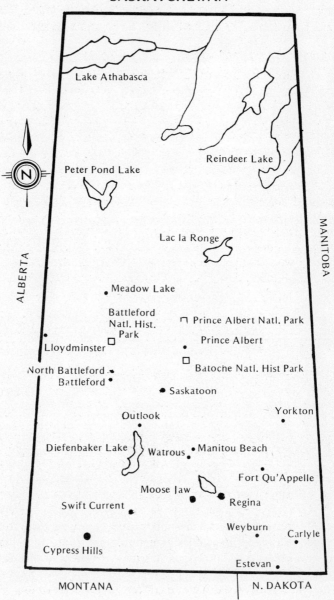

Lake Athabasca

Reindeer Lake

Peter Pond Lake

MANITOBA

ALBERTA

Lac la Ronge

Meadow Lake

Battleford Natl. Hist. Park

⊓ Prince Albert Natl. Park

Lloydminster

Prince Albert

Batoche Natl. Hist Park

North Battleford
Battleford

Saskatoon

Outlook

Yorkton

Diefenbaker Lake

Watrous Manitou Beach

Fort Qu'Appelle

Moose Jaw

Regina

Swift Current

Weyburn

Carlyle

Cypress Hills

Estevan

MONTANA

N. DAKOTA

contains some 1,000 islands in its 510 square mile area, and is a popular fishing spot. The town of La Ronge maintains the Northern Handicraft Centre and Museum, exhibiting Indian art objects. Cree Indians from the neighboring reservation act as guides for sportsmen.

HISTORIC SITES, MUSEUMS AND ART GALLERIES The Norman MacKenzie Art Gallery in Regina exhibits sculptures and art from Canada, the U.S.A. and Europe; open every day on the University campus. The Natural History Museum has a collection of provincial wild life. Open daily. The museum in the R.C.M.P. Barracks contains old photos, documents, firearms and Indian relics. **Saskatoon** The Mendel Art Gallery has Canadian and Eskimo works of art. The Western Development Museum (open every day) houses antiquated agricultural equipment, old harvesters, tractors, cars and carriages. Lloydminster's Barr Colony Museum at Weaver Park features items from the days of early settlement and exhibits of domestic wildlife. The renovated wooden church (1904) is open to the public. Fort Carleton, 45 miles northwest of Saskatoon, was the site of a Hudson's Bay Fort. Replicas of the original buildings have been furnished and can be toured. Battleford, Prince Albert and Fort Qu'Appelle have other museums. Cannington Manor, north from Carlyle and a bit east of Kenosee, was the site of an English aristocrat's settlement, begun in the mid 1880's. All Saints Anglican Church is part of the restored remains.

MUSIC AND THE THEATRE An International Band Competition is staged for three days in Moose Jaw each May. More than 70 bands and 5,000 musicians participate.

HUNTING AND FISHING Saskatchewan's forested north harbors black bear, caribou, mule deer, antelope, white-tail deer and moose. Waterfowl and upland game birds are pheasant, duck, ptarmigan, snipe, several varieties of grouse and geese and partridge. Main fish species are trout, Arctic greyling, perch, goldeye, whitefish, brown, speckled and rainbow trout, northern pike, sturgeon and walleye. Sportsmen encounter excellent fishing in the far north, at lakes so little known many remain nameless to this day. Current hunting and angling regulations are available from Saskatchewan Tourism and Renewable Resources, 3211 Albert St., Regina, Saskatchewan, S4S 5W5.

WINTER AND SUMMER SPORTS Winter recreational activities in the province are skating, hockey, curling and snowmobiling. There are nearly 100 public golf courses in Saskatchewan — in Regina, Saskatoon, Duck Mountain Provincial Park, Moose Mountain Provincial Park, Swift Current, Prince Albert, Moose Jaw, North Battleford and Maple Creek. Tennis is a feature of Prince Albert National Park. Swimming is safe at municipal swimming pools and in national and provincial parks. Little Manitou Lake, a short distance north of Watrous, is characterized by buoyant mineral waters; even non-swimmers can float. Lake Diefenbaker, Buffalo Pound Park and other provincial recreation areas and the province's extensive lake system provide opportunities for boating. Canoeing is excellent in the countless rivers and lakes to the north and trips mapped out on specified routes last from a week to 10 days. Horseback ride in Buffalo Pound, Moose Mountain, Battleford and Cypress Hills Provincial Park. Hiking trails are marked in Prince Albert National Park.

NATIONAL PARKS Prince Albert National Park in the north of the province is filled with forests, streams, lakes, prairie grassland, aspen parkland, camp sites and cabins in its 1,496 square mile area. Activities include game viewing, hiking, fishing, golf, boating and tennis. The park headquarters are in Waskesiu; the park is open all year. **Fort Battleford Historic Park** is the site of an early North West Mounted Police Post (1876). The original structures, stockade and museum are contained within the 40-acre park, open to the public from 9-5, May-October and on summer evenings. It's situated near North Battleford. **Batoche Rectory Historic Park** was the Métis headquarters at the time of the North West Rebellion of 1885. This was the scene of the final battle fought between the Métis, who were fur trappers, and the victorious Canadian government. See the rectory and exhibits on the period, May to the end of September.

FOOD AND DRINK Try bannock, if you can get it served (mostly in rural homes). It's bread prepared without shortening or yeast, served fresh from the oven or from hot coals. Berries native to Saskatchewan are the pinchberry, boysenberry and the Saskatoon, something like a blueberry. The legal drinking age is 18.

TRANSPORTATION IN SASKATCHEWAN Roads in the south of the province are good. If you are intent on driving without sightseeing, you should be able to cover a lot of territory — as much as 500 miles a day in the open, untravelled countryside. The Trans Canada Highway extends from Winnipeg in the east through to Regina and on to Calgary. VIA Rail Canada operates in the province. VIA's transcontinental service from Toronto to Vancouver passes through Saskatoon and Regina. Rail connections in a north-south direction are also scheduled. Bus service connects most communities to the rest of Canada. Bus tours originating from main cities such as Toronto include Saskatoon and/or Regina on their western itinerary. Car and passenger carrying ferries sail free of charge, offering regular crossings at several points along the North and South Saskatchewan Rivers. National and regional airlines fly to practically all parts of the province. Charter airplanes may be hired for hunting and fishing trips to remote northern lakes.

SHOPPING The Handicraft Centre of La Ronge in the far north sells wares produced by local Indians. Indian crafts are sold at stores operated out of a small number of Indian reservations. A provincial sales tax is levied on goods purchased.

ACCOMMODATION Moose Jaw Hospital Flag Inn, 405 Main North (306) 692-2301, 68 rooms, located downtown, each room has colour TV, radio and phone, fully licensed dining lounge, coffee shop, steam baths, indoor swimming pool, saunas, whirlpool. Best Western Downtown Motor Lodge, 45 Athabaska St. E., (306) 692-1884, 22 rooms and suites, laundry service, free parking, babysitting. **Prince Albert** Pines Motor Inn, 3245 2nd Ave. N., (922-1333), 78 rooms, extra large rooms available, colour TV, air conditioning, close to a major shopping centre, several restaurants close by, has own dining area, free parking, major credit cards accepted, near new police museum, open all year. **Regina** Sheraton Centre, 1818 Victoria Ave., (306) 569-1666, downtown near Legislative Bldg., and RCMP Museum, 251 rooms, 3 restaurants, 2 lounges, indoor pool complex, indoor heated parking, disabled facilities available, 40 non smoking rooms available. Seven Oaks Motor Inn, 777 Albert St., (306) 527-0121, 105 rooms, colour TV, air conditioning, free parking, dining room, programmes of entertainment on occasion, near downtown, weekend rates, major credit cards. Relax Inn, Hwy. 1 East on Service Road,

1110 Victoria Ave. E., (306) 565-0455, 190 rooms, with colour TV and air conditioning, indoor swimming pool, whirlpool, parking, water slide nearby. **Saskatoon** Northgate Motor Inn, 706 Idylwyld Dr. N., (664-4414), on Hwys. 16 and 11, close to airport and a few blocks from the downtown area, 56 rooms, colour TV, air conditioning, free local phone calls, free parking, ice machines, restaurant on premises, major credit cards. Relax Inn, 102 Cardinal Cres., near airport, 192 rooms, 24 hour gift shop, free parking. Holiday Inn Saskatoon, (306) 244-2311, 90 - 22nd St. E. at First Ave., downtown, next to Saskatoon Theatre for Performing Arts, 200 rooms, indoor swimming pool, programmes of entertainment, dining room, lounge, gift shop, weekend rates available, free parking, sauna, major credit cards accepted. Sheraton Cavalier, 612 Spadina Cres. E., (306) 652-6770, downtown, near museum, 250 rooms, 12 suites, coffee shop, 3 restaurants, lounge, entertainment, indoor heated pool, children's pool, sauna, giant water slides, whirlpool, pets permitted, disabled facilities available, non-smoking rooms available, parking. **Swift Current** Rainbow Motel, Hwy. 1 East, (306) 773-8351, 36 rooms, colour TV, air conditioning, phones, plug in parking, open all year, Visa and Master Card accepted, nearby are Dandy's General Store and OPA's Fine Eating Establishment, on 1106 6th Ave. N.E., specialties include German dishes, licensed, open daily. **Yorkton** Flag Inn, 110 Broadway East, (306) 783-9781, 92 rooms and suites, air conditioned, colour TV, phone, dining room, coffee shop, lounge, indoor pool, sauna, whirlpool, free parking. Corona Motor Hotel, 345 W. Broadway, (306) 783-6571, 85 rooms, air conditioned, radio, colour TV, restaurant, bar, entertainment, indoor swimming pool, sauna, golf course, beauty shop, free parking, laundry service, meeting and convention facilities.

MISCELLANEOUS

PROVINCIAL TOURIST BUREAU The Department of Tourism and Renewable Resources, 3211 Albert St., Regina, Saskatchewan, S4S 5W5.

VISITOR INFORMATION CENTRES are open in Lloydminster and Regina all year. Centres in Maple Creek, Fleming, North Portal, Diefenbaker Lake and Lac La Ronge are open in the summer.

Original home of John G. Diefenbaker, located in Wascana Centre, Regina

PERSPECTIVE

LOCATION When you realize that the Yukon Territory is bounded by Alaska to the west, the Arctic Ocean in the north and the Northwest Territories to the east, it's not difficult to appreciate that Whitehorse is about as remote from Cape Spear, Newfoundland in the easternmost part of Canada (some 5,7000 miles away) as it is from the state of Hawaii.

AREA 205,346 square miles.

BACKGROUND One of the first Europeans to explore the Yukon was John Franklin, who entered the region in 1825. The Hudson's Bay Company engaged in fur trading in the far northern area during the middle of the 19th century. Gold was discovered in the Yukon in minute quantities by adventurers and fur traders until a major strike in 1896 in the Klondike River sparked the most lucrative gold rush in history. More than $100,000,000 in gold was panned over the next five years, but by 1906 the precious metal began to peter out and a large part of the prospecting population drifted away. Ottawa created Yukon as a territory in 1898, but the territory has yet to be granted provincial status.

POPULATION About 25,000, the smallest of any of the provinces and territories.

CAPITAL Whitehorse, population 16,500. Dawson City is a community of 1,000.

LANGUAGE English.

TIME ZONE Yukon Standard Time. When the clock reads noon in Whitehorse, it is four in the afternoon in the Eastern Standard Time Zone.

WHEN TO VISIT June to September, when the summer days are pleasantly warm and sunny. Whitehorse, because of its extreme northern location, basks under 10 hours of Arctic summer sunshine a day in June and part of July. Daylight lasts about 22 hours a day in the summer.

YUKON TERRITORY

ALASKA HIGHWAY TO WHITEHORSE The highway begins at Dawson Creek, B.C. Local attractions of possible interest are World War II American Army buildings, the museum, Soap Box Derby competitions in June, the Fall Fair highlighted by rodeo contests and the curling bonspiel in July. You may wish to picnic by the 200 square mile man-made Williston Lake, created on the completion of the Portage Mountain Dam. The hydro plant operates tours. Hunting and fishing flourish in the region. Continue on the route past Fort St. John, Fort Nelson and Summit Lake to Watson Lake just over the border. Watson Lake is known for its huge collection of signposts pointing the way to myriad places around the world. A number of camping sites are situated off the road to Whitehorse.

WHITEHORSE, at mile 918 of the Alaska Highway, is famous for its associations with the Klondike gold rush of 1898. By 1905 more than $100,000,000 worth of gold was panned from the Klondike region. The M.V. Schwatka operates two-hour afternoon cruises of the Yukon River past Mile Canyon. The canyon commands a fine view of the Yukon River flowing past the gorge; many boats passing through here in '98 were wrecked. A suspension bridge provides a good angle for photos and a view of the canyon. Memories of the early Klondike days are relived by visiting the Klondike and other paddlewheel steamers anchored by the side of the river; the Klondike boat is open daily, June-September. Graves in the local cemetery are surmounted by little Indian style 'spirit' homes; the souls of the deceased are believed to return here. Other town sights are the MacBride Museum, Sam McGee's cabin nearby, the White Horse Rapids which have been dammed and the pioneer wooden church. Several of the country's highest peaks in the area tempt the climber.

TRIPS FROM WHITEHORSE Champagne is 41 miles west on the road to Haines Junction. The settlement is interesting for its nearly deserted trading post and views of the St. Elias Mountains. Haines Junction is situated 100 miles west of Whitehorse in the Shakwak Valley of the St. Elias Mountain Range, the most impressive on the continent. The ghost town of Silver City is 20 miles from Haines Junction. The Alaskan border is located at mile post 1202. Tetlin Junction, Alaska is at Mile 1301. **Dawson** was the centre of the gold

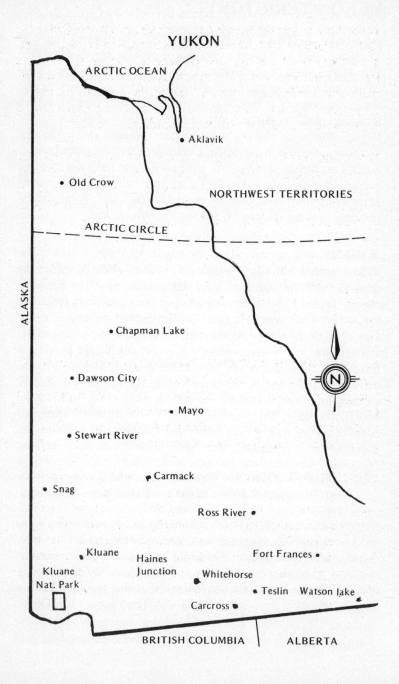

rush and you can still pan for gold in the Bonanza Creek. Buildings constructed during the era are the Palace Grand Theatre (1899), the Old Post Office (1901), Robert Service's cabin, Red Feather Saloon, Flora Dora Hotel and Madame Tremblay's. Dawson also boasts a legalized gambling casino. The summit of the mountain called Midnight Dome offers a panoramic view of the surrounding region. Mayo and Carmacks are mining centres. Carcross contains several 1890's wooden dwellings and other reminders of the period.

HISTORIC SITES, MUSEUMS AND ART GALLERIES The MacBride Museum in Whitehorse shows exhibits from the gold rush era, mounted animals, and photographs from the early days of the Yukon. Open daily from 9 a.m. to 9 p.m., from the middle of May to the second week in September. Sam McGee's cabin dates from 1899. He was a prospector from Tennessee, immortalized in Robert Service's poem, The Cremation of Sam McGee. The log Anglican Church, located at Elliott and Third Ave., houses displays on the early days and missions. Many buildings in Dawson City, including Robert Service's cabin, originate from the 1890's. Gold rush exhibits are on view in Dawson Museum. The S.S. Keno paddlewheeler may be viewed on conducted tours.

MUSIC AND THE THEATRE "The Gaslight Follies", entertainment reminiscent of the 1890's, is featured 8 p.m. to 10 p.m. nightly (except Monday) from the end of May through to September on the Palace Grande Theatre stage. Dawson City is also known for Diamond Tooth Gertie's, a gambling hall which features shows of can can dancing nightly in the summer months.

HUNTING AND FISHING Stone Dall sheep and grizzly bear inhabit the mountain regions. Other big game animals are moose, caribou, black bear and mountain goat. Game birds include duck, grouse, ptarmigan and geese. Non residents are required to hunt with a licensed guide. The Yukon's waterways, some of which have never been fished, yield Arctic grayling, kokanee and other types of salmon, northern pike, whitefish, rainbow and lake trout. Current hunting and fishing regulations are obtainable by writing Tourism-Yukon, Government of Yukon, Box 2703, Whitehorse, Yukon Y1A 2C6.

WINTER AND SUMMER SPORTS Whitehorse's Sourdough Rendezvous in February is highlighted by winter sports competitions, including dog team racing. Popular winter sports are cross country skiing, snowshoeing, curling, hockey and snowmobiling. Whitehorse offers tennis and swimming (in the municipal pool). You can boat and canoe far from civilization in mountain waterways; canoes are rented in Whitehorse. Mountain climbers are challenged by North America's highest peaks, including Mount Logan, 19.850 feet. Many others soar more than 10,000 feet. You can enjoy wilderness hiking at Kluane National Park in the summer.

NATIONAL PARKS Kluane National Park (8,500 square miles) features glaciers, alpine meadows, scenic beauties, mountains, icefields and wildlife, including moose, Dall sheep and grizzly bears. The park is a 2 hour drive from Whitehorse. Dawson City's Palace Grand Théatre and the S.S. Keno, a riverboat of the gold rush days, have been renovated and declared historic sites.

FOOD AND DRINK Two specialties of Whitehorse are steaks and Alaska King Crab. Liquor, wines and beer are sold in taverns and cocktail lounges, open daily, often to 2 a.m. Territorial outlets retail liquor in Whitehorse, Dawson, Haines Junction and Watson Lake.

TRANSPORTATION IN THE YUKON Avis, Hertz, Budget and Tilden car rental companies operate offices in Whitehorse. Gravel roads are adequate though it's wise to take along a second spare. **Atlas Tours** operates scheduled bus service between Skagway, Alaska and Carcross and Whitehorse. Atlas also offers sightseeing tours of the principal tourist attractions in the Yukon, including Whitehorse and Dawson. **Glacier Air Tours** offers trips by plane out of Burwash Landing over the beautiful Kluane National Park, noted for its soaring peaks, icefields and glaciers. Pleasure Island Restaurant Ltd. in Dawson City operates Yukon River tours from June to late August. Charter planes can be hired to get you to fishing and hunting areas.

SHOPPING Local specialties are Indian handicrafts, including parkas and mukluks, and rocks and jewellery. Excellent soapstone sculptures are on sale. Klondike gold jewellery can also be purchased.

ACCOMMODATION Eagle Plains Eagle Plains Hotel, 34 rooms, some with TV and direct dial phones, dining room, lounge, bar with satellite TV, free parking, gift shop, service station next door, open all year, all credit cards, campground, miniature golf, only hotel between Inuvik and Dawson. **Dawson City** Eldorado Hotel, a block from the Yukon River, 53 rooms with phones and colour TV, dining room with Yukon food specialties, lounge, live entertainment, open all year, friendly service, free parking. **Whitehorse** Edgewater Hotel, 101 Main St., (403) 667-2572, centrally located, next to Yukon River, 15 rooms with bath and satellite TV, central heating, dining room, lounge, free plug-in parking, gift shop, near sightseeing attractions, open all year, Visa and Master Card accepted. **Burwash Landing** Burwash Landing Resort, at mile 1093 Alaska Highway, 32 clean and comfortable rooms, dining room, overlooks Kluane Lake, lounge with pool table and video game, Kluane Museum nearby, open all year, sightseeing flights over nearby Kluane National Park can be arranged with the management, free parking, boat tours, well recommended.

MISCELLANEOUS

TERRITORIAL TOURIST BUREAU Yukon-Tourism, P.O. Box 2703, Whitehorse, Yukon Y1A 2C6.

VISITOR INFORMATION CENTRES operate in Haines Junction and Dawson City.

FRENCH CONVERSATION GUIDE

French and English are the official languages of Canada. French is spoken by approximately a third of the population of the country, but anyone can get along in English almost anywhere except in parts of Quebec. French is as much the medium of expression of Quebec City, Rimouski, Three Rivers and rural areas as it is in Paris. On many occasions, a French-language Canadian, while able to speak English won't — as a matter of pride. It's reasonable to accept that the majority of Quebecois prefer to speak French in their own province.

Personnel in hotels, restaurants and shops and customs, tourist and police officials in the province of Quebec will frequently first address you in French and make the switch to English courteously and automatically when it becomes evident that you are a visitor. The occasions when you will have to consult the French conversation section of this guide will be correspondingly fewer if you follow the grooves, the paths marked out by other visitors.

There will be times when the use of English won't be of any help — along the road, in out-of-the-way restaurants and inns, service stations and most often by the man on the street. You could get a parking ticket for leaving the car in a Montreal street designated "stationnement interdit" (no parking). Highway signs are written in French only. Inevitably, it will pay to brush up on your language skills.

Ninety per cent of the vocabularies listed in French language dictionaries are seldom, if ever, used in the course of a normal summer vacation. A basic 300-400 word vocabulary is sufficient to give oneself understanding of and to make oneself understood in any language. The following words have been selected to enable you to cope with day to day conversation needs. With a smile and a single word you can often get the message across, perhaps inelegantly, but at least effectively.

BASIC EXPRESSIONS AND COMMON WORDS

English	French
please	s'il vous plaît
thank you	merci
goodbye	au revoir
good day	bonjour
yes, no	oui, non
excuse me	excusez-moi
how are you?	comment allez-vous?
large, small	grand, petit
good, bad	bon, mauvais
in front of	devant
behind	derrière
more, less	plus, moins
before, after	avant, après
over, under	sur, sous
with, without	avec, sans
enough, too much	assez, trop
how much	combien
too much (market)	trop cher
when, where	quand, où

English	French
EN ROUTE	
baggage room	consigne
station (rail)	gare
ticket office	guichet
round trip ticket	aller et retour
one way ticket	aller
gasoline	essence
oil	huile
water	eau
fill the tank	faites le plein
greasing	graissage
change the oil	faites la vidange
car wash	lavage
to the left	à gauche
to the right	à droite
straight ahead	tout droit
police	gendarme
dentist	dentiste

242

EN ROUTE

English	French
doctor	médecin
pharmacy	pharmacie
hospital	hôpital

HOTEL

English	French
reception	réception
single room	chambre pour une personne
double room	chambre pour deux personnes
with bath	avec bain
without bath	sans bain
bed	lit
double bed	grand lit
cold water	eau froide
hot water	eau chaude
chambermaid	femme de chambre
elevator	ascenseur
laundry	blanchissage
hairdresser	coiffeur
pressing (ironing)	repassage
porter	porteur

HOTEL

English	French
shower	douche
cashier	caisse
telephone	téléphone
wake me at …	réveillez moi à …

POST OFFICE

English	French
stamp	timbre-poste
registered	recommandée
letter	lettre
post card	carte postale
envelope	enveloppe
writing paper	papier à lettre

IN TOWN

English	French
building	edifice
church	église
fountain	fontaine
garden	jardin
information	renseignements
mail box	boîte à lettres
market	marché

English	French
IN TOWN	
old town	ville ancienne
park	parc
statue	statue
street	rue
town	ville
town centre	centre ville
town hall	hôtel de ville
travel agency	bureay de voyages
ARCHITECTURE	
altar piece	retable
apse	abside
bell-tower	clocher
castle	château
cathedral	cathedrale
cave	grotte
ceiling	plafond
chapel	chapelle
choir	choeur
clock	horloge

English	French
ARCHITECTURE	
convent	couvent
cross	croix
crucifix	crucifix
dome	dôme
facade	façade
furniture	ameublement
interior	intérieur
library	bibliothèque
monastery	monastère
nave	nef
organ	orgue
paintings	peintures
pulpit	chaire
spire	fléche
stained glass window	vitrail
tomb	tombeau
tower	tour
wood carvings	sculptures sur bois
TOURING THE COUNTRYSIDE	
airport	aéroport

English	French
TOURING THE COUNTRYSIDE	
bay	baie
beach	plage
bridge	pont
cliff	falaise
coast	côte
country	campagne
customs	douane
frontier	frontière
harbour	port
hill	colline
island	île
lake	lac
lighthouse	phare
mountains	montagnes
river	rivière
rock	rocher
sea	mer
shore	rive

English	French
TOURING THE COUNTRYSIDE	
tunnel	tunnel
valley	vallée
village	village
woods	bois
NOTICES	
waiting room	salle d'attente
entrance	entrée
exit	sortie
open	ouvert
closed	fermé
prohibited	défense de
danger	danger
men	messieurs
women	dames
push	poussez
pull	tirez
occupied	occupé
free	libre

English	French
RESTAURANT	
dining room	salle à manger
menu	menu
wine list	liste de vin
breakfast	petit déjeuner
meals	repas
lunch	déjeuner
dinner	dîner
waiter	garçon
waitress	serveuse
knife	couteau
spoon	cuillère
fork	fourchette
plate	assiette
glass	verre
bottle	bouteille
ashtray	cendrier
bill	addition
tip	pourboire
BREAKFAST MENU	
bread	pain

English	French
BREAKFAST MENU	
butter	beurre
coffee	café
tea	thé
omelette	omelette
fried eggs	oeufs au plat
soft boiled eggs	oeufs à la coque
hard boiled eggs	oeufs durs
CONDIMENTS	
mustard	moutarde
vinegar	vinaigre
pepper	poivre
salt	sel
sugar	sucre
lemon	citron
SEA FOODS	
cod	morue
lobster	homard
oysters	huîtres

English	French
SEA FOODS	
salmon	saumon
shrimps	crevettes
snails	escargots
tuna	thon
trout	truite
MEAT AND POULTRY	
chicken	poulet
cutlet (veal)	côtelette
cold meat	viandes froides
duck	canard
grilled	à la broche
ham	jambon
lamb	agneau de lait
liver	foie
roast	rôti
sausages	saucisses
turkey	dindon
with sauce	en sauce

English	French
VEGETABLES	
asparagus	asperges
cauliflower	chou-fleur
cucumber	cocombre
french fries	pommes frites
peas	pois
green beans	haricots verts
mushrooms	champignons
onions	oignons
potatoes	pommes de terre
rice	riz
spinach	épinards
tomatoes	tomates
DESSERTS	
apple	pomme
banana	banane
cakes	gâteaux
cheese	fromage
cherries	cerises
fruit cup	fruits au sirop

DESSERTS

English	French
grapes	raisin
ice cream	glace
orange	orange
peach	pêche
pear	poire
pastries	pâtisseries

DRINKS AND BEVERAGES

English	French
beer	bière
cider	cidre
coffee	café
fruit juice	jus de fruits
mineral water	eau minérale
soda water	eau gaseuse
red wine	vin rouge
white wine	vin blanc
tea	thé

SHOPPING

English	French
film	film
pen	plume

SHOPPING

English	French
pencil	crayon
thread	fil
toothbrush	brosse à dents
toothpaste	pâte dentifrice
comb	peigne
hair shampoo	shampooing
insect repellent	insecticide
gift	cadeau
refund	remboursement
change	monnaie
sales tax	taxe de vente
shoes	souliers
records	disques
souvenir	souvenir
swim suit	costume de bain
blouse	blouse
skirt	jupe
gloves	gants
coat	manteau
hat	chapeau
sock	la chausette

English	French
SHOPPING	
raincoat	imperméable
handkerchief	mouchoir
shirt	chemise
jacket	veston
suit	costume
tie	cravatte
MISCELLANEOUS	
ski lift	remonte-pente
ski trail	piste de ski
fishing	pêche
hunting	chasse
red	rouge
blue	bleu
orange	orange
brown	brun
yellow	jaune
grey	gris
white	blanc
black	noir
Monday	lundi

English	French
MISCELLANEOUS	
Tuesday	mardi
Wednesday	mercredi
Thursday	jeudi
Friday	vendredi
Saturday	samedi
Sunday	dimanche
January	janvier
February	février
March	mars
April	avril
May	mai
June	juin
July	juillet
August	août
September	septembre
October	octobre
November	novembre
December	décembre
yesterday	hier
today	aujourd'hui

English	French
MISCELLANEOUS	
tomorrow	demain
one	un
two	deux
three	trois
four	quatre
five	cinq
six	six
seven	sept
eight	huit
nine	neuf
ten	dix
twenty	vingt
thirty	trente
fourty	quarante
fifty	cinquante
hundred	cent
thousand	mille